Choosing a CRUISE

A BRIT'S GUIDE

5th Edition

SIMON VENESS

foulsham
LONDON • NEW YORK • TORONTO • SYDNEY

foulsham

The Publishing House, Bennetts Close,
Cippenham, Berkshire, SL1 5AP, England

ISBN 0-572-02738-9

Other books in this series:
A Brit's Guide to Orlando and Walt Disney World, Simon Veness, 0-572-02744-3
A Brit's Guide to Las Vegas and the West, Karen Marchbank, 0-572-02746-X
A Brit's Guide to New York, *Karen Marchbank*, 0-572-02741-9

Printed in Great Britain by St. Edmundsbury Press, Bury St. Edmunds, Suffolk

CONTENTS

The *Daily Express* British Cruise Awards   Page 4

Acknowledgements   Page 5

Foreword   Page 7

Chapter One: Introduction   Page 9
Including: Changing the Image; Facts and Figures;
Looking Ahead

Chapter Two: What's It All About?   Page 21
Including: Debunking the Six Great Myths and
Misconceptions: Boredom, Relaxation, Seasickness,
Expense, Too Old, Too Formal; and Cruising for Newcomers

Chapter Three: The Indefinable Extras   Page 39
Including: Adventure Options; Honeymoons;
The Five Cruise Essentials: Facilities, Service, Entertainment,
Food, Ports of Call; and Types of Cruise

Chapter Four: Making Sense of the Variety   Page 73
Including: How Cruise Ships Rate; Big Ship v Small Ship;
Fly-Cruise v Ex-UK Cruise; Short v Long; Cruising for Singles;
The Disabled at Sea; Travel Agents v Cruise Consultants;
Portrait of a Typical Cruise; Ship-speak

Chapter Five: The Cruise Lines and Their Ships   Page 103
Including: African Safari Club, Airtours, Carnival, Celebrity,
Costa, Crystal, Cunard, Disney, Festival, First Choice,
Hebridean Island, Holland America, Island Cruises, Louis,
Mediterranean Shipping, Norwegian Cruise Line, Fred Olsen,
Orient, P&O, Princess, Radisson Seven Seas, Royal Caribbean,
Royal Olympic, Saga, Seabourn, Silversea, Star Clippers,
Star Cruise, Swan Hellenic, Thomson, Windstar;
Best of the Rest

Chapter Six: Where Can I Cruise?   Page 183
Including: Cruise Seasons; Where the World Cruises;
The Mediterranean and the Middle East; Northern Europe;
The Caribbean; The US West Coast (including Alaska);
The US East Coast (including Bermuda); The Far East;
Australasia; Indian Ocean and Africa; South America
and Antarctica

Chapter Seven: Hold the Front Page   Page 248
The Latest Cruise News;
The *Daily Express* British Cruise Awards

Index   Page 253

THE DAILY EXPRESS BRITISH CRUISE AWARDS

Choosing a Cruise has been instrumental in creating the UK cruise industry's first definitive awards scheme, the **BRITISH CRUISE AWARDS,** in conjunction with What Cruise magazine. They began as an idea in the first edition of this book six years ago and were quickly supported by the then-new What Cruise. With sponsorship from the Singapore Tourism Board, the awards took physical shape with a first presentation ceremony in 1997 at World Travel Market – the biggest holiday forum in the world – in Earls Court, London. The awards were such a success they were back in 1998, bigger and better than before, once again presented by well-known TV travel personality John Carter.

In 2000, the awards took a quantum leap forward under the aegis of the Daily Express, as we went to The Savoy with guest presenter Anne Gregg and very special guest Janet Anderson MP, the Minister for Tourism, opening proceedings. In 2001, we maintained the new-look style as the *Daily Express* continued to take the whole concept forward, with the full support of the British cruise industry as a whole.

The awards are also the work of 25 panelists, all experts in different fields of the business – from writers and researchers to cruise agents, consultants and specialists – who bring an unrivalled knowledge of the British cruise scene to the table.

Here's how they work: the panel identifies five categories of cruise style – Standard, Superior, Premier, Deluxe and Ultra-Deluxe – and there are awards for what we consider to be the best ship in each of those. Then there are awards for Best Family Ship, Best Specialist, Best River Cruise Line, Best Brochure and an Industry Contribution Award. We introduce the panel on page 249 and you can read the results of our deliberations there.

ACKNOWLEDGEMENTS

A book as broad in scope as this could never be the work of just one person, and so I am indebted to the help, research and advice of the following, and many others, who have all played a significant part in the creation of Choosing a Cruise.

The Passenger Shipping Association, the Passenger Shipping Association Retail Agent Scheme, the Seatrade Organisation, Cruise Lines International Association, Cruise Europe, MedCruise, the Guild of Professional Cruise Agents, Mundy Cruising, Cruise Club International, Page & Moy, P&O Cruises, Airtours, Crystal Cruises, Cunard, Disney Cruise Line, Festival Cruises, Norwegian Cruise Line, Princess Cruises, Royal Caribbean International, Thomson Holidays, Singapore Tourism Board, Cruise New Zealand, Caribbean Tourism Organisation, Hong Kong Tourist Association, US Virgin Island Tourist Office, the Port of Southampton, Harwich International Port and Dover Harbour Board.

In particular, I would like to thank the following individuals for going out of their way to assist, usually on numerous occasions: Christina Nedovich (Singapore Tourism Board), Lynn Narraway (Carnival/Holland America UK), Graham Dullop (Cruise Club International), Edwina Lonsdale (Mundy Cruising), David Dingle (P&O), Vicky Wilby (Airtours), David Selby and Rachel O'Reilly (Thomson), Eric Flounders and Michael Gallagher (Cunard), Ian Buckeridge (The Cruise Line Ltd), Tony Ripper (Cruise Advisory Service), Peter Pate (Mediterranean Shipping Cruises), Nigel Lingard (Fred Olsen), Patrick Ryan, Pete Williams, Michele Andjel and Kate Selley (Royal Caribbean), Aris Zarpanely and Steve Odell (Silversea), Peter Wild (GP Wild International Ltd), John Turgoose (Dover Harbour), Chris Hayman (Seatrade), Kate Jones and Louisa French (Weber Shandwick PR), Bronwen Griffiths (BGB & Associates), and Richard Bastow and Chris Coates (Cruise and Maritime Services).

My special thanks also go to my principal research assistant Carolyn Voce and Keith Cartwright at the *Daily Express*, plus the additional input of Gary Buchanan, Lucy Huxley, Patricia Piacente, David Mott, Peter Wild, Peter Milne and all the members of the British Cruise Awards panel.

By way of a quick 'plug,' I am also editor of **World of Cruising,** a quarterly subscription-only magazine, and would like to think this is also a compelling read for anyone wanting to increase their cruise knowledge. As well as a full range of news and ship features, World of Cruising highlights celebrity features (Barry Norman, Michael Aspel, Ellen MacArthur and Mary Nightingale have all featured in the last year), health and beauty, shopping, food and drink, and the history of cruising. Real-life Passenger Perspectives (who knows, it could be a chance for *you* to detail your latest voyage) are another feature, along with the View from the Bridge, which takes a look at the men in charge, plus insider gossip from The Admiral. There is a full, up-to-date Cruise Planner in every edition, not to mention some of the best photography we can get our hands on. All in all, it adds up to a neat and ultra-informative package and, at a mere £3.75 per edition (or £15 annual subscription, inc postage and packing) great value, too. To order a copy or place a subscription, call: 01273 833747.

FOREWORD

I guess I should blame my parents, really. After all, anyone who has done four Cape Town-Southampton voyages before their 17th birthday has little chance of avoiding the feeling later in life that cruising is somehow part of their life-blood, an essential requirement to well-being and happiness, a necessity.

Okay, that may be a slight exaggeration, but there is definitely something about cruising that gets under your skin and makes itself a vital component of your way of life. Put simply, it is addictive. Whether it be a two-day 'cruise to nowhere' or a luxury line voyage, life on the ocean wave is a heady mixture of excitement, enjoyment and, yes, even romance, that absolutely demands to be repeated.

Getting a taste for it so early in life (my parents, younger brother and I set sail for the first time from Durban in 1969 aboard the Union-Castle Line ship SA Vaal, when I had just passed my ninth birthday) was without doubt a watershed experience, not least because I was heartily seasick before we had even lost sight of land! Although I obviously did not realise it at the time, it was a formative experience whose memory would last long and strong.

So, what is it that makes this form of travel, which has subsequently become one of the fastest-growing holiday types, so deliciously habit-forming?

First of all, there is still the misguided certainty you are doing something exclusive and selective, that somehow you have a social advantage over all those non-cruisers of the world. There is also the theory that, as an island race, we Brits have an unbreakable affinity for the sea, but, in these days of instantaneous worldwide communications and high-speed travel, it is not one to which I subscribe. It is more subtle than that. Cruising does still represent a bygone age of elegance, sophistication and romance, and it is that feeling of enjoying such a rich heritage of travel experience that instils a cruise holiday with much of its mystique.

And, make no mistake about it, despite the ultra-modern appeal of the new build of cruise ships and their facilities, there remains a mystique about cruising which no other holiday type can capture or recreate. There is nothing in the wide world of travel which can compare with the feeling of sailing into a new port first thing in the morning, of seeing the lights go down and the sun come up over the source of new adventure and new experience, a wonderful thrill of possibilities gradually unfolding in magnificent surroundings.

On top of the mystique, there are many more tangible attractions to cruising, such as value for money, excellence of service, huge variety of appeal and the little-appreciated virtue of it being an ideal source of all-round family entertainment. This latter is something which all the major cruise companies are itching to exploit and, with few exceptions, is something they deliver with enormous success. I can certainly vouch for the inestimable youthful appeal of being in a world that caters specifically to kids' needs and delivers real excitement and facilities somehow divorced from adult life. I am equally sure my parents were similarly delighted my brother and I were safely off their hands for large parts of the day!

Having therefore become convinced of cruising's lasting appeal from so early an age, it was only a small, logical step to want to rediscover those well-remembered delights as soon as I could afford them myself (this was, admittedly, not for many years, being only a fairly run-of-the-mill journalist). Almost inevitably, it was in researching all the wonderful options for a modern cruise holiday that I became fascinated in exploring this rapidly expanding source of holiday appeal. So much so, in fact, I have now spent more than seven years interviewing cruise line staff, travel agents, ship crew and passengers, as well as visiting ship after ship to get the full flavour of the differences and attractions of the main lines (and, at the same time, thoroughly enjoying the occasional cruise!). During this process, the cruise lines and tour operators have co-operated fully with my research without once seeking to obtain a particular slant to a write-up or asking for the right to vet my material, which I believe speaks volumes for the quality of their service in general.

The days of line voyages and the Union-Castle Line are both firmly in the past, but in their place has sprung up a holiday industry that borrows heavily from cruising's elegant heritage while placing it firmly in a modern context. Gone are the days of the classic, class-structured cruise ships (with the one exception of the QE2), but instead has come a quickly-evolving new breed of vessels which can deliver the most flexible and varied experiences in some of the world's most beautiful areas. They retain their sense of style, but they have added a level of all-round comfort and sophistication (virtual-reality gymnasiums, anyone?) that almost defies belief. And the huge diversity of the product, from the small, luxury cruisers to the massive mega-liners means there is guaranteed to be something for everyone.

Happily, there remains, too, a sense of the industry's grand history. The debut in 1995 of P&O's new ship the *Oriana* brought a welcome sense of tradition and elegance back to the modern ship-builder and ensured, at least for my lifetime, the memories of Union-Castle will remain proud and strong. The last few years have seen a near-explosion of new tonnage of just about every shape and size, with Royal Caribbean currently holding the record for the biggest ships – the amazing 142,000-ton *Voyager* and *Explorer of the Seas* (twice the size of the QE2). P&O have a wonderful new flagship – Aurora – and the Disney company have joined in with some of the most remarkable family facilities of all.

I therefore dedicate this book to my parents in the happy knowledge there is still a world of holiday enjoyment and romance awaiting a new generation of cruisers. I urge you to go out and explore it – but, be warned, it IS highly addictive.

CHAPTER ONE

INTRODUCTION

Welcome to the big, wide world of cruising. Whether you are a cruise novice or an old salt, you cannot have failed to notice the amazing growth in the opportunities for holidays at sea. The cruise lines of the world now have a vast range of tantalising, high-profile offerings, and they are all firmly of the belief Britain is the place to sell them. It is a fascinating – but potentially hazardous – proposition, with a vast array of sweet-shop 'goodies' on display yet a series of pitfalls awaiting the unwary.

But, armed with this book, you can be safe in the knowledge you have all the necessary facts at your fingertips to make an informed and rewarding choice.

Cruising is a wonderfully thrilling way to spend a week or more, but it is still a highly complex and specialised field. Just trying to work out the average cruise brochure can still be a forehead-creasing experience, and the variety on offer is becoming wider and more bewildering all the time. There are more than 30 major cruise lines dealing in the British market, with in excess of 150 ships from which to choose. Newer, more dramatic and bigger vessels are being added all the time. It is a diverse, and multi-dimensional product. From the budget-priced basic cruise experience to the ultra luxury of the all-inclusive small specialist vessels, from the Caribbean super-liners to the individual adventure ships cruising the startling waters of the Antarctic, cruising is a breathtakingly broad experience.

So, let's start off with a few gentle facts to set the ball rolling (or the ship sailing, to be more precise). Britain is the second-largest cruise market in the world – a very distant second to America. Yet it is has grown incredibly fast from a small base and is one of the most dynamically healthy segments of the UK holiday industry. Put simply, the secret of the cruise holiday has finally been let out of the bag, and an increasing number of people have decided it is for them. And, once they have sampled its delights, they are equally reluctant to return to their old land-based holidays. For this happy yet still relatively small band, the secret they have discovered is that of an intensely rewarding holiday offering really terrific value for money – and it is a holiday with the highest satisfaction ratio of any on offer. Once bitten, nearly always smitten.

However, it is also an inescapable fact cruising has engendered more misconceived ideas and perceptions of its appeal than any other holiday type. To mangle a modern cliché, if I had a pound for every time someone asked me 'Why would you want to go cruising?' I would be a wealthy man (well, several hundred pounds better off, at least). Despite a veritable advertising barrage in the last three or four years, cruising still has an unfortunate image of being class- and age-conscious, not to mention it being something primarily for the well-to-do. **This is simply not the case.**

I am inclined to underline that statement as well, if only to get your attention from the outset. Henceforth, you will discard all preconceived notions of what cruising is and isn't, and you will be ready to enter a world of dramatic scale and appeal, not to mention magnificent value for money. Let me open up the world of cruising, therefore, with a detailed investigation of what it isn't, before moving on, in Chapters 2-5, to reveal the full, modern face of this holiday phenomenon.

For various reasons – and I will come to those shortly – cruising remains a bit of a mystery to the majority (a mystery formed from a bygone age of leisurely, long-distance travel peopled by the elderly, rich and titled), and its appeals are lost to the average holiday-seeker simply because it has yet to be properly explained. In the course of the next few chapters, this book will set out to destroy the myths, cut through the hype, explain the attractions and outline the wealth of opportunity that cruising really represents.

CHANGING THE IMAGE

To begin with, cruising's well-documented heritage, both in print and film, has helped to create this picture of it being exclusive and expensive. And, although the industry, particularly in this country, doesn't really like to be reminded, it is an image it is still struggling to dispel with the uninitiated. For many, the notion of taking a cruise holiday is one that just does not occur, hence the need to labour the point with all the subtlety of a cavalry charge. The modern face of cruising is so different to the common perception as to make the comparison almost funny. Not only is it so different, it is also hugely varied. That means, while there are still some bastions of cruising that remain staunchly faithful to past eras of bridge foursomes, ballroom dancing and high tea, there are equally up-to-date ships concentrating on totally youthful pursuits like video games, beer-drinking contests and teen discos. In between, you can enjoy bingo and art auctions, highbrow lectures and practical discussions on the best shopping, cordon bleu cuisine and all-you-can eat buffets, Las Vegas-style cabarets and ballet. And that is just a small sample. Hey, modern cruising is fun!

The other major area in which cruising has failed to sell itself in the past is through its travel agents. Until recently, your average high street multiple outlet of Thomas Cook, Lunn Poly, Going Places, Travel Choice, Co-Op or whoever has been woefully ignorant of all the merits, intricacies and options involved in a cruise booking. To be fair, the cruise lines themselves have not helped by producing brochures that have made selecting your average cruise about as easy as planning an expedition to the North Pole. In simple terms, the amount of specialist knowledge required for even a relatively straightforward cruise inquiry is far in excess of that needed for your average two-week package holiday. Therefore, the travel agents have notably failed in the past to provide much impetus for the cruise industry, leaving the field clear for the growth of specialist agencies dealing only in cruises. This is now changing as the big retail outlets bring out their own cruise-dedicated brochures and operate Cruise Clubs for past passengers. High street outlets have now caught up with the idea cruise holidays are good business for them and their customers alike and are training their staff in the necessary areas to understand and explain the product. I will return to this subject later as it has a number of implications when you sit down to debate the pros and cons of your cruise holiday.

IT'S BIGGER IN AMERICA

The basic truth remains, though, the British cruise industry as a whole is considerably underdeveloped when compared with America's. Herein lies the biggest contradiction, even allowing for the far greater numbers involved in the US tourist industry. To the average American, there is nothing prohibitive about going on a cruise, it is simply another holiday option. No drawbacks, no misconceptions, no problem. They do, of course, have the advantage of the world's biggest cruise playground, the Caribbean, virtually on their doorstep, but the essential idea of it being out of their reach for reasons of class or finance just would not occur to them. In Britain, on the other hand, it remains something for lottery winners, the retired or Lord and Lady Whoever. Joe Schmo from Chicago is *four times* more likely to take a cruising holiday than his counterpart in Birmingham or Manchester.

So let's knock this on the head once and for all – cruising is for absolutely *everyone,* young or old, active or passive, wealthy or not-so-wealthy. If you can afford two weeks on the Costa Blanca, you can certainly afford a cruise these days – and you'll get far better value for your holiday peseta. One of the most overlooked facts of a cruise holiday is how much it includes once you have paid your initial costs. To start with, it is full board (and then some), while all your entertainment, travel, transfers and, in some cases, even your shore excursions are also all paid for before you leave home. There are no hidden extras for meals, evenings out, discos, taxis or whatever. The only other expenses during your cruise are your drinks, ship-arranged shore excursions, beauty and health treatments, tips and, in a few cases, port taxes. There are even a few of the deluxe lines that are totally all-inclusive – you do not need to spend a single penny extra once you step aboard.

FACTS AND FIGURES

The message may seem obvious to anyone who has already sampled cruise life, but the basic facts and statistics still suggest it is getting through only slowly.

Back in 1986, the number of Brits who took a cruise holiday was barely 90,000. By 1990, Brits at sea had doubled to 186,000 and the annual rate of increase from 1995 to 2000 was almost 25 per cent. In 1998, the total was up to 634,740, but that still represents only a small percentage of the holiday market in overall terms – some 24 million Brits holidayed abroad in 2000 – and suggests the message is not coming across loud and clear. By comparison, the American cruise market currently numbers around 7 million.

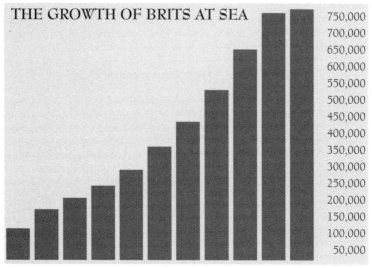

THE GROWTH OF BRITS AT SEA

91,500	152,140	186,490	219,200	270,000	340,000	416,000	510,000	634,740	746,000	754,000
1986	1988	1990	1992	1994	1995	1996	1997	1998	1999	2000

The evolution of the modern cruise industry is perhaps partly to blame for this since the likes of Cunard and P&O were slow to catch on to the developments of the American cruise lines, which seized this route in order to survive after the effective death of sea travel per se in the 1960s and 70s as Mr. Boeing and his friends sent their jets further and faster around the world. Instead of selling off their liners at a fraction of their worth, the most go-ahead cruise companies experimented with turning their ships into floating vacation resorts, following the sun year-round and offering a taste of previous class-orientated glories in modern, one-class comfort. The sunshine state of Florida became the centre of this burgeoning new tourist industry and Miami found itself the cruise capital of the world. Inevitably, America became the market leader. Fly-cruising became firmly established as the preferred method of holiday-making and, as the market became more sophisticated, California, Mexico and Alaska appeared on cruise itineraries. In the 1980s, cruising was given another boost with the visionary strides made by the Carnival Corporation under the control of owner Ted Arison and his son Micky. Their massive input in new cruise ships and aggressive marketing in making it appealing (and affordable) have ensured continued growth, not only in America, but worldwide. The arrival of the Disney company as a cruise line in 1998 has helped to enhance this process still further.

MEANWHILE, IN THE MED

In Europe, the Italian company Costa pioneered Mediterranean fly-cruising and the Greeks joined in, buying up old liners and turning them into island-hopping cruisers offering guaranteed sunshine. Britain, by contrast, was slow to exploit these developments, partly because Cunard and P&O still had worldwide traditional shipping commitments, and partly because of the obvious drawbacks of cruising from UK ports. Any company wishing to sail year-round from Britain had to contend with the winter and Bay of Biscay factors: firstly, you needed a fast ship to get your passengers into the sunshine quickly in the winter months, and secondly, you had to cross the notoriously rough Bay of Biscay (between Brittany in north-western France and Cape Ortegal, at the tip of north-western Spain) to get there, and hence your vessels had more design restrictions than the fair-weather liners. A crossing of the Bay in heavy weather and high seas is not for the faint-hearted, although many experienced cruise passengers do get a thrill from this sort of 'real' sailing!

The belated mass-market entry of Britain into the fly-cruise business in the late 1980s, plus the advent of P&O's *Oriana* in 1995, amazingly the first cruise ship purpose-built for the UK market, finally gave the British cruise industry the tools to expand its horizons. They are now after YOU – and your family. For, make no mistake, the future of cruising is considered very much in family terms, with ships demonstrating a sophisticated array of children's facilities as well as babysitting and child-minding services.

The other significant development now making Britain more cruise-conscious is the entry into the market of two of the biggest tour operators, Airtours and Thomson, plus First Choice, Direct Holidays and a new alliance between First Choice and the second-biggest American line, Royal Caribbean.

Airtours were first, in 1995, and, after sizing up what Carnival in particular were doing so well, they invested £52 million in buying up two existing ships and launching a new, mass-market product. Both they and Thomson, who chartered their own ship in 1996, make no bones about making cruising increasingly available for the budget-conscious as well as the traditional British package holiday-maker. It is a long-overdue development, but one eagerly greeted by (most of) the existing British cruise industry, who argue it will attract a host of first-time passengers to the market, a welcome influx who will surely want to investigate all the attractions of cruising much further in future. The few critics are worried the price-conscious nature of the new operations might devalue the product as a whole and actively discourage people from cruising. In reality, the impressive and whole-hearted approach of Airtours in particular has served to put cruising firmly in the travel agents' shop window like never before. The impact of the First Choice/Royal Caribbean operation which starts in summer 2002, called Island Cruises, could well add more impetus in this area.

LOOKING AHEAD

If that is the immediate past and present of the cruise industry, what of the future? Well, working on the theory bigger is better, Carnival, Princess and Royal Caribbean have all produced ships in excess of 100,000 tons for the first time, with an accompanying wealth of modernistic features that make the great liners of yesteryear look like closer relatives of the Ark than of these new ultra-mega-ships – there can be no other term for them. Prior to the 101,000-ton *Carnival Destiny* in 1996, the biggest previous passenger ship was the 84,000-ton *Queen Elizabeth,* launched in 1938. Typically, most modern cruise ships have weighed in at around 70,000 tons, while, by contrast, the average cross-channel ferry is a tiddler at 25,000. Royal Caribbean really pushed back the size boundaries with their 142,000-ton leviathan *Voyager of the Seas* in 1999, and will have no less than five such ships in operation by 2003. Both Star Cruises (in the Far East) and our own P&O also have plans to join the 100,000-ton-plus brigade, while Cunard (now owned by the Carnival Corporation) plan to regain the 'largest-ever' title in 2003 with their *Queen Mary 2* project.

In fact, the trend is increasingly to build either extremely big or rather small ships, working on economies of scale in the case of the former (where more cabins equals more people spending their money on board) and the attraction of all-inclusive, luxury service on the latter (where small scale means the epitome of the high-class, personal touch). There is also a tendency to build faster ships, which presents a fascinating throwback to the real glory days of the transatlantic crossings, when speed was everything, and the fastest ship was the best. The modern thinking behind faster ships, however, is not to win any particular award (as in the case of the Blue Riband, the cup awarded for the quickest transatlantic journey), but simply to get to more ports of call in any one holiday, and for longer in each case.

Sadly for traditionalists such as myself, the tendency of the modern ship design is increasingly towards the large, slab-sided floating hotel type, which does detract slightly from the true aesthetic enjoyment of being at sea. The evolution of the modern design is quite straightforward. Whereas the classic ocean-going liners of the pre-1970 era were designed for long-distance travel, and therefore needed to sail quickly, efficiently and smoothly, modern cruise ships have more in common with the major land-based resorts. Their clients demand a full range of on-board facilities, a choice of things like bars, lounges, restaurants and entertainment centres and an unimpaired sea view no matter where they are. As a consequence, features like dining rooms, which on classic ships used to dwell lower down in the vessel's deck hierarchy (for smoother service), are now brought up to become more of a feature, with big picture windows. A greater number of cabins are also placed much higher up on the ship's profile to allow for modern additions like balconies. Long gone are the days when a ship had passenger cabins below or on the waterline (and had other authentic touches like portholes instead of windows!). The overall result is a demand to build ships with a vastly increased public capacity and with much of it above the mid-point rather than below it. Hence, in the quest to fulfil these new criteria, the designers arrive at a more high-rise, box-like profile rather than the sleek, well-proportioned look of ships like QE2.

However, it is hard to argue the modern liners do not cater for every conceivable activity in magnificent style – multi-storey lobbies, glass-sided lifts, shopping malls, state-of-the-art theatres, 24-hour restaurants, wide-ranging health and fitness facilities and even rock-climbing walls and mini-golf courses are all regular features these days. And, while the outward appearance of a ship like *Grand Princess* is a touch monolithic, internally she is stunningly pretty.

The technology levels of the new build of ship are also a significant pointer to the way ahead. State-of-the-art sound systems, ever more sophisticated theatres, ice-skating venues, interactive games (virtual-reality golf and the rest) and service enhancements like in-cabin TV that can call up the day's menu, order your duty-free goods and even play poker with you (for real money!) are all the marine order of the day. The variety of such entertainment options will continue to be the envy of the rest of the holiday world, and it is also not uncommon these days to find ships well fitted out for business users, with conference facilities, faxes, photocopiers, internet links and even computer training facilities.

As if the massive level of hardware investment isn't enough (and there are 41 new vessels due to roll out of the world's ship-building yards before the end of 2004, totalling some £12 billion), the cruise lines are also seeking to develop new cruise areas. South America is seeing new ships sailing its waters all the time (including those of Fred Olsen), Hawaii is firmly on the charts of NCL, Holland America, Princess and others, the Indian Ocean-South African routes continue to be developed by Mediterranean Shipping Cruises, and Singapore and the Far East are seeing huge investment in ships and itineraries.

The only real cloud on the worldwide cruise market horizon is the steady growth of the industry's biggest players, often at the cost of some of the smaller ones. Several lines have gone bust in recent years (notably Regency, Premier, Commodore and Royal Cruise Lines in America and CTC in the UK), while others continue to struggle and face a rather uncertain future. Certain industry analysts can see this agglomeration of the most profitable companies (of which Carnival and, to a lesser extent, Royal Caribbean and P&O are the prime examples) only increasing through the rest of the decade, but there still seems a healthy market for the smaller, more focused lines like Crystal, Festival, Silversea and Fred Olsen.

Hopefully, by now, I will have answered the underlying question of this chapter and you will have cast off all preconceived notions of cruising's dated image and be prepared to explore more fully the delights and

THE WORLD'S LARGEST CRUISE SHIPS

Ship	Cruise Line	Built	Tonnage
Voyager of the Seas	Royal Caribbean	1999	142,000
Explorer of the Seas	Royal Caribbean	2000	142,000
Adventure of the Seas	Royal Caribbean	2001	142,000
Grand Princess	Princess Cruises	1998	109,000
Golden Princess	Princess Cruises	2001	109,000
Carnival Destiny	Carnival Cruise Line	1996	101,353
Carnival Triumph	Carnival Cruise Line	1999	101,509
Carnival Victory	Carnival Cruise Line	2000	101,509
Millennium	Celebrity Cruise Line	2000	91,000
Infinity	Celebrity Cruise Line	2001	91,000
Summit	Celebrity Cruise Line	2001	91,000
Norwegian Star	Norwegian Cruise Line	2001	91,000
Radiance of the Seas	Royal Caribbean	2001	88,000
Carnival Spirit	Carnival Cruise Line	2001	86,000
Carnival Pride	Carnival Cruise Line	2001	86,000
Costa Atlantica	Costa Cruises	2000	85,700
Disney Magic	Disney Cruise Line	1998	83,000
Disney Wonder	Disney Cruise Line	1999	83,000
Norwegian Sky	Norwegian Cruise Line	1999	80,000
Norwegian Sun	Norwegian Cruise Line	2001	80,000
Vision of the Seas	Royal Caribbean	1998	78,491
Rhapsody of the Seas	Royal Caribbean	1997	78,491
Sun Princess	Princess Cruises	1995	77,441
Dawn Princess	Princess Cruises	1997	77,000
Sea Princess	Princess Cruises	1998	77,000
Ocean Princess	Princess Cruises	2000	77,000
SuperStar Leo	Star Cruises	1998	76,800
SuperStar Virgo	Star Cruises	1999	76,800
Galaxy	Celebrity Cruises	1996	76,522
Mercury	Celebrity Cruises	1997	76,522
Aurora	P & O	2000	76,152
Norway (ex France)	Norwegian Cruise Line	1962	76,069
Grandeur of the Seas	Royal Caribbean	1996	74,100
Enchantment of the Seas	Royal Caribbean	1997	74,100
CostaVictoria	Costa Cruises	1996	74,000

NEW SHIPS BY THE YEAR 2005

Cruise Line	Ship Name	Tonnage	Delivery
Aida Cruises	AIDAvita	42,000	2002
Aida Cruises	Aida Club-class	42,000	2003
American Classic Voyages	Unnamed	72,000	2003
American Classic Voyages	Unnamed	72,000	2004
Carnival	Carnival Legend	86,000	2002
Carnival	Carnival Conquest	110,000	2002
Carnival	Carnival Glory	110,000	2003
Carnival	Carnival Miracle	86,000	2004
Carnival	Carnival Valor	110,000	2004
Celebrity	Constellation	91,000	2002
Costa	Costa Mediterranea	86,000	2003
Costa	Costa Fortuna	105,000	2003
Costa	Costa Majorca	105,000	2004
Crystal	Unnamed	68,000	2003
Cunard	Queen Mary 2	150,000	2003
Festival	European Stars	58,600	2002
Festival	Unnamed	70,000	2003
Festival	Unnamed	70,000	2004
Holland America	Zuiderdam	84,000	2002
Holland America	Oosterdam	84,000	2003
Holland America	Unnamed	84,000	2003
Holland America	Unnamed	84,000	2004
Holland America	Unnamed	84,000	2005
Mediterranean Shipping	Unnamed	60,000	2003
NCL	Unnamed	91,000	2002
P&O	Unnamed	109,000	2004
Princess	Star Princess	109,000	2002
Princess	Coral Princess	88,000	2002
Princess	Island Princess	88,000	2003
Princess	Diamond Princess	113,000	2003
Princess	Sapphire Princess	113,000	2004
Radisson Seven Seas	Seven Seas Voyager	50,000	2003
ResidenSea	The World	40,000	2002
ResidenSea	Unnamed	50,000	2003
Royal Caribbean	Brilliance of the Seas	88,000	2002
Royal Caribbean	Unnamed	142,000	2002
Royal Caribbean	Unnamed	88,000	2003
Royal Caribbean	Unnamed	142,000	2003
Royal Caribbean	Unnamed	88,000	2004
Star Cruises	SuperStar Sagittarius II	112,000	2003
Star Cruises	SuperStar Capricorn II	112,000	2004

attractions it can offer. Over the course of the book I shall attempt to steer you through the full complexity of what a cruise holiday has to offer, with explanations of the bewildering variety of styles and ship types, how a typical cruise shapes up and how you should go about booking one, taking advantage of the welter of discounts on offer these days. We shall take a detailed look at the main cruise companies dealing in the British market, and their hardware, and there is also a unique rating system that judges the cruise lines and their ships according to what they *really* offer, and not what their brochures claim. Finally, to complete the picture, you can get an idea of all the different cruise areas in Chapter Six.

WHAT'S NEW AND WHAT'S HOT

When it comes to the 'latest and greatest' in the wide world of cruising, there is always plenty to highlight. There are no less than 15 new ships on the market in 2001, following on from a similar number in 2000 – a record 30 glittering new vessels, the majority of super-liner size, all looking to impress.

The giant Carnival Corporation are again to the fore, with principal rivals Royal Caribbean, Norwegian Cruise Line and Princess not far behind. The **Carnival** line itself has two ships of a brand new class, *Carnival Spirit* and *Carnival Pride,* with the former offering summer cruises in Alaska and the winter in the Caribbean. These new 84,000-tonners also boast more outside and balconied cabins than any other Carnival ships, two-storey gymnasiums, wedding chapels and the line's first alternative dining option (the big buzzword in cruising these days). Carnival have also transferred one of their ships, the 1981-built *Tropicale,* to their European-owned line Costa, and are switching the *Westerdam* from their Holland America fleet to Costa, too.

Princess Cruises made a splash with a big UK showcase of their latest arrival, the second of their Grand-class ships, the 109,000-ton *Golden Princess,* which spends the summer in the Mediterranean and the winter in the Caribbean. **Royal Caribbean** have also made significant marketing strides in Britain with a Europe-only programme for their *Splendour of the Seas* and another new class of ship in *Radiance of the Seas,* while the 142,000-ton mega-liners *Voyager* and *Explorer of the Seas* (and *Adventure* in late 2001) have also proved to have loads of Wow! factor. Sister company **Celebrity Cruises** are also well to the fore with the second and third of their quite stunning Millennium-class vessels, *Infinity* and *Summit,* easily the most sumptuous and classy of the super-liners.

NCL have been particularly impressive with the introduction of their Freestyle on-board brand, particularly on new vessels *Norwegian Sky* and *Sun* (plus the dramatic-looking *Norwegian Star* in December 2001). This new concept, borrowed from parent company Star Cruises, gives a casual and wide-ranging style to ship-board life, with less of the formality and more choice – notably in dining – for all their passengers.

Elsewhere, **Festival** have taken another big stride with the arrival of their 58,600-ton new-build *European Vision,* a ship destined to promote their pan-European style still further with an excellent array of on-board facilities on a mid-sized ship (for a change). **Royal Olympic** are also likely to win new fans with the second in an even smaller series, the 24,500-ton *Olympic Explorer,* which offers a really tempting 7-day itinerary due to her high-speed design (plus the usual array of high-class creature comforts).

Things are equally competitive in the Ultra-Deluxe end of the market, with both Silversea and Radisson Seven Seas going head-to-head with magnificent new vessels. The *Silver Whisper* is the second of a 28,500-ton series for the European-orientated **Silversea**, a state-of-the-art, five-star floating resort which delivers outstanding service and cuisine. But the *Seven Seas Mariner* has upped the ante again, with an all-balcony ship (the first of its kind) which also delivers **Radisson's** most quality-conscious offering to date.

Looking ahead to 2002, the breathless pace of the business shows no sign of letting up, with another 12 ships on order and the start of a new line, **Island Cruises**. This latter is a combination venture between Royal Caribbean International and First Choice Holidays, with RCI's *Viking Serenade* being brought over to the Mediterranean and given a major face-lift to become *Island Escape,* with the intention of offering a more casual, laid-back style to appeal to the 30–40 age bracket. More ships for Island are believed to be in the pipeline.

Also in the UK, **P&O** have another major new project on their hands with the arrival of the *Oceana,* formerly the *Ocean Princess* of their sister company in the US. This newcomer should add a distinctly glitzy touch to the fleet, which has already benefited significantly from the 2000 debut of the wonderful *Aurora* – in my opinion, the best large-scale ship for the British market anywhere.

Go-ahead **Thomson Cruises** also look to have a number of new ventures up their sleeve for 2002, including a partnership with the two most recent ships of Festival Cruises and an imaginative summer cruise-and-stay programme based on the island of Corfu, making them the first British operator to offer cruises from Greece. And, while their own ships stick primarily to the Mediterranean, the Festival link means they will be able to offer cruise-and-stay Caribbean holidays, too, with a week's cruise linked to seven days in the Dominican Republic. The Corfu voyages will alternate two superb seven-night sailings on the smart little *Emerald,* the first taking in Venice, Trieste, Kefalonia, Dubrovnik and Split, and the second to Athens, Kusadasi (Turkey), Rhodes, Santorini and Gythion. As ever, there is a wide choice of departure airport from the UK (see also Thomson Cruises section, pages 172–4).

Carnival Cruises continue to push at the boundaries in America with a series of new cruises out of New Orleans, Galveston and Tampa. Their brand-new, 2,976-passenger *Carnival Conquest* will be based in New Orleans for seven-day voyages to Ocho Rios (Jamaica), Grand Cayman and Playa del Carmen/Cozumel (Mexico) from December 2002, while both *Sensation* (4- and 5-day) and *Inspiration* (7-day) will feature western Caribbean cruising from Tampa from August. The Galveston (Texas) scene will benefit from having two ships – *Jubilee* and *Celebration* – on the 4- and 5-day short-haul scene to Cozumel and Cancun from mid-August.

The distinctive discovery cruise style of **Swan Hellenic** will be going still further afield in 2002, with new adventures to the Norwegian Fjords and Arctic Circle, the Red Sea, Black Sea and North Africa, while they also look to offer more one-week voyages to entice the first-timer aboard their lovely little country-house hotel ship *Minerva*. There is also a 5-day 'sampler' cruise setting sail from Tower Bridge in London in July.

Finally, be prepared for an advertising and marketing broadside of epic proportions from **Cunard** as they gear up for the arrival of their *Queen Mary 2* in December 2003. This staggering 150,000-ton project aims to sweep the board in the mega-liner stakes, and all the early signs are that she will, indeed, be an immense proposition. The maiden voyage is reputed to be sold out many times over, but many details of her internal design had yet to be unveiled at the time of writing, so watch out for more throughout 2002 as they look to build awareness of this 2,800-passenger leviathan.

Hopefully, this taste of current – and future – trends now puts you in the mood to delve deeper into the great attractions of a life on the ocean wave as we sail into Chapter 2, What's It All About …

CHAPTER TWO

WHAT'S IT ALL ABOUT?

Having spent most of the opening chapter talking about what cruising isn't, it makes sense now to tell you more about what it is. To start with, it is a greater source of holiday excitement than any I have found, providing a much keener sense of anticipation and more wonderful reminiscences than anything else. But a full explanation of the modern cruise holiday also means identifying and dealing with the common objections to and misconceptions of it.

In basic terms, cruising is very much all things to all people. That is, it is so varied and flexible it can cater for all tastes and all types – provided you find the right ship and the right cruise line for you. That message cannot be emphasized enough, and is one of the essential reasons for reading this book. Even at budget level, a cruise still represents a significant expenditure, so it is vital you select the right one.

To that end, remember cruising can be either the ultimate relaxation or the height of holiday frenzy. You can be as lazy or as active as you wish, and you'll find plenty of facilities catering for both desires. You can also broaden the choice by selecting a cruise that either is port-intensive or features a predominant amount of open-sea sailing.

Indeed, what other holiday type guarantees to transport you from place to place, from one superb vista to another in total comfort – and with the huge advantage of having to unpack only once?

It is sometimes tempting to see the best value of a cruise in terms of the number of ports it visits, but beware! A seven-day cruise that boasts seven (or more, in some cases) ports of call can leave you in need of another holiday immediately afterwards. The itinerary of any ship is one of its most attractive features, but, if you have never cruised before, these port-intensive trips will not give you the best view of cruising, simply because they are so demanding. Of course, you can just stay on the ship, but it is difficult to ignore the charms of a new port completely, and you can quickly lose track of where you have been if you try to cram in too much. This is a particularly American affliction – our transatlantic cousins usually don't get as much holiday time as we do and therefore prefer itineraries that show them as much as possible in as short a time as possible. Hence, at the end of seven days and eight ports of call, it is not uncommon to find them debating among themselves: 'Honey, was that Antigua or Dominica on Monday?' Believe me, it happens. And, after all, your holiday is supposed to be a stress-free environment, so you need those sea days to be able to relax and get properly attuned to your nautical nature.

TRAVEL TIP

It is a notable fact British passengers DO prefer a higher number of days at sea to their American counterparts. The most comfortable ratio – especially for first-timers to cruising – is roughly one day at sea for every port of call.

Ultimately, the amount of hectic port-visiting anyone can reasonably enjoy is a matter of personal preference, but you do risk failing to take full advantage of your floating home if you insist on a port-intensive itinerary, and, in most cases these days, you will miss out on one of the primary attractions of your holiday. For, make no mistake, the modern cruise ship is a wondrous vessel for the activity-conscious.

The vast range of facilities should destroy, well and truly, Myth Number One: I Will Get Bored On Board.

From early-morning aerobics to late-night discos, you are guaranteed a full daily programme of events, and there will always be a choice of things to do at any given time, from organised deck sports and games, to bridge, bingo, lectures, art auctions, karaoke or even dance lessons.

These daily programmes (many of which are common to all the main cruise lines) also hint at the vast array of on-board facilities which modern ships can boast – and which are becoming more sophisticated with the launch of every new vessel.

To illustrate these points, I have taken the example of a typical day in the life of the cruise ship that carries more British passengers than any other, P&O's flagship super-liner *Aurora*. The programme is taken from their daily on-board news-sheet, *Aurora Today,* and highlights the wide range of activities available from early morning to late at night (and this is all before you visit your first port of call!).

Typically, a cruise ship will consist of the following standard features, designed to further broaden your choice of what to do at any given time: a beauty salon, massage treatment rooms, sauna and steam room, modern gymnasium (with a full range of weight-training and exercise equipment), disco, observation lounge, a wide range of bars (as many as 15 on *Voyager of the Seas*), restaurant, buffet-service dining rooms (both inside and out), casino, swimming pool(s), jacuzzis, sun deck, deck sports, showlounge or theatre, library and video library, video games room, children's playroom (and night nursery in some cases), self-service launderette and medical centre. Boredom doesn't have a chance!

AURORA TODAY

7.00am: Continental Breakfast

8.00am: Oasis Beauty & Health Spa open (to 8pm)

8.00am: Main Restaurant Breakfast

9.00am: Fitness Centre – Gentle Stretch Class

9.00am: Shops open (to 10.30pm)

9.00am: Children's Clubs open (to 10.00pm)

9.45am: Port Talk (Malaga and Malta)

10.00am: Line dancing

10.30am: Golf Simulator Open Morning

10.30am: Morning Coffee with entertainment team

10.30am: Deck Quoits tournament

10.30am: Gymnasium Induction

11.00am: Hair Workshop

11.00am: Shuffleboard Competition

11.15am: Handicrafts

11.30am: Short Tennis tournament

12 noon: Buffet Luncheon

12.15pm: Open Sitting Luncheon in main restaurants

2.00pm: Bridge class

2.30pm: Cinema Feature Film – The Patriot

2.30pm: Cricket

2.45pm: Dance class

2.45pm: Whist Drive

3.00pm: Learn to make … soft toys

3.00pm: De-stress Seminar

3.00pm: Learn to play blackjack, roulette and poker in the Casino

3.00pm: Fitness Centre – Body Conditioning

3.30pm: Art Auction

3.30pm: Table Tennis tournament

4.00pm: Football

4.00pm: Afternoon Tea

4.15pm: Jackpot Bingo

5.15pm: Children's Tea

5.30pm: Fitness Class – Legs, Tums and Bums

6.00pm: Individual Quiz

6.00pm: Cocktail Music

6.30pm: First Sitting Dinner

8.15pm: Cinema Feature Film – Chicken Run

8.30pm: Second Sitting Dinner

8.30pm: Classical Concert

8.30pm: Casino Tables open (until late)

8.30pm: Roy Walker and Stadium Theatre Company

9.30pm: Evening Dancing Begins

9.45pm: Bridge Competition

10.30pm: Roy Walker and Stadium Theatre Company

10.30pm: Syndicate Quiz

10.30pm: Pub Night in Champions Bar

11.00pm: Late Night Music

11.45pm: Breakthru – Freddie Mercury tribute show

12.30am: Disco Date

≡≡≡≡≡≡≡ TRAVEL TIP ≡≡≡≡≡≡≡

For the best array of British sports and deck games, P&O take some beating. On my last cruise aboard *Aurora,* I barely had time to fit in my shore excursions around games of cricket, football, short tennis, shuffleboard, table tennis, volleyball and deck hockey, plus visits to the gym (well, how else can you afford to fit in your fifth meal of the day?).

GET WITH THE THEME

As if all that is not enough, many cruises are increasingly 'themed' to cover a whole range of activities, from sport and music to cooking, gardening, art, astronomy and even *The Archers.* Norwegian Cruise Line, for example, offer a Dive-In programme giving you the chance to learn to snorkel in some of the most idyllic locations for underwater adventures, while P&O now even have a brochure on their themed cruises, covering 18 different topics. Other notable themes and their cruise lines include bridge (P&O, Orient, Page & Moy, Fred Olsen, Saga, Cunard), Country & Western (NCL, Holland America, P&O), golf (Seabourn, Silversea, P&O, Royal Caribbean, Crystal, Fred Olsen, Radisson, NCL), wine-tasting (Holland America, P&O, Seabourn, Orient, Crystal, NCL, Swan Hellenic, Airtours, Windstar, Saga, Cunard), ballroom dancing (P&O, Airtours, Holland America), classical music (P&O and Saga), jazz (Mediterranean Shipping Cruises, NCL, Crystal, Holland America, P&O), antiques (Airtours, Orient, P&O), photography (Orient), gardens (Saga) and topical or historical lecture programmes (Swan Hellenic, Seabourn, Radisson, Fred Olsen, Orient, Crystal, Cunard). Scuba-diving lessons are offered on a host of ships, while Holland America have even an education experience in their 'University at Sea' programme and Crystal also offer a Computer University@Sea course.

Having set all that on the credit side, Myth Number Two now rears its ugly head: I Won't Be Able To Relax If I'm Surrounded By The Hectic Hordes!

Okay, so relax. There are few better places to feel really at peace with the world than sitting on deck with no sight of land. The new build of cruise ship features huge expanses of open deck space with ample opportunity to find a quiet corner to read a book or just soak up some rays. Don't get the idea, either, you are likely to be rail-roaded into joining in any of the deck sports or activities against your will – there is never any pressure to take part and there are no Redcoats at sea to make sure you have fun whether you like it or not (although on some of the more high-density, fun-orientated ships – notably the American Carnival Line vessels – it is sometimes hard to relax in the presence of so many dedicated, non-stop party-goers). Equally, if the big-ship style doesn't take your fancy, there are a number of smaller, more exclusive vessels which are geared totally towards a more refined, laid-back approach, offering fewer facilities but more chance to unwind in a sophisticated environment.

TRAVEL TIP

It is well worth taking the time to do your homework and find the cruise line that suits you best. Do you want lots of facilities or relatively few? Are you looking for older, more reserved fellow passengers or young and lively? Even the ship's nationality makes a difference, whether it's British, American or European.

GO WITH THE FLOW

Arguments of feeling confined on the modern cruise ship are similarly wide of the mark. Admittedly, the average cabin is still smaller than a typical hotel room or holiday apartment, but you actually spend so little time in it, it is more a question of the provision of public space around the ship and the way passenger flow is designed to prevent large numbers building up where they are not wanted. The latter has become a real art form, and you can be sure the newest ships will all have sophisticated design factors which prevent their 2,000-plus passengers arriving at the same place at the same time (this is notable aboard the new mega-liners like Princess's *Grand* class and Royal Caribbean's *Voyager* series), where the huge range of lounges and other facilities ensure the majority hardly ever meet up at one time). Chapter Five, The Cruise Lines and Their Ships, deals with these matters more specifically, looking at the Passenger/Space Ratio. This is a rather arbitrary figure that provides a sliding scale helping to separate the good from the not-so-generous in on-board space terms. Basically, you divide a ship's gross registered tonnage by its maximum number of passengers and get a figure between 12 and 60. The nearer 60 you get, the better off you should be for space throughout the ship (although this doesn't take into account if a ship is only half-full or if its passenger flow is poor).

The size of the ship, therefore, is not the paramount concern, it is the number of passengers it carries that defines the Space Ratio. For instance, Crystal Cruises' up-market 50,000-ton ship *Crystal Symphony* can carry as many as 960 passengers and has a Space Ratio figure of 52, while Cunard's *QE2* is much bigger at 70,327 tons but has a Space Ratio figure of 40.1 because she carries as many as 1,750. Similarly, Airtours flagship *Sunbird* is smaller at 37,584 tons but carries up to 1,432 customers, giving her a Space Ratio figure of only 26.2.

TRAVEL TIP

Gross registered tonnage isn't actually a measurement of a ship's weight, but rather of the amount of enclosed space within a ship's hull and superstructure. One gross registered ton = 100 cubic feet of space. Fascinating, huh?

Still on the subject of relaxation, this is also, remember, a relatively hassle-free zone in terms of all your 'domestic' arrangements: your meals are laid on, transport is taken care of, there is rarely a rush to do anything and there is nearly always a choice. So, if it is relaxation you are after rather than an all-action holiday, cruising is still definitely for you.

TRAVEL TIP

Be warned, however: the one area where all the large cruise liners fall down – and even some of the higher-density smaller ships – is when it comes to one-off activities. Embarkation and disembarkation are traditional bugbears of the mega-ships as queues are common, and you can also have lengthy waits at the Shore Excursion Desk or Purser's Office.

Myth Number Three is rather more basic and simply insists: I Can't Go Cruising, I'll Get Seasick.

There are three main reasons why this is not the case. One: ships are getting increasingly larger in size, and that immediately makes for more stable sailing. Two: all passenger ships are equipped with stabilisers which take the edge off rough seas. And Three: there are several ready remedies to seasickness which will be available on any ship (or which you can easily take with you). Dramamine is the most commonly-taken motion-sickness tablet, while the use of pressure bands worn on the wrists (called either Sea Bands or Aquastraps) is also quite widespread and comforting. Both are excellent protection against all but hurricane-force weather, and, in extreme cases, the ship's medical officer will be able to offer you a Dramamine injection that goes to work even faster.

Quite often, the best cure for that slight nauseous feeling, which is simply your inner ear adjusting to the unusual motion of the ship, is just to get out on deck, put your face in the breeze and stare off to the horizon. Stroll the promenade deck to let your body get used to the new motion (it is called getting your sea-legs) and you will find the fresh air works wonders.

TRAVEL TIP

Don't be tempted to try to settle a slightly sea-upset stomach with a big meal. Eat a little, but stick to plainer foods. I have particularly vivid memories of being seduced by the aroma of a tempting Goan fish curry on one P&O cruise, only for my stomach to tell me it wasn't such a good idea an hour later!

The bottom line is seasickness is primarily a psychological worry, and it is really a thoroughly unnecessary concern for the majority, especially when you remember the accuracy of modern weather forecasting allows ships to steer clear of any really nasty weather. And, to be honest, there are so few areas of cruising's mass market that stray out of calm waters, seasickness is just not a major issue in shipboard life these days. It may help to remember that according to the statisticians, it affects barely three per cent of all passengers on any cruise. The chances are you are more likely to be treated for sunburn than seasickness – it is amazing how many people think they can sit out in the Caribbean sun for a few hours without using a high-factor sun cream, especially when they are in and out of the pool.

TRAVEL TIP

The one exception to the rule, and an unpredictable one at that, is the Caribbean during hurricane season, which lasts from June to October. A few notable storms have hit the headlines in recent years, but it is only because they affect the cruise industry so rarely that they make headlines.

If, after all my cajoling words, seasickness remains an issue, you should consider cruising aboard one of the classic, older vessels which offer a rock-steady ride (they have deeper drafts and are designed for the open seas), like NCL's *Norway* or *QE2,* or the radically different, twin-hulled *Radisson Diamond* (one of the most stable craft ever built), and then opt for an area which doesn't stray into 'real' seas that much. The typical Alaskan Inside Passage cruise rarely encounters anything other than millpond waters, the eastern Mediterranean in summer offers dead-calm sailing and the Caribbean in spring and early summer is similarly docile. Finally, if you select a cabin which is centrally situated and on one of the lower passenger decks, this reduces what little movement there is likely to be and should guarantee a worry-free voyage.

Myth Number Four has already been touched on in the opening chapter, but I might as well beat it to death here because some people still claim: Cruising Is Too Expensive.

It may well seem at first glance your average cruise is likely to set you back as much as a week's wages for a Premiership footballer (okay, that may be a touch extreme – no one spends *that* much on a cruise), but the main mistake people make in comparing a cruise to a land-based holiday is in looking at the price only as a starting point and imagining there will be much more to pay. However, once you realise what is included in the cruise package compared with an equivalent land-based option, you soon realise why there is such an apparent price difference to start with.

The simple truth is cruising represents much better value for money than most typical packages because you pay the vast majority of the cost straight away and there are no real hidden extras once you are on board. On your usual land option, you can easily end up doubling the starting price by the time you add on your meals, entertainment, taxis, etc. And that's before you take into account the extras a cruise provides in the form of organised children's facilities, in-between meals and the convenience of everything being under one roof. The only areas where you start to push up the cruise cost are in gratuities (which are added in many – but by no means all – cruises, and which can tag on £25-£40 per person per week), very occasionally in the sneaky add-on of port taxes (you have had to look in the small print for these in the past, but there has been such an outcry about the inequity and inequalities of this largely unquantifiable extra that most lines now include them as well), your on-board drinks and any shore excursions you may take. The latter two, of course, are entirely up to you, and it is perfectly possible to keep those expenditures down to a minimum.

You will also find the quality of ship-board life, whether it be in the facilities, food or service, of a higher standard than the same type of holiday on land. In many cases, you would need to spend considerably more on a brochure package to the more expensive parts of the Mediterranean or the Caribbean than you would pay for the cruise equivalent. Consider the example drawn up below for two comparable Caribbean products using Norwegian Cruise Line as a typical ship option.

HOTEL v CRUISE

	Long-haul Tour Operator	Norwegian Cruise Line
Hotel/Ship:	Rex St Lucian	*Norwegian Sky*
Resort:	St Lucia	Eastern Caribbean: Miami-St Thomas (US Virgin Islands)-San Juan (Puerto Rico)-Bahamas (NCL's private island)-Miami
Meal basis:	Accommodation only; choice of 2 restaurants in resort	Full board – up to seven meals a day; choice of seven restaurants
Taxes	£9 (departure tax)	None
Duration:	Seven nights	Eight nights
Entertainment:	Local entertainment	Every night, including Broadway shows, live music, comedians, cabaret, casino and disco
Activities:	Water sports, sightseeing, tennis, swimming pool, jacuzzis, shopping plaza	Dive-In snorkelling programme, fitness programme, golf clinics, deck sports, dance classes, arts and crafts workshops, kids' clubs for 3-17s, backgammon, bridge, fashion shows, art auctions, quizzes, films, beauty salon, sports talks, shore excursions, shopping, etc.
Departing:	March 2001	March 2001
Adult price:	£869	£1,042 (with 25% early booking discount)

Although the cruise option starts slightly more expensive, it is easy to see where your expenses would mount up on the land-based example. Eating out is not usually a cheap option in St Lucia, and then you would have extras like taxi or car hire, night club entrance fees and any kids' facilities or child-minding services. Start adding on the cost of a few drinks in these more up-market Caribbean resorts and your initial outlay can easily more than double, while your cruise ship, on the other hand, will generally charge usual bar prices for your drinks. Your only other outlay in the ship-board version is then how many organised shore excursions you take. And, in the Caribbean especially, there are few really unmissable excursions which will demand your money.

TRAVEL TIP

One of the biggest rip-offs in the cruise world is that of shore excursions which simply aren't worth the money. The best rule of thumb here is to consider only those options which you couldn't do on your own, e.g. submarine rides in Grand Cayman, and NOT a half-day tour of Nassau in the Bahamas (which you can easily walk around).

All the major cruise lines are currently desperate to ram home this message of price comparability and value for money, and the last couple of years have seen a surge in discounting, which is bad news for the industry but great news for the consumer in the short term. With newer and bigger ships being added all the time, capacity is still easily out-stripping demand in the mass market (mainly in the Caribbean and, to a lesser extent, the Mediterranean), and many operators have been forced to freeze or even lower their starting prices. This means there has never been a better time to take advantage of the numerous deals on offer by the likes of P&O, NCL, Costa, Festival, Airtours, Thomson and others. Airtours also made the whole business much more price-conscious when they entered the market in 1995 offering a seven-day cruise with a lead-in price (i.e. their lowest brochure price) of just £399. Even in early 2001, that temping lead-in had increased to just £499.

TRAVEL TIP

Don't expect to be able to pick up a cheap cruise anywhere in the world. Alaska and the Far East manage to sell well without much discounting, but real bargains can often be found in the Caribbean, especially if you can go out of the main holiday seasons.

You need only look at the weekend travel sections or flick through the pages of Teletext to see just how widespread cruise holiday discounting has become, and it is likely to last for another year or two yet as the big lines continue to slug out their price wars and some of the smaller ones inevitably sink out of sight. In the short term, therefore, it is a real bonus for anyone looking for a bargain. In addition, virtually every line offers early-booking discounts and repeat-passenger special offers which often come on TOP of a discount you might get at one of the specialist cruise consultants that sell cruises (see Chapter Four).

HAPPY FAMILIES

The subject of children on holiday is another area where you can add to the value of a cruise, at the same time as removing some of the inevitable worry of keeping kids happy for the duration. Here's a question for all dads: how many times do you put your hand in your pocket for ice creams, sweets and other snacks for your brood? Just a few, I bet. Well, with so many ships now including complimentary ice cream bars and hot-dog or hamburger grills *as well as* the normal meal-times, you can blissfully wave goodbye to those pocket-tugging cries of 'Dad, can I have …?'. Add to this the amazing programme of organised children's activities on nearly all the main-stream cruise products (there are exceptions, but I'll go into those later), and you can quickly see how cruising represents outstanding value for the family market.

This leads on to the issue of general safety, and is just another area where cruising scores heavily over its rivals. There are few more secure environments than a modern cruise ship in the normal course of events, and, when you are travelling around potentially hazardous or troubled parts of the world (some areas of the Caribbean, like Jamaica, plus the Far East and South America spring to mind), the reliable sanctuary of your ship becomes that much more valuable to your peace of mind. A laughable minor myth believed by the totally uninitiated says something like: 'My kids will fall overboard or find some other way of hurting themselves.' The reality, of course, is that, unless your children are total

TRAVEL TIP

As the family market becomes increasingly sought-after, so the cruise lines pay more and more attention to children's facilities and supervision. Disney Cruise Line and P&O issue pagers to parents checking their offspring into the kids' clubs, as well as maintaining the highest ratio of counsellors to children at sea, while both Carnival and Princess offer an ever more high-tech range of fully-supervised activities. P&O's night nurseries are another feature to provide mums and dads with peace of mind, as well as evening freedom.

maniacs or you abandon all measure of parental control, your nearest and dearest are not likely to take a swallow-dive off the nearest handrail. The big family-orientated ships all employ full-time children's counsellors (not to mention nurses and child-minders) to keep a watchful eye on the youngsters in their charge as well as master-minding a full programme of events and activities to keep them occupied practically all day if you wish. Chalk up another success to the attraction of cruising. As an additional note on safety, all modern ships are specifically designed with children's safety in mind.

I recently took a P&O cruise on *Aurora* en famille (children aged two and four) and came away hugely impressed by the level of facilities, the range of daytime activities, the care of the children's centre staff and the real bonus of the night nursery for the under-5s. The children's teas were another big hit for all concerned, as were the pools and jacuzzis. In fact, the hardest part was getting them to come *out* of the kids' clubs for meals and *off* the ship at the end of the voyage!

The bottom line is cruising drastically reduces the 'hassle factor' for family holidays. Obviously, on smaller ships facilities are more limited, so you should always check for the availability of kids' clubs (some run only in school holidays) and the age ranges, and the provisions for babysitting – some are on a first-come, first-served basis and therefore are not always guaranteed. Once again, P&O and Disney score high marks all round.

It should also be noted the international cruising industry has some of the strictest safety criteria to which it must adhere. Central to seagoing safety issues is the United Nations body, the International Maritime Organisation, which monitors a number of regulations, foremost among which is the SOLAS (Safety of Life at Sea) convention. Any ship not conforming to these criteria is simply not allowed to sail, and this has meant many of the lines with 'veteran' ships have been looking closely at their viability. It also goes without saying the industry cannot afford the bad publicity poor safety standards would bring. There has not been a single reported death on a cruise ship due to a marine incident in the last 14 years, enhancing cruising's reputation as one of the safest modes of transport. Even the unfortunate collision of the *Norwegian Dream* with a container ship in the Channel in August 1999 served to underline the integrity of their emergency procedures and the structural safety of the vessel in such an extreme situation. While the ship was badly damaged, there were no serious injuries on board.

This message was underlined at a Seatrade Cruise Shipping Convention in Miami where the president of Princess Cruises pointed out: 'A cruise ship is intrinsically a very safe place with a substantially reduced threat of personal violence or loss of personal property. The ship is the maritime equivalent of a "gated community", third parties may not access the ship without authority, all members of the community (the crew) are known to each other and have been interviewed and recruited by the owner, a perpetrator of a crime has nowhere to hide and there is a disciplinary presence on the ship trained to supervise the security of the ship, its passengers and crew. A cruise ship is one of the most secure ways to visit the less developed countries of the world. There is limited exposure to airport or hotel crime, and shore excursions are undertaken in a controlled and supervised environment.' Enough said.

> The discussion on personal safety and comfort leads neatly on to Myth Number Five, another familiar one, which states: **Cruising Is For The Blue Rinse Brigade.**

Now, it certainly isn't my aim to be in any way ageist, but there is little doubt the world of the cruise liner was once the primary preserve of those folks who are slightly more advanced in years. Not any more. As you will surely have recognised by the emphasis on the family market, cruising is now a very different kettle of piscine creatures. The latest Passenger Shipping Association figures for the cruise market as a whole reveal the average age for passengers to the Caribbean is down to just 42 and, on some of the three- and four-day fun cruises, it can average 28. Across the whole scene, the average age of British passengers has dropped from 60-plus to under 55 in just six years. There are, of course, variations in the overall picture and so you will find many more families at sea during the school holidays than at other times, but the likes of P&O have set their stall out firmly to attract the family market and are doing an impressive job of delivering the right product.

Naturally, if there are cruise lines offering great deals for the family market, there are equally others serving different areas just as successfully, which is one of the reasons why studying the world of cruising is so fascinating and rewarding. The QE2, for example, remains a bastion of the bygone age of class-conscious cruising in the most stately of surroundings; the Holland America line caters in only a limited manner for children (on their Caribbean and Alaska sailings during school holidays, although all their cruises are slowly becoming more youth-friendly) and also retain the elegance of yesteryear. The Brit-popular Fred Olsen Line still averages between 50 and 60 years of age in its passenger profile and also handles children in only a limited fashion (although they are now encouraging more families); Saga, the over-50s tour operator, has its own cruise ship; Swan Hellenic, with its smart purpose-designed vessel *Minerva,* outwardly discourages young children on its voyages, which offer a rich cultural and heritage-orientated programme around the Mediterranean, Baltic and Red Seas and into the Far East; and P&O, for all the fact they cater so well for kids, still draw their passengers from the full age spectrum (and the average age definitely goes up out of season).

TRAVEL TIP

P&O are possibly the best example of across-the-board social and age mixing, catering superbly for the full range of tastes, from classical concerts to teen discos, and theatre to bingo.

In addition to these general differences between the lines, there also tends to be a different age profile according to the length of the voyage. Hence, a seven-day cruise may attract a good number of families while a ten- or 14-day cruise would see the number of youngsters aboard reduced, quite drastically in some cases. And, when it comes to the major line voyages, the round-the-world trips which a few companies specialise in, you see an even greater preponderance of older folk aboard for the obvious reason it is usually only the retired or very wealthy who can afford to spend a month or three at sea!

The table on the following pages, compiled by the Passenger Shipping Association, serves to highlight these issues for the biggest cruise lines who deal in the British market.

Of course, the age profile is intended only as a general guide, especially as it is one of the areas of biggest change in the cruise world as more and more people are sold on its appeal. There are also variations according to season of the year and even the location of the cruise (Alaska, for example, tends to attract an older customer than the Caribbean, while the Baltic Sea passenger is, on average, older than the Mediterranean variety), but it does serve to give an indication of the huge variation on offer, and about which there will be much more detail in Chapter Five. Once again, cruising can truly be said to offer something for everyone.

> **Everyone, that is, except those who still insist on Myth Number Six: Cruising Is Much Too Formal For My Holiday Taste.**

This is possibly the most-heard objection among the younger set, who envisage nights of black-tie dinners, ballroom dancing and bridge foursomes. And yes, it is perfectly possible to find a cruise where formality of this type is still the order of the day, but the simple fact about the mass market is it has moved miles away from its old image. Once again, the cruise companies themselves have been slow to deliver this message, but it is nonetheless true for all that. There is also another essential difference between the traditional British and American passengers here. As a general rule of thumb, Brits are keener to dust off their DJs and posh frocks for the occasional formal evenings, while our transatlantic cousins prefer a more relaxed style.

TRAVEL TIP

Another easy way to gauge the level of formality on any given cruise is simply to weigh up the length of the cruise and the number of days at sea. More days at sea = greater formality, with cruises in excess of seven days becoming distinctly more formal than their shorter version options.

Of course, there are still people who are attracted to cruising just because it gives them a chance to dress up and show off, and the industry is just as happy to cater for them as well. On most seven-day cruises you will therefore find a pleasant mix of the formal and informal (and also what the cruise industry likes to call 'casual'). You will probably find that two nights of a seven-night cruise are designated Formal, three or four are termed Casual (usually the days in port) and the other one or two are Informal. For practical purposes this means: Formal, a dinner jacket,

CRUISE LINE PROFILES

Cruise Line	Typical Age Profile	Nationality
Airtours	Across the board	British
Carnival	20–50	American
Celebrity	Across the board	American/European
Costa	30–60	American/Italian
Crystal	Couples/singles 40–60-plus	American
Cunard	Couples/singles 30–60-plus	European/American
Disney	Familes/Couples 30–50	American
Festival	Across the board	European/British
First Choice	Across the board	British
Holland America	40–60	American
NCL	Couples/singles 30–60	American

Reduced Rate for Kids Sharing with Parents?	Children's Facilities
Yes (up to 15)	Kids' clubs for 3–6s and 7–12s on all sailings; (organised teen activities in holiday periods)
Children pay 3rd and 4th occupancy rate	Kids' clubs for 2–5s, 6–8s, 9–12s and 13–15s; children's playroom, teen club disco; group babysitting for under 12s
Yes (up to 11)	Programmes for 3–17s; children's playroom; teen club on newest ships; group and individual babysitting (c. $6/hour)
Yes (up to 11)	Programmes for 3–6s, 7–12s and 13–17s in Caribbean and peak-season Med sailings; children's playroom; teen centre on *Classica*, *Victoria* and *Atlantica*; group babysitting available
Yes (up to 11)	Programmes and counsellors on sailings with 10 or more children; limited facilities
Children pay 3rd and 4th occupancy rate	Programmes and facilities on QE2 and *Caronia* with 10 or more children
Yes (up to 11)	Kids' clubs for 3–4s, 5–7s, 8–10s and 11–12s; extensive facilities; teen lounge; night nursery and group babysitting available
Yes (up to 17)	Programmes in high season; children's facilities on all ships; teen club on *Mistral* and European *Vision*
Yes, two children (up to 12)	Kids' programmes for 3–6s, 7–11s and 12–15s
Yes (2–8)	HAL programme of kids' clubs for 5–8s, 9–12s and 13–17s; children's menus and Alaska shore excursions; group babysitting available
Yes (up to 11)	Kids' clubs for 3–5s, 6–8s, 9–12s and 13–17s; children's playrooms; group and individual babysitting available (c. $4/hour)

Cruise Line	Typical Age Profile	Nationality
Fred Olsen	Average 50–60	British
Orient	40–60-plus	British/American
P&O	Across the board	British
Princess	Familes/couples 40–50-plus	American/British
Radisson Seven Seas	Couples and singles, 40 plus	American
Royal Caribbean	Across the board	American
Saga	50-plus only	British
Seabourn	Couples 40–60-plus	American
Silversea	Couples 40–60-plus	American/European
Swan Hellenic	Couples 30–60-plus	British
Thomson	Across the board	British
Windstar	Couples, 30-plus	American

Reduced Rate for Kids Sharing with Parents?	Children's Facilities
Yes (up to 16)	Programmes on busy sailings; children's playroom on *Black Watch*
Children pay 3rd and 4th occupancy rate	Not generally suitable for children
Yes (up to 17)	Kids' clubs for 2–5s, 6–9s, 10–13s and 14–17s; playrooms (not *Victoria*); teen disco; night nursery (for 5 and under); and baby-listening; daily children's teas; no children accepted on *Arcadia* from May 2002
Yes (up to 11)	Kids' clubs and facilities for 2–12s and 13–17s on all but *Royal* and *Pacific*; extensive activities on *Sun, Dawn, Sea, Ocean, Grand* and *Golden*; Group babysitting available ($4/hour)
Not applicable	Not suitable for children
Yes (up to 11)	Kids' clubs for 3–5s, 6–8s, 9–12s and 13–17s; children's playroom babysitting available ($4/hour)
Not applicable	No children allowed
Yes (25 per cent of adult)	Chilren tolerated rather than welcomed
Yes (varying percentage)	Children tolerated rather than welcomed
50 per cent for under-25s	Not suitable for children
Yes (up to 12)	Kids' clubs (2–3 hours per day) for 3–7s and 8–12s; teens' area on *Topaz*
No	Not suitable for children

tuxedo or business suit for men, and cocktail or evening dress for the women; Informal usually means jacket and tie for the men (although I often get away with just a smart shirt and trousers – I'm a bit of a rebel!) and most things for women (the Americans are keen on highlighting 'pant suits' for women on Informal nights, for some reason); Casual means just about anything goes (except T-shirts and shorts in the dining room). I find the majority of people, even if they start off a bit reluctant, do actually enjoy wearing their glad rags occasionally, and the odd formal evening does add a really splendid appearance to the ship-board scene. Equally, you will not be keel-hauled for wearing the wrong attire on the wrong night or if you are really not comfortable being fully suited up. The formal element is also less noticeable in the mass-market American cruise world (on lines such as Carnival, NCL and even Disney), as well as being more low-profile on Thomson, Airtours and Fred Olsen than P&O and Cunard. A welcome new addition is that of themed or even fancy dress evenings. These can vary from obvious eras like the Fifties and Rock 'n' Roll to more modern fads such as Country and Western and more geographical themes like the Caribbean (where the brightest, most flowery clothes suddenly become chic). P&O typically have a Black and White evening while the Italian line Costa make a feature of their final evening Toga Parties.

CRUISING FOR NEWCOMERS

In addition to cutting down on the formality in a bid to attract the first-time cruiser, there are a few lines which also go out of their way to set up a cruise experience for beginners. These generally go under the heading of Newcomers' Cruises and can feature such pertinent extras as a special host to welcome first-timers and help them to settle in; a Newcomers' cocktail party to meet all your fellow rookies and ask any urgent questions (like, 'What time is the midnight buffet?' Don't laugh, it happens!); a bottle of Welcome Aboard champagne waiting in your cabin; a free shore excursion to get you into the swing of things; and sometimes a certain amount of free on-board credit (say, $50 per person) to encourage you to get involved with things like the beauty salon or health treatments. Princess Cruises are one of the most switched-on lines for newcomers, dedicating a number of attractive cruises to first-timers with all of the extra benefits mentioned above, while several QE2 sailings offer free first-class rail travel to Southampton or free car parking at the port, a first-timers' cocktail party, a newcomers' courier, free shore excursion and £100 of on-board credit per cabin. It is also now a feature of some P&O, Saga and Fred Olsen cruises.

Right, now we have established the ground-rules for enjoying your cruise holiday, let's see what else we can tempt you with …

CHAPTER THREE

THE INDEFINABLE EXTRAS

So, we should by now have established cruising as something that is both leisurely and up-tempo; that is highly safety-conscious and no longer a seasickness risk; that suits all budgets and all social types; that is for children as much as the retired; that now cuts down on formality and raises the entertainment stakes; and that offers a really exciting alternative to land-based holidays. What more can it produce to satisfy our ideals of the perfect holiday?

FROM ALASKA TO ZANZIBAR

Well, how about the chance to visit some of the most remote and picturesque places on earth, the possibility of romance, the unquestionable air of mystique and the opportunity to eat yourself silly?

The fact cruising has become so popular so quickly has inevitably led to the demand for more alternative itineraries and ports of call, and it is perfectly possible these days to sail just about anywhere in the comfort of your mobile home, from Alaska to Antarctica, Japan to the Galapagos Islands, Russia to Zanzibar, and nearly all points in between. Chapter Six will deal more fully with the various cruise areas of the world, but suffice it to say here there is a mouth-watering choice, and there is an increasing demand to explore the more out-of-the-way places. The Far East, in particular, is seen as an area of up-and-coming cruise potential, while Alaska has experienced an incredible boom since the start of the 1990s and the Red Sea and Arabian Gulf are just beginning to be explored by some of the main Mediterranean operators as an alternative for the winter months.

In fact, the *where* of this business should be among your first questions. In some respects, it is more important to have an idea of where you would like to go before you consider which cruise line is the right one for you. The right choice of region and itinerary can easily be three-quarters of the way to a memorable voyage.

There is also a growing demand for adventure cruises – voyages that avoid the normal routes and levels of comfort and strike out to the more far-flung outposts of the world. Typically, there are even different types of adventure options, from the 'soft' version of cruise lines like Orient, who operate the 22,000-ton *Marco Polo* in a fair degree of luxury to areas like

Antarctica, to the real basic, close-up experience of purpose-built exploration vessels such as the *Kapitan Dranitsyn,* operated by Quark Expeditions. Also, for those inclined to an even earlier age of cruising, there are a number of sailing vessels (Windstar and Star Clippers) where you can participate in the raising and lowering of the rigging or just sit back and watch, if you want, and generally enjoy a more laid-back, leisurely approach to life at sea. These offer an outstandingly different cruise experience for the more discerning traveller and a much less structured atmosphere.

THOSE WEDDING BELLS

The subject of the romance of sea travel is also close to my heart, in both general and specific terms, and I can heartily vouch for the extra appeal which this aspect of cruising can afford to both singles and couples alike. Anyone familiar with the long-running but cringe-inducing American TV series The Love Boat (which actually did a major promotional job for Princess Cruises) may find this hard to believe, but there is a genuine romantic feel to many aspects of modern cruising. To start with, it is one of the most popular and natural choices for honeymooners, and most of the cruise lines offer some fantastic extras for newly-weds, from champagne, flowers and cake to more practical items like cabin up-grades, special portrait photographs and on-board credit. There will usually be a special get-together for all the honeymoon couples aboard (upwards of 100 couples on some Caribbean cruises is not uncommon), and the staff often go out of their way to make you both feel extra-special at the start of your married life.

Equally, both established couples and mums and dads (with the kids safe in the hands of the ship's babysitters for the evening) can enjoy each other's company so much more just watching the sunset on deck, going for a late-night moonlit stroll or dancing the night away as they used to do in their courting days. It is also a distinctly civilised and tranquil setting in which to catch up on how much you really appreciate your partner. So much so, in fact, there is a successful trade in anniversary packages and even the renewal of wedding vows at sea. Sadly, the ship's captain can no longer perform the marriage ceremony itself, either in port or at sea, but several cruise lines (notably Princess, Carnival, Celebrity, NCL and Royal Caribbean) offer the chance of a wedding on board at the departure port before setting sail on honeymoon (with some of the wedding guests in many cases).

TRAVEL TIP

Honeymooners take note. When you book that dream wedding holiday, make *sure* with your travel agent the cabin you choose has a double bed – some still have twin beds that do *not* convert into doubles!

The cruise company can coordinate the whole event for you, down to the provision of a cake, and I defy anyone to conjure up anything more romantic than sailing off into the sunset on your first wedded night together ...

All this may sound as if it precludes singles from getting the full benefit of their cruise, but that is most definitely not the case. Cruising is a genuinely easy and enjoyable way to make new friends, and it is certainly not unknown for people to meet that one special person in the wonderfully heady, almost tailor-made atmosphere of ship-board life. Many lines hold singles' parties to help break the ice, but the general run of events is usually sufficient to throw people together to find out if they enjoy each other's company.

TRAVEL TIP

Quite often, it is the daytime events like organised sports and other social activities that can be as instrumental in sparking romance as the evening events. Singles are just as likely to hang out in the gym as in the bar.

Several lines (notably Cunard, Crystal, Fred Olsen and Orient) also offer a Gentleman Host programme for unaccompanied women, providing company at meals, dances and other social occasions.

Once again, it all helps to add up to the general mystique of cruising that is ultimately hard to explain in plain language, but which, even in this age of the high-tech mega-liners, still adds an air of magic to the whole experience that is just impossible to reproduce on land.

TRAVEL TIP

The cruise world caters extremely well for single women travelling alone, both in terms of providing social activities and a genuine measure of security and safety that is hard to match on land.

DINNER IS SERVED

Of course, an additional item that goes hand in hand with romance (well, sort of), is food. I am sure the majority of us enjoy the chance to dine out, and it is now a well-established legend of life at sea that mealtimes are an essential part of the experience – up to seven times a day if you have the capacity. Obviously, the standard does vary from line to line (even if every brochure does try to make out every meal is a five-star gourmet experience), but there isn't a ship afloat that doesn't make a feature of every meal, and, in some cases, they can be hugely extravagant. Scarcely an hour goes by at sea without the chance to indulge yourself in some sort of gastronomic exercise or other, and the only difficulty can be in deciding whether to dine out on deck or in the dining room, to enjoy a late breakfast or early lunch, or to see if you can fit in afternoon tea as well as dinner. It is even possible in many instances to enjoy 24-hour room service (at no extra cost, of course, on the majority of lines) or, on the more up-market ships, to take advantage of waiter-service dining in your own cabin. If your cabin also has its own balcony, you are back into serious romantic territory once more, with all the possibilities for moonlit dining *al fresco*.

TRAVEL TIP

Beware. Your cruise can really take its toll – on your waistline. Typically, the average passenger puts on a pound a day in weight, and a quick turn round the Promenade deck will *not* be enough to stave off the danger of an expanding waistline. This is where those well-equipped gyms can come in handy.

CHECKING YOUR CRUISE ESSENTIALS

In all seriousness, however, food is just one of the five essential principal elements of any cruise, all of which you need to study fairly closely to make sure you find the right cruise for YOU. All of the brochures proudly claim to have Luxury This, or Five-star That, but the reality is there are only a handful of lines who can truly claim to be at the Ultra-Deluxe end of the market. And this will be reflected in these key areas of **Facilities** (essentially the ship's hardware), **Service** (or the software, the ship's crew), **Entertainment** (the mix of daytime activities and evening shows), **Food** (as outlined above) and the **Ports of Call** (their number, variety and the choice of shore excursions).

You will probably by now be aware of the vast differences that exist in the make-up of the 140-plus cruise ships operating in the British market. They can be anywhere from 3,000 tons (more of an overgrown yacht, really) right up to the 142,000 tons of *Voyager* or *Explorer of the Seas;* they can be anything up to 45 years old or the latest thing out of the ship-building yards of Europe; they can be high-density (in the mass market) or they can be immensely personal (with a high Space Ratio figure on the true Ultra-Deluxe vessels); and they can offer a wealth of user-friendly facilities that put you more in mind of a small town than of a mere ship.

I have already listed the standard array of on-board **Facilities** which you can expect from the modern cruise ship, but it also makes sense at this point to highlight some of the current developments in ship-building that are shaping the way forward and offering a continually changing emphasis of features.

The obvious main development is to build bigger and ever more impressively. The race to the first 100,000-ton monster was won by Carnival with the launch of their *Carnival Destiny* in October 1996, but Princess promptly topped that in 1998. And Royal Caribbean have now gone further still with the amazing *Voyager* series. Also, no new cruise ship is now complete without at least one multi-storey **atrium lobby** down the centre of the vessel, complete with glass-sided lifts, specially commissioned artwork and cascading waterfalls. It almost seems in some cases as if ship designers are trying to compete more with the grand land-based hotel resorts than with their marine predecessors in terms of the amount of glittering, large-scale architecture they can incorporate in the newest examples of their work. The *Sun, Dawn, Ocean* and *Sea Princess* possess the most breathtaking four-storey central atrium, full of gleaming marble, bright chrome and bronze railings and ceilings, panoramic lifts, a stained-glass skylight and a magnificent sweeping, circular staircase. Costa's 75,000-ton *CostaVictoria* includes a novel four-storey forward observation area that adds another dimension, while Royal Caribbean's sextet of *Legend, Splendour, Rhapsody, Enchantment, Grandeur* and *Vision of the Seas* all feature a seven-storey atrium rising up to the ships' trademark Viking Crown Lounge at the very top of each vessel. *Carnival Destiny, Victory* and *Triumph* boast a truly cavernous central atrium full of the line's characteristic bold neon designs.

One of the most recent innovations which has quickly been copied by others is *Oriana*'s full-scale, West End-quality theatre, complete with revolving stage and full orchestra pit. Its detail includes excellent all-round sight-lines and individual air-conditioning on all the seats. Celebrity, Royal Caribbean and Carnival have all refined this theatre-at-sea concept to the point where the venues are works of art in themselves.

Celebrity have also pioneered the development of dramatic new sound systems for their ships, in partnership with the Japanese electronics firm Sony, and it is this willingness to embrace new technology which is now characterising a lot of ship design. Notably, Celebrity (and, inevitably, others) have incorporated clever new facilities with their in-cabin TVs that allow you to order room service or duty-free items on screen, peruse the day's menus and even read about and book shore excursions. Already, there are virtual-reality exercise bikes aboard several of these new vessels, along with state-of-the-art golf simulators, and the advent of *Grand Princess* added virtual-reality adventure rides, a 'film' studio that puts YOU in the picture and a swimming pool with its own current for serious swimmers. NCL's *Norwegian Sky* in 2000 pioneered worldwide web access at sea, with the first ocean-going Internet Café at sea, and the other major lines all quickly followed suit with elaborate computer facilities for passengers to be able to access their e-mail and go cyber-surfing. All cabins now come complete with their own Internet access socket.

Alongside these twenty-first-century innovations, the enhancement of existing facilities is rather more mundane but nonetheless important for all that. **Health and beauty facilities** of the highest standard are now demanded on all ships as a matter of course as passengers become increasingly body-conscious (as a result, no doubt, of those seven meals a day). They expect exercise equipment incorporating all the latest in aerobic design as well as an increasing range of treatments like massage, hydrotherapy, reflexology, aromatherapy and even mud treatments and acupuncture, on top of the more common features like saunas and steam rooms. The average health centre's beauty salon will also be able to offer the latest in hair care and other treatments like manicures and facials. Celebrity's AquaSpas are a veritable Aladdin's Cave of top-class treatments and worth seeking out in their own right. NCL and Silversea have even recruited Far East specialists Mandara Spa to take their on-board pampering a step further.

TRAVEL TIP

It is easy to get carried away with the enjoyable extras of massage and other beauty treatments, but remember they are *extras* on any cruise (although you shouldn't pay more for a cut or perm than you do at home).

As the average age of the cruise passenger comes down, so the demand for fitness facilities increases, and every ship now carries fully-trained gymnasium staff to supervise all these excellent facilities and to advise on and arrange comprehensive aerobic and other exercise programmes. These can be tailored to individual requirements in many cases (this could be the moment finally to knuckle down to that proper exercise routine you could never quite find time for), and there are usually programmes to analyse your aerobic capacity, fitness level and even body-fat content (for a small charge). For those happy just to do their own gym thing, there should be a full range of equipment like exercise bikes, rowing machines, stair-climbers and treadmills, plus the ever-popular multi-gyms and weights for weight training.

TRAVEL TIP

Newcomers to the cruise world never cease to be amazed at how quickly a ship's beauty salon fills its appointments book. The trick is to get in EARLY and usually to book a visit to coincide with one of the formal evenings – experienced cruisers have got this off to a fine art.

From comprehensive health facilities, the demand increasingly is also for **children's facilities**, and the main cruise lines have not been slow to incorporate features especially for the youngsters. P&O's *Aurora* is a wonderful example of this, with purpose-built rooms for 2–5s (Toybox), 6–9s (Jumping Jacks), 10–12s (Quarterdecks) and 13–17s (Decibels), plus video games, an outdoor play area and paddling pool. The aft deck area also becomes the exclusive preserve of the younger passenger on school holiday cruises, when up to 300 children on board is not unknown.

The incorporation of specialised areas like health and children's facilities is also being extended in more general terms just to provide an increasing number of options throughout the modern cruise ship. The early days of the super-liner were characterised by building along gargantuan lines when it came to public rooms. Nowadays, the tendency is towards providing an alternative rather than trying to be size-impressive, and you will find a greater variety of lounges and bars, many of which are designed to provide an intimacy that the early super-liners lacked.

With this tendency towards high-tech, it is easy to overlook the appeal of more simple facilities like traditional **deck games**. Even on the newest ships, there is still an element of these and it will be a sad day for cruising if ship designers decide to do away with them altogether. Happily, that is certainly not the case yet as recent vessels like *Aurora,* Princess's newest sextet, *Crystal Harmony* and *Symphony* and all of Celebrity's new-builds have continued to incorporate 'proper' deck sports. Indeed, the *Century* and Celebrity sisters *Galaxy* and *Mercury* all boast 62,000sq ft of open deck space to provide for table tennis, basketball, volleyball and jogging as well as just lazing in the sun. *Oriana* and *Aurora* both boast great cricket nets (I kid you not, and it is very popular), as well as short tennis, football and the usual array of traditional games like shuffleboard and quoits. And the likes of Crystal and Princess both incorporate good-sized paddle-tennis courts that provide an excellent social focus as well as a chance to show off your sporting prowess. Inevitably, technology and the designers' imagination have led to further variations on the games theme, with *Voyager* and *Explorer of the Seas* both sporting the first rock-climbing wall at sea (which Festival have since copied for *European Vision*) and in-line skating tracks. As I have already insisted, there is no way you will be bored on a cruise!

Of course, having extolled the virtues of cruising as one of the really great inclusive holidays, I have to say more on-board variety means more opportunities for the cruise lines to try to persuade you to part with some extra money. And it is this area of on-board spending where lines attempt to recoup some of the money they have lost in the discounting wars. Therefore, you can expect all ships, particularly the newer ones, to include a dazzling array of **shopping opportunities**, including duty free, to beguile you into running up your on-board credit. Again, Royal

The cashless society

All cruise ships are operated on a cashless basis to make the day-to-day running that much simpler (and remove the hassle of having to carry money on board). You are given your own on-board credit card or account as soon as you step aboard (usually in exchange for a swipe of your credit card at the Purser's Desk, although you can opt to pay by cash or cheque at the end of the cruise) and you then use this to sign for every purchase, whether it be in the bar, beauty salon or one of the shops. If you opt for the credit card method, you need only check the final itemised bill that is sent to your cabin on the last evening. If you have opted to pay by cash or cheque you will need to settle up in person at the Purser's Desk before you disembark – and, believe me, you won't be allowed off the ship unless you do!

Caribbean have taken this a step further on their biggest duo, with a fully-fledged shopping *mall* down the centre of both ships.

On the subject of losing money (well, I always do, anyway), the **casino** is now an absolutely fundamental requirement of all ships (except Disney's). The Americans in particular love to gamble because it is illegal in most of the USA, and you will frequently find this facility dedicated primarily to them. The casinos aboard Carnival ships in particular are massive affairs, and they are nearly always decorated in the best Las Vegas style with a major assault on the visual senses from flashing lights, neon signs, fruit machines (or 'slots' as the Americans call them) and other gaudy designs. A typical casino will offer roulette, poker, blackjack (or pontoon), standard fruit machines and machine poker and, on the American lines, a dice or craps table.

TRAVEL TIP

The casino can be a daunting place for newcomers to the world of gambling, but don't be afraid to watch. They are frequently much more friendly than land-based varieties and some hold classes in poker or blackjack playing. Holland America even have a themed poker cruise.

In total contrast (and not, this time, a popular feature of American ships) is the still widespread provision of a **library** at sea. Quite often these days it is accompanied by a video library on the more up-market ships. This is a feature that really does hark back to the days of cruising's traditional style, of long voyages when there was often little else to do than settle down with a good book. Happily for British cruise passengers it is a tradition still keenly maintained by the likes of P&O, Fred Olsen and Swan Hellenic. The library aboard the *Oriana* is one of the most tastefully elegant public rooms on the ship, but, be warned – the first day or two of any voyage sees the book equivalent of a horde of locusts descend with the end result that the library's shelves can be seriously depleted before some passengers have even discovered it. By the same token, the **card room** is still a common feature of even the newest ships and some can also be quite elegant. However, they may also have to double up as a conference or business centre.

Every ship will also have its own **photographic services**, with a decent range of film and other equipment to buy or rent, plus several ship's photographers whose job it is to circulate regularly and take a variety of snaps of you enjoying the cruise.

In a similar vein, all cruise ships carrying more than 36 passengers are required by maritime law to provide proper **medical facilities**, with at least one doctor of GP standard and a nurse. Typically, the newest vessels can boast better health care than some hospitals, with ships like *Oriana* having full surgical capability as well as more practical, common items like a pharmacy, X-ray machines and cardiac arrest units. Each medical centre will keep particular surgery hours, but the medical staff are on call

24 hours a day for any emergencies and cabin visits. Of course, medical treatment is neither free nor cheap, but provided you have proper travel insurance, you will be fully covered.

TRAVEL TIP

Another word of warning here. You may well want to collect the full set of ship-taken photographs ('This is us at embarkation', 'This is us at the Captain's cocktail party', 'This is us with a drink by the pool', etc.), but at up to £14 a time, they are *not* a cheap alternative to using your own camera. Also, a ship is an expensive place to buy film. Stock up before you sail.

The final key area in this discussion of shipboard facilities and their development is **cabins**, and it is an area which causes most confusion and concern for cruise first-timers. The first concept to understand with a ship's accommodation is it is not like a hotel room, i.e. large and uniform. You do not specify a particular room when you book a hotel, but that is what you usually do with a ship.

To start with, unlike most hotels, there are different categories of cabin, which is a product of the evolution of the cruise ship and something which only the most modern of the larger ships are trying to standardise. On the classic old cruise ship, the categories were decided by the amount of space in the cabin and on which deck it was situated (another throwback to the old days of class-orientated cruising when the more you paid, the higher the deck your accommodation was on).

This profusion of cabin choice gives rise to an unfortunate side effect which is perpetuated for some reason best known only to the cruise lines themselves, and this is that the average cruise brochure can often resemble something akin to a page of algebra when it comes to trying to select your accommodation. A bewildering array of types, sizes and formats makes for a daunting task for the uninitiated, and even the average travel agent can find it tough sorting out this complexity of choice. On older ships in particular, the configuration of the decks increases this confusion, and it is only the modern way of ship-building that has helped to simplify matters (although both the *Grand* and *Golden Princess* are a bit of a throwback – I mean, 36 cabin categories. Help!). Instead of being built from the hull up and filled out accordingly in one homogeneous build, the new cruise ship is constructed from prefabricated blocks, almost like a giant Meccano kit, which allows for units like cabins to be 'bolted on' in a standardised fashion, so most cabins conform to much fewer types.

Using *Oriana* as a prime example, here's how a typical deck plan of a modern cruise ship will look, showing how the accommodation decks are kept largely separate from the public areas and how the different cabin categories are shown from the highest deck down.

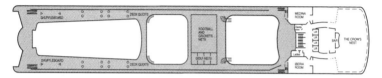

SUN DECK (Deck 13) Outdoor decks, deck sports, observation lounge

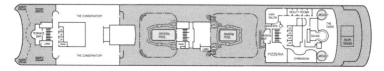

LIDO DECK (Deck 12) Outdoor decks, buffet dining, pools and health and fitness centres

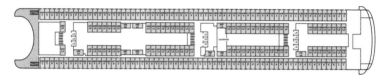

A DECK (Deck 11) Two-berth inside and outside cabins, 20 singles

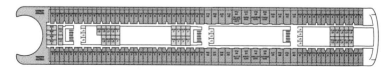

B DECK (Deck 10) Balconied staterooms, suites, a few inside singles and doubles

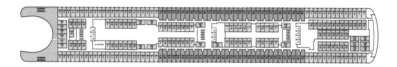

C DECK (Deck 9) Staterooms, inner and outer doubles, 42 singles

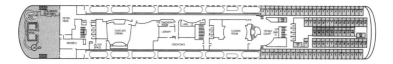

D DECK (Deck 8) Public rooms, children's facilities, one-, two- and four-berth cabins

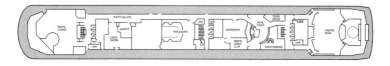

PROM DECK (Deck 7) Public rooms, including Theatre Royal and Harlequins nightclub

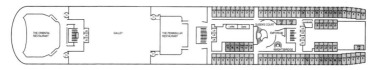

E DECK (Deck 6) Restaurants, one-, two- and four-berth cabins

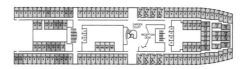

F DECK (Deck 5) Two-, three- and four-berth cabins, eight for disabled passengers

G DECK (Deck 4) Hospital and night nursery

≋ TRAVEL TIP ≋

Don't be fooled by the cruise lines who insist on calling cabins by the more grand title of Staterooms. There is rarely anything stately about them. It is just another case of brochure jargon.

As a general rule of thumb, your cabin will be notably *smaller* than a typical hotel room. The arrival of the super-liner in the late 1970s and early 80s increased this tendency as the emphasis was on squeezing in as many small, identically-built cabins as possible. Some cabins, particularly those on lower passenger decks, resembled little more than glorified cupboards as the then-current perception insisted passengers spent only a tiny amount of time in their cabin.

≋ TRAVEL TIP ≋

Newcomers to cruising are often worried about the possibility of having a cabin down in the ship's bowels or even below the water line. This is never the case, but it can actually pay to pick a cabin on a lower deck if you are worried about seasickness as it minimises the effect of the ship's movement. The same also applies to cabins that are centrally located amidships.

It is really only in post-1980s ship-building that designers have fully come round to the idea of providing passengers with a bit of elbow room in their cabins, as well as solving one of cruising's most ticklish problems, that of providing proper double beds! There is also, at long last, an increasing move towards standardisation of cabin design to reduce the unnecessary volume of variety. Usually, cabins can be arranged to accommodate two to four people with the use of convertible settees or fold-down bunks, while several lines (notably Royal Caribbean) are experimenting successfully with purpose-built family cabins that have a second bedroom for the children. This should be the full range of extra choice beyond a standard two-berth (where berth is just ship-speak for bed), but check the small print to see if those twin beds definitely convert to a double as there are still instances where they don't.

INSIDE OR OUTSIDE?

So, just what should you expect from a typical cabin these days? Well, one of the most straightforward distinctions is that of either an inside or an outside cabin (and no, an outside or outer cabin doesn't mean outside the ship! That may sound absurd, but I can assure you it is a not uncommon query among those unfamiliar with ship terminology). Thankfully, modern designers have gone a long way towards making this differentiation almost unnecessary by building cabins of identical size whether they are outer (with a window or porthole, though the latter, sadly, is becoming a rare feature) or inner (usually with a curtained mirror in place of the window). There is still, of course, a substantial difference in price between the two types, but, unless you suffer from claustrophobia, the inner cabin on a modern cruise ship represents excellent value for money – you pay less, yet you still benefit from all the facilities and public rooms outside your cabin door, you eat the same food and enjoy the same level of entertainment. Royal Caribbean introduced an interesting variation on this theme with *Voyager of the Seas* – inside cabins with a view, over the grand central atrium promenade.

The only other cabin distinction of note is the suite, which should have more than one room (a sitting room as well as a bedroom) and a higher level of facilities all round.

TRAVEL TIP

Given the choice of a lower-rated ship and a higher category of cabin or a higher-rated ship and a lower cabin category, take the latter option. Your overall cruise experience will be much more rewarding.

A second rule of thumb says you find steadily increasing cabin space the higher up in the ship you go, and this holds true for nearly all but the most recent designs. This, of course, means you pay more on a higher deck than a lower one, but again, I would caution against automatically opting for the bigger cabin, especially if price is the most important factor to you. In many cases, the extra space is negligible and you should consider carefully if you will feel the benefit of, say, a two-seater settee – or an extra £200 to spend. Of course, if money is not the prime consideration, the top levels of cabin can offer an attractive alternative to the standard varieties. A typical suite will provide a sitting room as well as a bedroom (and, more often than not, a queen-sized bed), more generous cupboard and drawer space (provision of these can be pretty limited lower down) and a proper bathroom. The latter should be stressed because standard cabins are usually equipped with a shower only and, while they are perfectly adequate, there is still no better way to relax in the bathroom than in a well-filled tub. Many up-market cruise lines (and the top-level cabins on the middle-range ones) may also boast a whirlpool bath.

In addition to the size and configuration, the facilities of the cabin may vary slightly as you go through the range, but once again this is something which is gradually being phased out. In the past, the standard cabin's extras may have amounted to little more than a coffee table or an additional chair. Any cabin on a cruise ship launched today will include a TV (and occasionally a video recorder), a proper dressing-table, some sort of extra seating (be it an armchair or a settee), a hairdryer and a coffee table or bedside table in even its lowest-grade cabins. The 'extras' at the other end of the scale now usually consist of refrigerators or mini-bars, video recorders, full seating area, and even a whirlpool bath. In-cabin safes have also become a common feature across the board.

Other considerations to bear in mind when selecting your cabin are the proximity of the busier public rooms (you need to avoid the nightclub or casino if you are an early-to-bed type), the occurrence of jogging on the promenade or sun deck (you do not want to be directly underneath them when the early-morning fitness fanatics take to the deck), the position of the ship's lifeboats (which can obscure the view from your cabin window in some cases – typically, these cabins should come at a lower rate than those with unimpaired views) and location at one of the business ends of the ship: the stern is usually worst for a slightly enhanced vulnerability to engine vibration, while the bow houses the anchors – and there is nothing like the sound of a heavy-duty anchor being released as your ship docks in the early morning to act as an instant alarm call!

TRAVEL TIP

No matter what the level of modern sound-proofing or the situation of the cabin itself, you are travelling on a *moving* object so there is bound to be some kind of background noise, some kind of creak or groan (and we're not talking about the honeymoon couples here!), usually low-level but quite noticeable to cruise newcomers. This is not usually a reason to complain (as some newspapers might have you believe when relating stories of imaginary cruise horrors) but is simply the nature of the beast – and part of its charm.

TO BALCONY OR NOT TO BALCONY?

Finally (and this is a final Finally), comes the question of the feature which is beginning to dominate cabin design – that of whether or not to have a balcony.

In every ship that rolls off the production line these days, the percentage of cabins with this extra outdoor facility – however small – is increasing all the time. When *Grand Princess* made her debut in 1998, her owners proudly proclaimed 55 per cent of her cabins as having balconies; more than half of the up-market *Crystal Symphony*'s cabins come complete with balcony; the same proportion of outer cabins on *Carnival Destiny* can boast this feature; and the new *Seven Seas Mariner* of Radisson Seven Seas has opted for an industry first with *every* cabin boasting the luxury of a balcony. Luxury? Well, yes and no. It usually adds a substantial amount to a standard cabin price and is therefore not something I would recommend to the price-conscious. But – and it is a fairly big But – if you can afford the step up, you really will feel the benefit.

If there is one thing the average cruise ship cannot guarantee, it is your own private outdoor space. But, with a balcony, that problem is immediately solved. And, once you have tasted the sea air and watched the world sailing slowly by from your own little private enclave, you will wonder how you ever managed to stay in a normal, enclosed cabin. For all the fact cruising is no longer the preserve of the privileged few, there is something wonderfully exclusive about sipping a pre-dinner drink on your own cabin balcony and luxuriating in your splendid, individual isolation!

SERVICE WITH A SMILE

If that gives you the lowdown on a ship's hardware, the second important element in your choice of cruise line concerns the **Service** you will receive on board and the people who provide it.

The most significant factor to bear in mind is the passenger/crew ratio, which provides a good indicator of the level of attention you can expect. The nearer 1:1 it approaches, the more pampering you can expect. At the luxury end of the scale, both Seabourn and Silversea vessels boast this near-perfect ratio. The standard, mass-market ships all operate on ratios of upwards of 2:1. This has an inevitable effect on the quality of the service as well as the personal nature of it, yet there is rather more to the enjoyment of this aspect of your cruise than the simple logistics involved. For instance, the cruise lines take care of their crews in different ways, and often this is reflected in the style and friendliness of the service you receive; a happy crew makes for a happy cruise. Celebrity, Crystal, Orient and Seabourn all have excellent reputations for looking after their staff and consequently their care really does pay off in the attitude that is picked up by the passengers. By the same token, the older ships have fewer facilities for their crew, and therefore they have a higher staff turnover and lack that efficient edge which is noticeable only in its absence.

Equally, several lines go out of their way to ensure the service their passengers receive is that bit more memorable or special. All of the up-market lines guarantee this as standard, but it is noticeable in one or two others where they work wonderfully hard at producing an atmosphere that is efficient without being too formal and friendly without being too familiar. Swan Hellenic, Orient, Holland America, Festival, Celebrity and even the budget-priced Thomson and Airtours all excel at producing a level of service above and beyond the norm.

Indeed, in some cases, the ship's 'software' can make for some of the most memorable cruise experiences and can be one of the primary reasons why people return again and again to that particular ship. Indeed, my research assistant Carolyn Voce rates the fairly down-to-earth (in terms of facilities) *Pacific Princess* one of her most memorable cruises primarily because of the happy, family atmosphere generated by the crew. Otherwise, it is the bar steward who always remembers your favourite drink, the friendly deck hand who somehow knows your name or the member of the entertainment staff who goes out of his way to ensure you feel involved, that are all regular examples of the personal touch which cruising does better than most hotels.

A ship's crew can be a pretty varied bunch, too, in both their country of origin and the function they perform on board. As the world's cruise fleet continues to expand, an ever-greater number of people are required to crew them and a typical nationality profile may encompass men and women from the Philippines, India, Pakistan, Europe (especially eastern Europe these days), the Caribbean, USA, Canada and Latin America. It is a real United Nations at sea and often requires a degree in international diplomacy by the ship's hotel director, who is in charge of the majority of the service staff. The need for cruise lines to cast their nets ever further afield to find the necessary staff has meant something of a drop in the general service standards of the big, mass-market product as the lines struggle to train people up to the required level and encounter problems with language.

There are six main groups who make up a cruise ship's staff.

Cabin staff

Usually, the steward or stewardess who is assigned to your cabin for the duration of the cruise. This is the individual you may well see most of, busily attending to a number of cabins on your deck and responsible for making sure each one is kept clean every day. He or she makes the beds, ensures the bathroom is kept stocked with the necessary toiletries and will attend to your extra requirements such as room service, laundry and shoe-cleaning. Your steward or stewardess will almost certainly make contact with you soon after you have settled into your cabin for the first time and will appreciate being called by name – if only to make sure you know who to tip at the end of the cruise! Occasionally, there can be more than one steward/stewardess to each cabin and on the most up-market ships there may also be a butler.

TRAVEL TIP

Unless you are used to having your own servants at home, the presence of a butler can be faintly embarrassing. It may sound like a quaint idea in theory, but, in practice, there isn't really a lot extra a butler can provide which your steward can't.

Deck staff

This is the most varied and multi-purpose staff group of all, combining the function of on-deck waiters and waitresses with that of general cleaners and tidiers. Very often they are assigned areas of the deck, and you will quickly become familiar with a particular face or two as you develop your own routine on board.

Restaurant staff

Like your cabin steward, you will soon be familiar with your restaurant waiter and assistant waiter (referred to as the busboy on American ships) who you will also see on a daily basis. This duo will play a vital role in your enjoyment of mealtimes, and cruise lines are now extremely adept at selecting some of the best characters for the dining room as well as those with a good understanding of the food itself. They will often be keen to discuss your day at the evening meal, offer advice for the next port of call and make sure you enjoy every course. I vividly recall a Costa Rican waiter on one ship who introduced himself as Earl the Pearl and who was, indeed, a real gem at mealtimes. And a Turkish duo called Attila and Ilhan who turned every meal into 'Showtime!'. In addition to the waiters, you will also be looked after by the dining room's maître d' and be able to order drinks from the ever-present wine waiter or waitress.

TRAVEL TIP

When it comes to the end-of-cruise tipping, waiters/waitresses and their assistants should figure highly in your estimation. However, don't feel it necessary to tip the maître d' unless he (or she) has arranged some special service for you, while the wine waiter/waitress will have benefitted from every order you have made during the cruise as drinks usually carry an automatic service charge.

Take a tip from me

As a minor digression, having stumbled into the oft-misunderstood realms of on-board tipping, it is worth pointing out several things. Tipping is part and parcel of virtually every cruise, especially on the American ships where it is as natural as breathing. Brits, on the other hand, have a hard time with what is, after all, just a way of saying 'Thank you' for good, polite service. We are either embarrassed, ignorant or simply don't see the need for it. All of these reactions are easily overcome. There should certainly be no need for embarrassment these days as every cruise line makes it clear what the recommended daily gratuity rate is for the three main people who are most deserving of your cash – your steward, waiter and assistant waiter. You simply calculate the recommended rate (and more than 90 per cent of passengers do adhere to the cruise line's recommendation) over the number of days of your cruise and then deposit the amount in the handy envelopes that will inevitably be left in your cabin on the final evening. The Purser's Desk will have spares or extras should you need them. As a general rule, American lines recommend around $3.50 per person, per day for your waiter and steward, and half that for the assistant waiter. P&O put forward a slightly more pocket-friendly recommendation of £3 per person per day for all your tips.

The matter of ignorance of this shipboard custom is important to deal with as the stewards and waiters rely to a large degree on tipping for the bulk of their income. They work long contracts for a relatively low standard wage, and it is therefore up to them to provide the right level of service to encourage their passengers to be generous at the end of each cruise. Someone who simply forgets this custom at the conclusion of their holiday is unwittingly taking advantage of the individual workers concerned. Some people will argue the practice of tipping is rather objectionable and is only a way of allowing the cruise lines to keep their wages low. 'Why should I be required to help pay someone's salary?' is a remark I have heard. But it misses the point. Tipping is a perfectly respectable way of rewarding good service and it hurts only the innocent party if you decide not to. Of course, if you haven't received the right level of service you are perfectly at liberty to withhold your gratuity. But, if you really do experience bad service, it makes more sense to see the Hotel Manager first.

However, having said all that, the cruise industry is aware tipping is not popular and is trying to change things. Firstly, an increasing number of lines now allow you to pre-pay all your tips at the time of your main payment. Then, instead of filling an envelope with cash at the end of the cruise, you are given a voucher to hand over instead. By far the better option – and something many cruise lines (notably Thomson and Airtours) are introducing is to abolish tipping altogether and actively discourage it on board. You may end up paying slightly more to start with, but it does remove the one constant bugbear for many people.

As hinted at above, your bar staff and waiters are likely to benefit with every drink you order through a practice that is, to my mind, slightly more annoying. This is the American ship custom of adding an automatic 15 per cent service charge. In reality, it adds only a minor sum in the overall scheme of things, but it is a dubious automatic expectation. By far the better practice (and, I'm happy to say, a hallmark of British-run ships) is for the waiter or bar steward to leave the total blank on your bill and allow you to supply the tip which you think is warranted. That way, you get to reward particularly good service, or your favourite waiter/waitress, in suitable fashion.

Bar staff

You will already have picked up the message the bars and lounges are run by regular staff who will endeavour to have your drink ready before you have ordered it. Again, you will find some of the biggest characters responsible for dispensing the alcoholic beverages, and it is easy to be lulled into having that drink or three too many!

Cruise staff

This is again a multi-purpose group of people who are those most directly responsible for making sure you enjoy the cruise. They consist of the entertainers who put on the evening shows and, in some cases, organise the daily events; they man the Purser's Desk and they take the shore excursion bookings; they give talks on the ports of call and have titles like Port Lecturer and Social Hostess; they introduce the shows and are always there to make sure you Have a Nice Day; in short, they are the main interface between the ship and its passengers. The cruise staff *do* get paid a decent wage and therefore do *not* get tipped.

The officers

Headed by the Captain, these are the people who actually run the ship. It is their job to ensure it gets from place to place safely and on time, that the engines run smoothly, the air-conditioning works, the tele-communications links stay open, and, through the doctor and nursing staff, that everyone stays healthy.

The Captain is The Boss. In the overall chain of command he sits right at the top and oversees the running of the ship and its crew. His immediate aides are the Staff Captain and Chief Engineer, who between them oversee the day-to-day operation of the ship itself. Under the Staff Captain come the Chief Officer, the First, Second and Third Officers and the Radio Officers. The Chief Engineer runs the engine room and all the electrical facilities with a staff of Deputy, Second and Third Engineers, and the Chief Electrician and his Junior Electricians.

TRAVEL TIP

On board the American ships, if you find yourself yearning for a bit of British company and the rest of the passengers are all from Detroit or Chicago (unlikely, but possible), it is worth knowing that several ship concessions are staffed almost exclusively by Brits at sea. These usually include the photographers, the beauty salon staff (often a Steiner Transocean concession), casino staff and some of the entertainers.

However, the running of a large, modern cruise ship is now such a specialised business in itself that further top staff are needed and so the Staff Captain and Chief Engineer are joined in their rank of responsibility by the Hotel Manager, or Director, who oversees all the other groups of the crew. The Hotel Manager's chain of command also has five distinct links, and increasingly it is he (or she) who is primarily responsible for a successful cruise (although the Captain maintains the ultimate responsibility for the ship, crew and passengers – an important distinction). Under the Hotel Manager come: the Head Chef and a team of assistant chefs, galley staff and storekeepers; the Deputy Hotel Manager, who controls all the restaurant staff from the maître d' to the busboys; the Food and Beverage Manager and a team of bar managers, bar staff, waiters and waitresses; the Cruise Director, who fulfils another vital liaison role with the passengers, along with the Deputy Director, Social Host and Hostess, Stage Manager, Cruise Staff, Entertainers and Children's Counsellors; and the Purser, the previous supervisor of 'domestic' matters before a Hotel Manager became necessary, with a staff of Assistant Pursers, Printers, Stewards, Stewardesses and, importantly, the outside operators or concessions who run the health and beauty facilities, shops, casino and photographers. It sounds like a cast of thousands but does in fact number only hundreds in most cases.

THAT'S ENTERTAINMENT

The third vital component of an enjoyable cruise is the multi-faceted one of **Entertainment**, and this is an area where the larger, more up-market ships all score big marks.

From early-morning aerobics to the late-night disco or nightclub, a ship's entertainment staff work almost non-stop to provide you with a range and quantity of attractions that often leave the cruise newcomer amazed. As already mentioned, the appeal can be as wide as bingo to antiques, napkin-folding to art auctions, karaoke to classical concerts, family variety shows to even adults-only comedians. In many cases, the entertainments staff are hire-contract professionals doing short-term bookings for just one or two cruises. These people will include singers, musicians, comedians, magicians and variety acts. The majority are not big TV or theatre names, but have a solid background in live entertainment and are often more fun than big-name stars.

In addition to the imported entertainers, each ship will also have its own theatre company or dance group who will put on a series of ostentatious song and dance shows during the course of the voyage. On the new ships with big-stage capability, these shows can be highly elaborate indeed, drawing on material from the big West End productions or, in the case of the American ships, their Broadway or Las Vegas equivalent. On the smaller or busier ships (notably those of Airtours and P&O), the dance company also organise a lot of the daytime activities and sports, and it is a nice way of getting to meet them, too. By the nature of this diversification they need to be more flexible and so will often be good all-rounders rather than outstanding at any one type of performance. *Choosing a Cruise* researcher Carolyn Voce also notes the enthusiasm of the theatre cast on *Victoria* as an outstanding feature.

With the growing development of the theatre-at-sea idea, it is true the majority of lines are lavishing an increasing amount of attention on these big-scale production shows to the point where they are now usually the main focus of the evening's entertainment. However, they may not be to everyone's taste and hence there will nearly always be an alternative form of evening entertainment in the ship's secondary lounge (once again, the new mega-liners go one better in having at least three main evening venues – a vital factor with more than 2,600 people aboard – and even the relatively modest *Mistral* of Festival boasts seven showrooms or lounges). The main show will usually be repeated for the benefit of second-sitting diners on the larger ships, and so once again your only worry will be what to choose (although you shouldn't miss the big-production shows on the new-look NCL vessels).

Another relatively recent addition is that of art auctions. As a complete art duffer, I can assure even the most non art-minded they will find these an unexpectedly good source of entertainment, as well as providing an interesting insight into the art world. There is rarely any pressure to buy, and the patter of the auctioneer can be highly amusing (especially if he turns out to be Scotsman Gavin Watson, one of the busiest art auction men at sea and a very humorous guy as well).

Obviously, the actual programme of entertainment varies from cruise line to cruise line and some do things better than others (P&O, Disney and Royal Caribbean are certainly three of the best), but the overall quantity and quality should not leave you without amusement, especially when you add in the omnipresent events such as port lectures, bingo sessions, bridge competitions, dance classes, films, quizzes, singalongs, and board games. Once again, I defy anyone to get bored.

IT'S MEALTIME (AGAIN!)

Without wishing to over-stress the importance to a good cruise of the **Food**, it is quite instructive to examine just why it features so prominently in the brochures and advertisements (and on passengers' waist-lines!).

To start with, mealtimes are one of the principal social occasions of ship-board life and the likelihood for couples is you will find yourself sharing a table with two or more people you haven't met before. Some find this thought a little off-putting, but it is true in nearly all cases that it is a wonderful way of making friends and discussing the day's events and other cruise experiences, and the chances are you will want to keep in touch with your new-found companions once the cruise is over. Occasionally, it is possible that two couples really do not get along together, and then you are perfectly at liberty to seek a change of table, or even of sitting, with the restaurant's maître d'.

TRAVEL TIP

If you are offered a table for six or more, take it. It both reduces the chances of being stuck with any cruise bores and enhances the social ambience which a ship's restaurant creates, making every meal an occasion. Tables for two are relatively rare (although not with P&O).

The standard practice, when you first join your ship, is to be offered the option of first or second sitting in the main dining room (unless you are on one of the handful of truly up-market ships which offer open-seating dining at your convenience). Traditionally, first sitting will be 8am for breakfast, 12 noon or 12.15pm for lunch, and 6.30pm for dinner, with second sittings at 9am, 1.30pm and 8.30pm. On some ships, breakfast and lunch will be open seating in the main restaurant due to the reduced demand, and this will often be the case all round when a ship is in port. Alternatively, there will always be a buffet option away from the main restaurant for both breakfast and lunch, with the chance to experience one of life's real pleasures – cruise ship dining al fresco. Your choice may be slightly reduced in the buffet option, but the added bonus of enjoying your meal on deck more than compensates. There will also usually be at least one featured buffet lunch, with a regional food theme such as Italian or Chinese, where the ship's chefs really go to town with visual as well as culinary style. P&O's on-deck barbecue buffet is another winner here, while *Aurora* also features a splendid Indian menu alternative dinner.

For those just wishing to pig out and get the maximum value for their cruise pound, here is a typical example of the full run down of how your Seven Meals a Day line up: from 6am, Early Riser's Breakfast (usually pastries, fruit juice and coffee on deck); 8-10am, Full Breakfast (in the restaurant or the buffet alternative); 10.30-11.30am, Bouillon (not literally broth, but a savoury mid-morning snack comfortably eclipsing elevenses); noon-2pm, Lunch (again in either the restaurant or buffet); 3.30-4.30pm, Afternoon Tea (and a chance to snack up on sandwiches and cakes in the best British traditions); 6.30-8.30pm, Dinner (up to seven courses in some cases); and finally, a Midnight Buffet for those who can take it.

Having detailed the culinary experience in deliberately general terms, it should be evident the quality of the food and service will vary from line to line according to the individual style (and the price) of that line. At its most basic, you are likely to miss out on some of the finer points of content and service and the accent will be on hearty portions rather than finesse. At its best, the top cruise lines can rival the best restaurants in the world for their quality and presentation and you can expect a meal fit to grace the table of any top London chef.

These differences will be discussed in more detail in the next couple of chapters under the subject of rating the cruise lines, but it serves here to highlight two particular examples of the type of menu you can expect, using P&O's mass-market *Oriana* and the top-of-the-range *Crystal Harmony* (see pages 61-3).

TRAVEL TIP

To get the maximum enjoyment from your meal, opt for second sitting if given the choice because you will rarely be hurried to finish and you will get more chance to make the most of the social setting, something which British passengers are much keener to do than their American counterparts.

Increasingly, too, cruise lines are concerned with providing a full-time alternative to the main restaurant, be it only a hot-dog or burger bar or a small, specialist restaurant, again all at no extra charge (apart from the occasional tip). Princess Cruises feature pleasant, well serviced (and highly popular) pizzerias, while NCL ships each offer a bistro dining experience and an afternoon or late-night chocoholic's buffet (not for the faint-hearted – the Americans take mealtimes seriously at the best of times, and there is a positive stampede for this). Crystal's claim to fame in this department is the addition of two intimate, themed restaurants (Japanese and Italian), while Holland America can boast outdoor taco, pasta and ice cream bars. Put simply, the bigger the ship, the more eating alternatives there are (nine on *Grand Princess,* seven on *Carnival Destiny*

ORIANA DINNER MENU

Appetisers
Smoked Scottish Salmon with Lemon and Brown Bread

Half Avocado filled with strips of Parma Ham, Celeriac and Apple Mayonnaise

Spinach Risotto with Marsala and Parmesan
****

Soups
Cream of Asparagus Soup with Chive Cream

Consommé of Beef Jardinière
****

Main Courses
Fillet of Cod with Champagne and Saffron Sauce

Roast Sirloin of Scottish Beef with Yorkshire Pudding and Rosemary Gravy

Steamed Breast of Chicken with Winter Vegetables and an Arran Mustard Sauce

Stir-fried Fragrant Pork with Shiitake Mushrooms, Water Chestnuts and Soft Noodles

Fusilli Pasta and Winter Vegetable Bake

Today's Cold Cuts served with a selection of Salads and Dressings

Side Orders
Selection of Market Vegetables
****

Desserts
Sticky Toffee Pudding with Butterscotch Sauce

Traditional Sherry Trifle

Rich Dark Chocolate Terrine with Grand Marnier Sauce

Fresh Fruit Salad

Vanilla, Strawberry and Peach Ice Creams

Passion Fruit Sorbet
****

Selected British and Continental Cheeses with Biscuits and Fruit

Espresso/Decaffeinated/Filter Coffee

After Dinner Mints

Fresh from the Bakery: White, Wholemeal, Granary and Garlic Rolls

CRYSTAL HARMONY DINNER MENU

Appetisers

Iced Caspian Sea Sevruga Malossol Caviar with Traditional Trimmings, Melba Toast

Blackened Fresh Sea Scallops with Tropical Fruit Relish

Truffled Chicken Liver Parfait with Warm Brioche

Chilled Assorted Fruit in a Half Coconut Perfumed with Honeydew Melon Liqueur

****

Soups

Fresh Mushroom Soup 'Cappuccino-style' with Whipped Cream and Paprika

Clear Oxtail Soup with Barley and Chester-sesame Sticks

****

Salad

Captain's Salad
Medley of Selected Crunchy Field Lettuce with Cherry Tomatoes and Eggplant Chips

Dressings available in the traditional favourites plus today's specials:

Fat-free Honey-lime or Low-calorie Carrot-cucumber Yoghurt

****

Sherbet (Sorbet)

Refreshing Peach Champagne Sherbet

****

Main Courses

Broiled Lobster Tail 'Madame Butterfly'
Served with Light, Creamy Lobster Sauce, Steamed Baby Vegetables and Truffled Pilaf Rice

Grilled Fresh Halibut Fillet
With Fennel Vinaigrette, Assorted Baby Vegetables and New Potatoes

Chateaubriand
Sliced Black Angus Beef Tenderloin with Port Wine Sauce,
Baby Vegetable Mix with Asparagus Spears and Stuffed Baked Potato

Sautéed Medallions of Veal Loin
With Light Tarragon Sauce, Steamed Green Asparagus
and Angel Hair Pasta with Tomato Confit

****

Side Orders

Garden Fresh Baby Vegetables   Green Asparagus Spears
Truffled Pilaf Rice
Stuffed Baked Potato   New Potatoes   Angel Hair Pasta with Tomato Sauce
****

Desserts

Chocolate Fantasy – Crunchy Chocolate-almond Sticks with Grand Marnier
and Fresh Berries; Tartelette Pavlova – Meringue Shell with Lemon Cream;
Sugar-free Tiramisu; Freshly Frozen Non-fat Hazelnut-amaretto Yoghurt;
Plantation Truffles and Petits Fours from the Chocolate Treasure Chest;
Assortment of Seasonal fruit and Selection of International Cheeses with
Crackers and Biscuits

and even as many as six on the more modestly-sized *Norwegian Dream* and *Wind*), while a 24-hour dining option is also increasingly in favour, and *Norwegian Sky* offers a Chinese-Italian restaurant option, Ciao-Chow. A further feature of most ships is the Midnight Buffet, one last chance to indulge your taste buds. Watch out in particular for the Grand or International Buffet, where the chefs serve up a positive extravaganza of culinary temptation, complete with set-piece displays of magnificent ice and butter carvings.

There is one further element which has emerged just recently from two different directions. Firstly, P&O's *Aurora* is the first ship in the fleet to offer a 24-hour bistro – the wonderful Café Bordeaux – that provides both an evening alternative to the main dining room and a late-night snack outlet, replacing the need for the midnight buffet. This will surely spread to the rest of the fleet in time. And then there is the development pioneered by NCL's parent company Star Cruises and swiftly copied by several of their rivals, notably Princess. NCL's new on-board Freestyle regime promotes a refreshing open-seating policy at all times, and Princess have been quick to add their Personal Choice Dining, which also offers this eat-when-you-like theme. Thomson Cruises will argue that they pre-date all of this with their all-inclusive *Topaz*.

It may come as something of a relief to the more dimensionally well-endowed among us after all this emphasis on quantity to know most lines also now provide a low-fat menu, along with low-sodium, vegetarian and even kosher offerings.

YOUR PORTS OF CALL

The final key element in weighing up the cruise product on offer is, of course, where your ship takes you, how many **Ports of Call** it visits and your options for **Shore Excursions** while you are there. The actual areas the main cruise lines visit will be discussed in detail later in the book in Chapter Six, but here it is a good idea to make yourself familiar with the kinds of standard itinerary on offer.

First of all, it is another fairly basic difference between ourselves and our American cousins at sea that we take rather more interest in the ports of call once we are there. We want to be well informed on the sights to see, the local culture and the people we are going to meet ashore, as well as knowing all about the shopping opportunities (which often seems to be an American's raison d'être on a cruise). Therefore, we take more care over our choice of itinerary and, as a result, the predominantly British cruise lines tend to put together more packages that have those tastes in mind. Fred Olsen have acknowledged this trend and now offer trips to the Far East and South America in addition to their more traditional Scandinavian and Canary Island itineraries.

Having said that, it is now an established fact of modern cruising that there is an increasing demand to get off the beaten track, to explore new itineraries and new areas ... to boldly go where no cruiser has gone before! Well, almost. The Caribbean remains the Number One cruise destination worldwide, with the Mediterranean still a strong second, but the fastest-growing area of cruise interest over the last few years has been Alaska, and most of the main companies now offer some very attractive packages to America's largest yet most natural state.

The Far East is seen as the next big area of growth, while there are also increasing amounts of cruise traffic to South America (especially the Amazon River), the Indian Ocean and Australasia. In fact, with the emergence of the adventure cruise ships, there are now few areas which cannot be explored by sea.

As the mass market increasingly switches on to the potential and excitement of cruising, there is an inevitable standardisation of the main products, and these can be summed up in several ways.

TRAVEL TIP

Something of which the majority of cruisers are unaware but which is in the small print of *every* brochure, is the cruise line's right to change a given itinerary at little or no notice for operating reasons. The two big Caribbean hurricanes of 1995 are the best case in point as they gave rise to some hysterical newspaper stories – passengers complained bitterly of missing out on ports of call simply because they were being hit at the time by 120mph winds! Be warned, therefore, a ship's itinerary is not set in stone and, if you have your heart set on one particular port, double-check it for adverse weather conditions before you book.

Most significant for the UK market is the huge predominance of seven-day cruises. In most cases these are geared for the American market because the US does not enjoy as much holiday time as Europe and so they will rarely devote more than a week at a time to their 'vacations'. This means on the majority of fly-cruise trips (the Caribbean being the prime example) we are travelling a long way for just a week's holiday when we are far more used to taking two weeks at a time. A typical American seven-day cruise can also be pretty port-intensive due to their taste for cramming in as much as possible in their vacation time. This can leave the average Brit at sea just a little bit breathless after such a long-distance but short-duration dash. Happily, the cruise companies have quickly realised they have a wider audience to appeal to, and so there are now plenty of packages that offer cruising as just half or part of your overall holiday. There is a wealth of opportunity for a week's stay on one of the Caribbean islands in addition to your seven-day cruise, and several lines also offer an individual tailor-made packaging service – NCL, for example, can marry up any of their Caribbean cruises with visits to most resorts in the region or even the USA – in addition to the ship-board half of your holiday. P&O started offering cruise-and-stay packages for the first time for their 1999/2000 season while Airtours, Thomson and First Choice have had well-organised programmes linked with a stay on Majorca or Cyprus right from the word go.

WALT DISNEY WORLD AND ALL THAT

As Florida is still the biggest long-haul market for British holiday-makers, the main tour operators have also cottoned on to the possibilities of offering a week's cruising as well as a week in the theme park wonderland of Orlando or one of the coastal resorts of the sunshine state. This is potentially one of the biggest growth areas of the UK fly-cruise holiday business, and it will soon be common procedure for Caribbean cruising to be featured quite prominently in Florida brochures, the theory being so many Brits going there are now repeat visitors they are likely to be looking for something different to do. Cruising does offer a terrific value add-on to a week's theme-parking in many cases. The Walt Disney company themselves have joined this trend with their own high-quality cruise option, which they expanded in 2000 from just 3 and 4-day short-haul cruises to proper week-long voyages, which are well worth investigating if you are planning a Disney World visit.

First-timers will also be tempted into the cruise world in this area by the increasingly well-advertised prospect of only a three- or four-day cruise in addition to their land-based week or ten days. Now, these shorter cruises are an excellent way of finding out if cruising is really for you without going to the full expense of the whole cruise experience, and Florida is the centre of this particular cruise activity, again focusing on the vast numbers of holiday visitors there. The only comparable British cruise activity of this kind are a handful of three- or four-day cruises out of Southampton with P&O or Cunard visiting either France, Holland or the Channel Islands. The three- and four-day cruise market is big business with the Americans, but somehow it has more limited appeal to the British market, perhaps because we are not comfortable with the idea of going all the way to Florida for such a short cruise. But it will become a regular feature of our holiday brochures, and it is certainly worth considering if you don't fancy going the whole hog straight away.

CHOOSE YOUR TYPE OF CRUISE

A discussion of this short-duration style of cruising leads on to a breakdown of the FOUR main types of cruise which are the staple fare of any cruise brochure. Every cruise will conform to one of these formats, and they all affect the ship's itinerary in different ways.

Circular cruises

These are the most common in the mass market. They start and finish at the same point (in the case of the mass-market Caribbean, usually Miami or Fort Lauderdale in Florida or San Juan in Puerto Rico) and visit the same ports of call every week or ten days. The ports are always ready for the ship when it arrives, the facilities will be guaranteed and the shore-side organisation is well-grooved to the point of being humdrum. The chances are you will be in port with at least one other sizeable ship and, in some cases like the US Virgin Islands, it is not uncommon for there to be six liners in at once, meaning BIG crowds in all the main shore-side tourist spots. The seven-day cruise is absolutely tailor-made for the circular style and it usually runs like clockwork, even in places like Alaska (round-trip from Vancouver). The three- and four-day versions are similarly of the circular variety, and are run even more on bus-like lines. They are the most informal types of cruise and nearly always have the youngest age profiles, with plenty of couples and plenty of children and teenagers. In many cases, if you feel seven days is just not enough, a circular cruise can also be taken back-to-back with a complementary itinerary that turns it into a figure-of-eight cruise. For example, Celebrity Cruises offer a 16-night package that takes in first a seven-day circuit of the western Caribbean and then, after returning to the home port, a seven-day circuit of the eastern Caribbean. This can also be done with Costa, NCL, Princess, Holland America and Royal Caribbean or by changing ships at the end of seven days with Carnival. You should also get a decent mix of sea days and port days, remembering that you don't want a surfeit of ports of call unless you are really keen to see every island.

TRAVEL TIP

Cruising remains the best way of sampling the Caribbean because many of the islands would not keep you actively interested for a full two weeks, while a day's visit is just enough to give you a good taste of what's on offer (plus, there is a school of thought that says one island paradise looks much like another after a while).

P&O operate the best examples of circular cruises out of the UK (along with Fred Olsen) but the very nature of sailing out of British waters demands a longer voyage, hence you will rarely find any seven-day cruises in this area. Airtours and Thomson were instrumental in creating Britain's first mass market in circular cruising, with summer itineraries out of

Palma in Majorca and Limassol in Cyprus, but the Italian firm Costa were the pioneers of Mediterranean fly-cruising and they still have some of the best itineraries in this field, sailing out of Genoa and Venice, along with Festival and MSC. Airtours also joined in with ex-UK sailings in 2000, which gave them another attractive string to their bow.

Linear cruises

These tend to operate on a back-and-forth basis and are as well-grooved as the circular variety. The best example is the trans-Panama Canal route, which sees ships sail from Miami, Fort Lauderdale or San Juan through the magnificent Canal to Acapulco or Los Angeles, and then retrace their steps eastbound with a new set of passengers. The minimum length of time for a linear cruise is seven days, and ten- to 14-day varieties are not uncommon. The latter will have more days at sea and will therefore tend towards the more formal, with a slightly older passenger profile (say, 50-plus) and fewer children. Linear cruises also include transatlantic crossings on a regular basis, which used to be the real essence of life at sea. The QE2 is now the only ship offering a regular transatlantic service, and, as there are no ports of call as such (Southampton at one end to New York at the other), the formality is high. But although tending towards the older, the age range can be quite broad (especially as the ship has good children's facilities).

Irregular cruises

The more up-market lines all operate on a less bus-like basis and, therefore, offer more intriguing itineraries that are rarely repeated. These work solely for cruises of at least seven days, and usually longer, and so are likely to be more formal. A typical example is the way the Crystal ships work their way around the world, offering various segments as they move around South America, the Panama Canal and Caribbean, Alaska and Canada, the Far East and then back to Europe to start the whole slow cycle over again. Usually, these provide the most fascinating itineraries as they specialise in getting off the beaten track, although they do also feature some of the world's main ports, like Sydney, Hong Kong, Rio de Janeiro and San Francisco. The length of this type of cruise (upwards of seven days) means the passenger profile will again tend towards the older (50-plus) range with few children and fewer children's facilities. An alternative version of the irregular cruise is the repositioning cruise, where one of the mass-market lines moves one of their ships from one main cruise area, for example the Caribbean, to another like Alaska or Europe. This will be a once or twice a year occurrence and offers the chance to sample the ship for longer (and more formally therefore than is usual) and through more varied ports of call. There is an extra spontaneity about repositioning cruises which makes them highly popular, and they also often represent especially good value for money.

World cruises

These were an all-but-dying breed until the up-market lines managed to create a new market for the ultimate in ship-borne extravagance in recent years. Cunard's QE2, P&O's *Canberra* and a couple of similar classic liners of equal maturity were virtually the sole representatives of the round-the-world fraternity until the likes of Crystal, Holland America, Germany's Hapag-Lloyd, and, more recently, Saga rediscovered the demand for a leisurely month or three. They represent the last word in ocean-going formality because of the length of time you spend at sea, and it is almost unknown to encounter children on a world cruise. World cruises specialise in the grand destinations and offer an extra level of glamour that goes with the huge expense which spending this long at sea represents. Increasingly, they can also be purchased in smaller segments, from two weeks to a month, and these are another growth area in the cruise world, with Holland America, for example, offering their 99-day voyage in 13 sectors from 13 to 31 days. Silversea have also joined the World Cruise throng, and have quickly proved there is a market for the small, Ultra-Deluxe ship here as well. With more than 40 ports in 25 countries spread over 95 days, they have proved unarguably the world cruise IS here to stay.

Orient Lines have added another twist to this theme with a series of Grand Voyages of 30-plus days to destinations like Australia, Hong Kong and across the Pacific. In fact, these world-type voyages have really caught on in recent years, with Royal Caribbean pioneering a long round-trip from the Mediterranean to the Far East and back and Crystal modifying their world cruise in 2002 to a Circle Pacific Itinerary. Princess Cruises have a Grand Adventure series of from 33 to 67 days, visiting South America, Africa and the Far East.

Once again, cruising has shown adaptability and innovation in its attempts to be both attractive and varied, and there are even more long-distance options when you explore the world of working ships and one-off vessels like the cargo/passenger RMS *St Helena*, which operates out of Cardiff to the south Atlantic and South Africa, with sailings from 35 to 39 days. The PSA offers a fact sheet on working ships (tel 0207 436 2449), while The Cruise People Ltd (0207 723 2450) are the UK's leading specialist travel agents in this field. For more information, the British-based Freighter Travel Review is published six times a year (cost £30, tel 01206 503798) with everything you need to know on this subject.

ALL ASHORE

The facet of a cruise that goes hand-in-hand with your ports of call is that of the **Shore Excursions** which your ship will offer. This is an area that can make or break your cruise, particularly on a port-intensive one. In theory, every cruise ship should have a qualified Port Lecturer on board to give you the full rundown on your next port of call the day before you get there. In conjunction with the daily lectures, there should also be a full explanation of the range, nature and cost of the shore excursion options open to you right at the start of the cruise. It is easy to miss the shore excursion talk, so try to make a note of it as soon as you board and make sure that at least one member of your party attends. It is usually better to attend en masse as that makes it easier for you to formulate a coherent plan of campaign for your excursions – and in most cases you will need a plan. In many cases, the excursion talks are now repeated on your in-cabin TV, so you get several chances to tune in!

Your shore excursions will take the form of three or four possibilities for each port of call, with the cruise line or their land-based agent providing all the necessary transport, transfers, tickets and guides. You simply buy each excursion as a package from the ship's Excursion Desk and the total cost is added on to your ship-board account. If the cruise line supplies a brochure of the excursion options with your tickets before you board, study it carefully and draw up a provisional list of what appeals to you. The ship should also provide on-board literature on all the ports of call, highlighting the most interesting tourist points. Once you have digested as much of the written information as possible, go along and listen to the shore excursion talk aboard the ship, fill in the form you will be given with your choices and hand it in at the Excursion Desk in person or post it through their letter box. Be warned also, the Shore Excursion Desk frequently has the longest queues (or lines, as the Americans call them).

TRAVEL TIP

Try to get in as early as possible with your excursion requests. Many are on a limited number basis and it is easy to miss out on the best tours by leaving it too late. It is occasionally possible to pre-book excursions when you get your cruise tickets, and this is an even better solution.

It is quite easy to get carried away with the number of excursion options you will be offered and end up with a huge bill on top of your other cruise costs. The best advice is to stick to no more than one excursion per port of call and try to weigh up what you are really getting: if the half-day island tour of Barbados costs £30 per person and includes a rum punch lunch, you can probably get better value by doing your own tour of the port of Bridgetown first, calling in at one of the island's information points for a list of any comparable tours and prices, return to the ship for lunch (it's already paid for – why pay for an extra meal you don't really need?) and then see if one of the local excursions takes your fancy. In nearly all cases, it will be cheaper to take the local option provided you are confident enough to deal with the local agents or taxi drivers. Your daily port talks should give you an idea of how safe it is to venture off on your own, and don't hesitate to ask for up-to-date safety advice or other local travel tips. The only real benefits of taking the ship-bought excursions are that they occasionally come up with tours you would not be able to do on your own (like white-water rafting or helicopter flights in Alaska – these are not to be missed!), they allow you to budget in advance and they should provide an in-built element of extra safety which is important to some people. As a general rule, all shore excursions are designed for people completely new to the area, so, if you have been before, you are likely to be better off on your own.

It is hard to be more specific about the excursions themselves, other than to say that the Caribbean has the fewest examples of the 'Must-try' excursion. They tend to be unimaginative and rarely anything you couldn't do on your own, especially as English is widely spoken.

TRAVEL TIP

In ports where English is not the first language and you want to go off on your own, make sure you have the name and address of the ship and the harbour written down to be able to show a taxi driver to get you back to the right place and on time. I nearly came unstuck in Turkey without that essential information!

Greece and Turkey frequently offer the best guides with ship-bought shore excursions, while parts of the Far East and South America are also best done in large groups for safety reasons.

In Russia and other parts of the former Soviet Union, you need to apply for a separate visa in advance if you wish to go exploring on your own as the ship's visa covers only the organised excursions.

Just keep your common sense with you at all times when you leave the ship and you should be fine.

As an additional note on the Caribbean, the Port Lecturer is your best friend for up-to-the-minute local shopping. The main cruise lines now take in advertising from the bigger and better stores ashore, and these will be recommended by the lecturer as they carry a guarantee for all your purchases. By all means shop around to compare prices, but rest assured that the days when the Port Lecturer (or more likely the Cruise Director) got a kick-back for shop recommendations are long gone.

TRAVEL TIP

Sadly, you are unlikely to unearth any real bargains in the well-trodden paths of the Caribbean ports. There will be plenty of claims of the Best Price for this or that, but the chances are you will get just as good value from the airport duty-free shop on the return home (Hong Kong, Singapore and other parts of the Far East are a different story).

Finally, when it comes to buying things ashore, the US dollar is an almost universal unit of currency. The majority of ships (the major British lines being the main exceptions) all run on the dollar and, while they will offer a bureau de change on board (usually with the rate of exchange heavily weighted in their favour) to allow you to collect some local currency for Jamaica, Curaçao or wherever, you can usually rely on the power of the dollar to do most for you in the main towns and ports of call. If you do want to take some local change with you (a good idea, in particular, for taxis) change only a limited amount as it can be difficult to re-convert to dollars or sterling. Major credit cards – Visa, Mastercard and American Express – are also widely accepted and offer their own built-in safeguards, too.

Having said your ports of call can be a make-or-break feature of your cruise, it might make sense at this point to get some inside track on the best places to visit in the eyes of the people most in the know – the various ship captains and their staff. My assistant Carolyn and I regularly check the favourite ports of call with the officers whenever we are at sea, and here is our unofficial Top Ten of their recommendations:

1) Sydney Harbour, Australia – an unforgettable entrance
2) Rio de Janeiro, Brazil – another totally spectacular setting
3) Hong Kong – splendour, hustle and bustle – and shopping!
4) Venice, Italy – even more romantic to visit by cruise ship
5) New York, USA – the ultimate city skyline
6) Tahiti, South Pacific – a jewel in the Polynesian Islands' crown
7) San Francisco, USA – another stunning port entry
8) Singapore – main Far East gateway and superb city
9) Portofino, Italy – picture-postcard pretty village resort
10) Santorini, Greece – one of the most amazing island ports

Now, not having been to all of the above (Sydney certainly remains top of my 'wish' list), I can't vouch personally for their validity, although you can be pretty sure of a great experience in each one. Other ports to receive multiple votes were Skagway in Alaska (for scenery, walking and fishing), Montreal (for its nightlife), Nagasaki ('Just because it is Japan,' Carolyn was told), Wellington (New Zealand's pride), Monte Carlo (and not just for gamblers), the Geiranger Fjord in Norway (one of the most picturesque places in a thoroughly scenic country) and Hobart in Tasmania, Down Under.

For what it's worth, my own Top Ten would be:
1) Cape Town, South Africa – with its breathtaking backdrop of Table Mountain
2) Vancouver, Canada – gateway to Alaska and a really happening city
3) Istanbul, Turkey – a fascinating city at the historic crossroads of civilisation
4) Santorini, Greece – ditto the reason above
5) San Francisco, USA – as above, but also for its great city style
6) New York, USA – the only way to enter this great metropolis is by sea
7) Oslo, Norway – simply because it's one of my favourite cities
8) Glacier Bay, Alaska – not really a port but a thrilling location
9) Livorno, Italy – the gateway to Florence and living history
10) Portofino, Italy – just can't get enough of that Italian style.

In all, that's a list of 23 vastly contrasting ports. I could add Barcelona (another wonderfully chic city), Palma de Mallorca (splendid old town), Madeira (beautiful island), Amsterdam (especially with the entrance via the Ijmuiden Lock and North Sea Canal), Guernsey (real, old-fashioned charm), Key West (just so artistic, darlings), Juneau in Alaska (superb setting, plus the Red Dog Saloon!) and Kusadasi in Turkey (for the chance to visit the unmissable ancient site of Ephesus). So, if you manage to take in half a dozen or so of these, you will have ensured a good helping of port memories and provided yourself with an essential part of the cruise experience.

That concludes this review of the principal features of your everyday cruise. Let's now look closely at some of the more specific aspects of cruise ships, including who the main players are, how their ships rate and what a typical cruise experience is all about ...

CHAPTER FOUR

MAKING SENSE OF THE VARIETY

Up until now, I have been dealing with cruising largely in general terms. Now it is time to start talking in specifics and discuss some of the more practical issues, like how to choose the right cruise for you. This involves rating the main cruise lines, how a typical cruise shapes up, how to book it and the main considerations involved.

Having frequently mentioned various lines and some of their ships in the opening chapters, it makes sense at this point to take a more detailed look at the ways in which the cruise companies differ, and to formulate an easy-to-understand guide to the main types. Now, just the merest perusal of your average brochure might lead you to think everyone is offering the same luxurious standard of holiday indulgence, the level of pampering you will receive will be uniformly high and the five key elements of the cruise experience (Facilities, Service, Entertainment, Food and Ports of Call) will be of guaranteed five-star standard. Unfortunately, that is just not the reality. Along with the Six Big Myths listed in Chapter Two, it is also wide of the mark to imagine all cruise products are largely equal. They might want to make you believe this is the case, and the cruise industry is certainly one of the worst for the over-use of such terms as Luxurious, Top Class, Five-star Plus and Supreme Quality, but in truth things are extremely different.

Basically, there are FIVE distinct levels of the cruise experience and once you have grasped the essential requirements of each you will be in a much better position to make your choice. These categories have evolved and been refined over the last few years in conjunction with the British Cruise Awards panel.

STANDARD

This is the budget-minded entry level of all modern-day cruising. The product will basically be a no-frills operation where the accent is on value for money rather than finesse. The ships will tend to be high-density (with a low Space Ratio figure, nearer the 20 mark than the 50 which represents the true benchmark for a spacious ship) and of the older variety (pre-1970 in nearly all cases). Therefore some facilities, like modern gyms, theatres and fancy lounges may be missing; service will still be with a smile but will lack the personal touch; on-board entertainment will be broad-based rather than star quality and choice will be more limited; food will tend towards the hearty rather than the gourmet; and the ports of call will be the more standard, well-known destinations rather than anything particularly exotic. In short, it is a great introduction to all that cruising has to offer – and usually at an excellent price, but don't expect a lot of finesse and certainly no hint of 'luxury'. In hotel terms, they are a three-star product.

SUPERIOR

This is the category that has developed most quickly in the modern era as lines have either spruced up older tonnage (in the case of Airtours' *Sunbird*) or where ships that were state-of-the-art not so long ago now don't quite live up to their newer brethren (like Fred Olsen's *Black Watch*). Space Ratio figures are still relatively low, but there is greater attention to detail in service and cuisine. More recent ships in this level boast a bigger range of facilities (like Festival's recent *Mistral*) while the more veteran category members (like P&O's classic *Victoria* and the *Pacific Princess* of Princess Cruises) may lack the modern touch but still retain a charm and warmth that mark them out as above average. In all cases, they represent some of the best value for money in the cruise world, as discounts are fairly common but they still offer a quality experience. If they were hotels, they would rate three-star-plus.

PREMIER

The next level up sees some of the biggest operators and some of the newest, glitziest ships as the cruise companies look to tempt the first-timer into something rather more extravagant, and the repeat passenger into a new, more glamorous experience. The mass market is also firmly involved in this level through the sheer size of the ships (rarely anything below 30,000 tons), and so you can expect the full range of facilities, a friendly, if occasionally less than totally efficient, service (simply because of the large numbers involved), a varied package of entertainments with some high-powered main shows, a more extensive menu, but still the more tried and trusted ports of call. The average age profile is showing the biggest change in this area through the efforts of operators like Royal Caribbean, NCL, Costa, Princess and P&O to attract the family market. Discounts are at their most common at this level as the cruise companies find themselves directly in competition with the cost-conscious Standard and Superior level ships and with the other lines competing for a larger slice of the huge volume which there now is in Premier cruising. They would be four-star in hotel terms.

DELUXE

Here you find the widest range of cruise options in terms of the hardware, from the small sailing vessels, through the niche products like Hebridean Island Cruises, to some extremely grand new designs that offer the latest in cruise technology, but still deliver an above-average service ethic. Size therefore varies enormously, but the Space Ratio figure should still be good, at least 35 if not better. This is also the more classic, stylish version of cruising, with less emphasis on casinos, non-stop fun and glitz. Service will always be attentive and personal, albeit with a slightly more formal style than in previous categories. Entertainments will be less the likes of bingo, karaoke and organised sports and more lectures, art auctions and so forth, with the occasional ballet show or classical concert as well as the Broadway-style spectacular. The food will be more varied, with the smaller ships of this type able to score heavily for quality. Your fellow passengers will be widely travelled and the itineraries will consist of some truly outstanding ports of call. In some instances, the age profile can be wide here, with Deluxe cruising attracting the wealthy, retired types as well as the younger go-getters and jet-setters, but the cruise experience will be primarily a formal one. Discounts are rare but not unknown and can therefore provide some of the best value for money. In hotel terms, we are talking four-star-plus.

ULTRA-DELUXE

There are more claims for this true luxury distinction than any other, but few lines match up to the proper definition of the word. Consequently, with few exceptions, the Ultra-Deluxe ships are small, boutique-type vessels, catering with supreme style of service and food to the most discerning passenger. The Space Ratio figure will be at least 50 and cabins will be particularly spacious, with a high proportion having balconies. In many cases, it is not so much cruising as pampering of the highest quality that just happens to be at sea. Competition in this part of the market is therefore as much with the top land-based resorts and hotels as with the rest of the cruise world. By the nature of the ships being smaller and more exclusive, the level of facilities will therefore be fewer (although there are a couple of notable exceptions – see the tables on pages 78–81), but everything is maintained to the highest standards. Service will be of the white-glove, silver-service variety and the food as good as anything you can get in the best restaurants of the world, with the great benefit in most cases of open-seating dining (the chance to eat when you want with who you want). Entertainments are distinctly low-key, with the accent more on social discourse than big-production shows. These ships also operate only irregular or world-type cruises, hence the ports of call are the most exotic you will find. The level of formality is high (but not stiflingly so) and the age profile older than most. Extras like gratuities, drinks and shore excursions are often included, and the Ultra-Deluxe cruise therefore attracts some seriously wealthy passengers. Discounting is virtually unheard-of by the necessity of keeping this level exclusive. The one real exception is Crystal Cruises, who operate the two largest Ultra-Deluxe ships in the world, which are both 50,000 tons and therefore, to my mind, more versatile. They don't offer single-seating dining (which some claim knocks them out of this category) or any fully-inclusive packages, but they do offer big-ship facilities with small-ship quality of service. Truly, these are the five-star hotels of the cruise world.

MIX 'N' MATCH

In some cases, it is possible for a cruise line to have ships in more than one of the five categories as they try to cater for as wide an audience as possible or as they introduce newer ships which knock their older stock down a peg or two. A typical example of this is the Italian line Costa Cruises, where their older ships are definitely in the Standard or Superior brackets but their newest ones are most certainly in the Premier range. It should also go without saying, the price scale increases steadily through each of these five levels. A week's cruise on a Standard ship may cost as little as £500 and seven days on a Premier product might set you back only £900, but a week on board a Deluxe vessel will take you into the four-figure region and the Ultra-Deluxe class goes well beyond that.

The other essential difference between the main lines has been hinted at in several places already but should also be dealt with in its entirety here, and that is the fundamental distinction between the American companies and the British and European ones. With almost 7 million Americans at sea compared with barely 750,000 UK passengers, it stands to reason the majority of cruise lines cater primarily for US tastes and styles. This can be slightly off-putting for someone who has never travelled on a ship full of Americans (and there can be more than 2,000 of them at a time, remember), but the reality is they are no better or worse than 2,000 of any other nationality. The American tourist abroad tends to get a rather unfortunate press, and, while it is true there will always be one or two who will conform to the loud, garishly-dressed, camera-bedecked stereotype, the vast majority are of a different type altogether. I have made many transatlantic friends in the course of my cruises and have never had any worries about being surrounded by American accents. There is always the fact, of course, cruising tends to attract the more cosmopolitan, thoughtful tourist in the first place, rather than the brash variety. It also, therefore, tends to attract like-minded souls who enjoy similar social tastes, and so there is usually nothing to be gained or lost in social terms by opting for the all-American variety of cruising.

The differences in style should be fairly obvious, and it is the matter of your own personal taste in these areas that will lead you to decide whether the American way is more appealing than the British way (even allowing for people who prefer simply to travel among their own). The American style is, of course, slightly more ostentatious and showy, and this can be easily seen in the elaborate design of many of their ships where they tend to go for immediate visual impact. The British (and

European) way is to be rather more restrained, almost formal, and to hark back to the more traditional era (hence the preference for proper promenade decks). The Americans make no bones about their lack of any class differentiation, while British cruises can still have an element of class-consciousness. When it comes to entertainment, the US tendency is for the big, glitzy production shows while the British version is somehow just that bit more reserved (although this difference is diminishing all the time). American tastes in comedy are definitely different (but don't ask me to define how), and so if the likes of Cheers!, The Golden Girls and Seinfeld leave you cold, then you are probably going to be better off with British entertainment. By the same token, if you are a meat-and-two-veg type of eater, you will probably yearn for a proper meal by the end of an American cruise. Once again, US tastes are for quantity in terms of courses (a salad course is ever-present, for example), a glamorous touch in presentation and, ultimately, a kind of universal blandness in their treatment of anything spicy. It is no coincidence the menus displayed in the brochures for Thomson and Airtours both feature a good old roast, while the typical American version would highlight Lobster Thermidor or Filet Mignon. For some reason, however, Baked Alaska is a universal dessert on every cruise ship.

TRAVEL TIP

As a final note on Anglo-American differences, it remains true that the average US cruisers are more adept at complaining than their British counterparts. We tend to keep our niggles and worries to ourselves and whinge about it to each other. An American will tell the person in charge straight up – 'This isn't right and I want it changed.'

The European style of cruising, as practised by the likes of Costa, Mediterranean Shipping, Festival, Royal Olympic and Louis, offers an alternative change of emphasis. Less structured than us Brits, more formal than the Americans, occasionally rather raucous but usually quite chic, the Italian or Greek influence remains strong and surprisingly appealing, and the only real drawback is the need for repetitive multi-lingual announcements. Festival's newest ships *Mistral* and *European Vision* are wonderful examples of modern European design.

But, if that is the broad picture of the different types, how does this work in real terms? Well here is the most honest Who's Who appraisal of the main lines in the main cruising areas of the world, arranged, roughly, in ascending order.

WHO'S WHO (AND WHERE) IN THE CRUISE WORLD

	Ships	Rating	Caribbean (inc the Bahamas)	East Coast USA (inc Bermuda)	West Coast USA (inc Alaska)
Louis	9	Standard			
First Choice	1	Standard			
African SC*	1	Standard			
Clipper	4	Standard	YES	YES	YES
Thomson	2	Standard	YES		
MSC**	3	Stand/Sup	YES		
Royal Olympic	12	Stand/Prem	YES		
Fred Olsen	3	Stand/Sup	YES		
Airtours	3	Stand/Sup	YES		
Festival	4	Stand/Sup	YES		
Costa	9	St/Sup/Prem	YES		
Carnival	16	Sup/Prem	YES	YES	YES
P&O	4	Sup/Prem	YES		
NCL***	7	Premier	YES	YES	YES
Star Cruises	8	Premier			
Royal Caribbean	14	Premier	YES	YES	YES
Star Clippers	3	Prem/Deluxe	YES		
Princess	10	Sup/Pr/Del	YES	YES	YES
Saga	1	Premier	YES		
Swan Hellenic	1	Premier			
Orient	2	Premier			

The Med	Northern Europe	Atlantic (inc the Canaries)	Indian Ocean	Far East	South America	Others
YES						
YES						
			YES			
YES	YES			YES	YES	Transatlantic, Panama Canal, Antartica
YES						Transatlantic
YES		YES			YES	Transatlantic
YES	YES	YES			YES	Transatlantic, Panama Canal
YES	YES	YES	YES		YES	Transatlantic
YES	YES	YES				Transatlantic
YES	YES	YES				Transatlantic
YES	YES	YES				Transatlantic
						Panama Canal
YES	YES	YES				Transatlantic, World Cruise
YES	YES				YES	Transatlantic, Hawaii, Panama Canal
				YES		
YES	YES		YES	YES		Transatlantic, Hawaii, Panama Canal
YES				YES		Transatlantic,
YES	YES		YES	YES	YES	Transatlantic, Hawaii, Panama Canal
YES	YES	YES				Transatlantic, World Cruise
YES	YES		YES	YES		
YES	YES		YES	YES	YES	Transatlantic, Panama Canal, World journeys, Antarctica

	Ships	Rating	Caribbean (inc the Bahamas)	East Coast USA (inc Bermuda)	West Coast USA (inc Alaska)
Windstar	4	Deluxe	YES		
Renaissance	10	Deluxe	YES		
Holland America	10	Deluxe	YES	YES	YES
Cunard	2	Deluxe	YES	YES	
Celebrity	8	Deluxe	YES	YES	YES
Hebridean Island	2	Deluxe/ Ultra-Deluxe			
Hapag-Lloyd	4	Super/Deluxe/ Ultra-Deluxe			YES
Radisson	5	Deluxe/ Ultra-Deluxe	YES	YES	YES
Seabourn	5	Deluxe/ Ultra-Deluxe	YES	YES	
Silversea	4	Ultra-Deluxe	YES	YES	
Crystal	2	Ultra-Deluxe	YES		YES

*SC = Safari Club   **MSC = Mediterranean Shipping Cruises

The Med	Northern Europe	Atlantic (inc the Canaries)	Indian Ocean	Far East	South America	Others
YES						Transatlantic, Panama Canal, Costa Rica, New Zealand
YES	YES		YES	YES	YES	Transatlantic, South Pacific
YES	YES				YES	Transatlantic, Panama Canal, Hawaii, World Cruise
YES	YES	YES			YES	Transatlantic, Panama Canal, Hawaii, World Cruise
YES	YES				YES	Transatlantic, Panama Canal, Hawaii
YES	YES		YES			
YES	YES				YES	Antarctica, North-west Passage
YES	YES	YES	YES	YES		Transatlantic, Panama Canal, South Pacific
YES	YES	YES	YES	YES	YES	Transatlantic, Panama Canal, South Pacific
YES	YES		YES	YES	YES	Panama Canal, South Pacific, World Cruise
YES	YES			YES	YES	Panama Canal, South Pacific, World Cruise

***NCL = Norwegian Cruise Line

If that is the full rundown of the main cruise lines working in the British market, it is also informative (not to mention quite an amusing game with which to annoy party guests) to try to list the Top Ten lines worldwide in order of their size. Obviously, this is a fairly inexact process at the best of times because of the continual changes occurring in the cruise market, with companies selling off old stock, acquiring new ships or simply going bust. But, with the main ones, it is at least possible to come up with a table something like this.

THE TOP 10

SHIPPING LINE	NO. OF SHIPS	TONNAGE
Carnival Corporation	**46**	**2,327,019**
Carnival	16	1,179,571
Holland America	10	540,845
Windstar	4	31,854
Costa	9	441,505
Seabourn	5	38,425
Cunard	2	94,819
Royal Caribbean International	**22**	**1,817,875**
Royal Caribbean	14	1,227,159
Celebrity	8	590,716
P&O	**14**	**968,385**
Princess	10	730,665
P&O	4	237,720
Star Cruises	**18**	**770,205**
Star Cruises	8	284,251
NCL	7	429,624
Orient	2	56,330
Louis	**21**	**292,491**
Louis	9	114,236
Royal Olympic	12	178,255
Renaissance Cruises	**10**	**250,845**
Disney Cruise Line	**2**	**166,000**
Festival Cruises	**5**	**154,040**
Radisson Seven Seas	**5**	**122,729**
Crystal Cruises	**2**	**100,404**

It is fairly clear four lines dominate, with Carnival now owning around one third of the world's total cruise capacity. Royal Caribbean have kept pace, with the surprise acquisition of Celebrity in June 1997, and P&O and the youthful Star Cruises (now owners of NCL) remain the other mega-lines. However, in sheer profit terms, no one can touch Carnival's $965.5 million in 2000, from a total revenue of some $3.78 billion.

The picture for the Mediterranean – where the majority of British passengers can still be found – is rather different and has undergone a radical re-shaping since 1995. Italian line Costa, now owned by Carnival after a 1997 takeover, is traditionally the biggest carrier, with some 160,000 passengers in 2000 (Cyprus-based Louis Cruise Lines actually have more capacity, but the majority of their voyages are only two or three days), while Royal Olympic are a strong second (around 140,000) with their mix of two to seven-day cruises. Airtours have claimed a sizeable chunk of the market with around 80,000 passengers in 2000, followed by P&O/Princess with some 77,000, while the rapidly-developing and Brit-popular Festival and Mediterranean Shipping are in the 50,000 region. Thomson Cruises scaled back their operations in 2000 to limit their capacity to around 45,000, but remain one of the biggest British operators, while American lines Royal Caribbean (45,000), Holland America (39,000), Orient (26,000), NCL (24,000) and Windstar (20,000) are all significant.

When it comes to the major British-carrying lines, the top three are easy to identify, even allowing for the fact lines are pretty cagey about the figures they release. Airtours and P&O are firmly established as the Top Two, with worldwide figures of close to 100,000, while Thomson are a strong third (around 50,000), and this trio accounted for around 32 per cent of the total domestic figure of 754,416 passengers in 2000. The growing European presence of Royal Caribbean (including Celebrity) and NCL (including Orient) means these two have consolidated their position as the biggest British-carrying American lines, while Princess reckon to carry upwards of 30,000 UK passengers a year, putting them sixth. Carnival are making big strides with an increased profile through a marketing tie-up with Airtours (which has the integrated support of high street travel agent Going Places), while they also figure in an increasing number of brochures with other tour operators like Virgin Holidays and British Airways Holidays. As indicated above, Festival are a growing source of British passenger popularity, as are the Far East operations of Star Cruises, while Costa typically draw about 10 per cent of their customers from the UK. In more traditional vein, Cunard, Fred Olsen and Swan Hellenic remain solid bastions of British-ness at sea.

The more up-market lines of Holland America, Crystal, Silversea and Seabourn have also targeted the UK market in the last few years to the extent it is now pretty rare to find a sailing of even the most Ultra-Deluxe, exclusive line without at least a few Brits aboard.

BIG SHIP v SMALL SHIP

As well as the inherent differences between the lines, there is also a fair bit of variety to choose from when it comes to the size of the ships themselves, and so it is possible to set out some additional criteria which further help to focus your choice.

Big is not necessarily always best for some folks, even allowing for the fact the super-liners now have excellent passenger flow designs and will seldom make you feel you are at sea with as many as 3,000 fellow cruise devotees. The statistics show you can pick a ship as small as 3,000 tons (Star Clippers, Abercrombie & Kent) with as few as 96 passengers aboard, while you can go up to *Voyager of the Seas'* immense 142,000 tons and 3,600 passengers. I have already noted the need to study a ship's Space Ratio figure in order to assess its relative level of comfort; the other aspects of ship size are relatively obvious, but worth pointing out nonetheless.

The most basic difference is in the facilities on offer, and to a lesser extent the style of the ship as a consequence. Small ships in the sub-20,000-ton category seldom offer a large range of sporting activities, apart from water sports, and so if you are of an active persuasion and enjoy the social aspect of the likes of paddle tennis, shuffleboard and modern gymnasiums, then the larger ships will be more your cup of marine tea. However, the smaller ships score higher marks for a more personal level of service, greater relaxation potential and a more unstructured approach to life at sea. They also have the potential (sometimes overlooked) to get into the intimate nooks and crannies of the cruise world which their bigger brethren cannot squeeze. This means more imaginative itineraries, greater variety and the bonus of usually being able to dock alongside a pier rather than having to ferry passengers ashore by tender, which is common practice with the bigger ships in some ports of call and is a minor nuisance because of the extra time it can take as well as the question of accessibility it poses. The latter is of more concern to older passengers who may feel disinclined to tackle steep ladders and moving decks, as well as passengers with disabilities, but I will say more about those aspects later on.

In cruise terms, bigger (in the 50,000-ton-plus range) also tends to mean more modern, so you can be sure of state-of-the-art technology on offer by way of in-cabin TV, health facilities and video games, as well as much greater emphasis on children's activities, even to the provision of kids' swimming pools and on-deck play areas.

FLY-CRUISE v EX-UK CRUISE

Another key area where your cruise selection is important is deciding from where you cruise. This may sound absurdly obvious, but many people do not take the opportunity to consider the advantages of sailing out of a British port rather than flying to pick up your ship, and vice versa.

The choice is straightforward. Fly-cruising is the big area of growth in the British cruise market and offers far more variety and possibilities. The most recent PSA figures for British passengers show a ratio of almost 3:1 in favour of fly-cruising. The world is genuinely your lobster (to quote TV's Arthur Daley) and the full range of cruise line and ship choice is yours. The likes of Airtours, Thomson and First Choice also have an extensive choice of regional airports in use with their Mediterranean cruises, which adds to the flexibility of their packages. If you live in Newcastle, say, you have a much closer gateway to the port of Palma (Majorca – centre of the Mediterranean cruise world) than you have by travelling down to Southampton. However, it does not appeal to everyone, simply because not everyone is happy with the idea of flying, and there is inherently more hassle involved in a fly-cruise than with the ex-UK variety. You are more limited in the luggage you can take (flight allowances tend to be 20-25kg per person) and there is more of a let-down if you have a long journey home from, say, San Juan or Vancouver, than if you sail back into Southampton or Dover. The real beauty of ex-UK cruising, which gives you the choice of Southampton, Dover, London, Harwich (in the case of Royal Caribbean and Holland America) and Oban in Scotland (in the case of Hebridean Island Cruises), is you have to make only one journey to the docks – and both Southampton and Dover now have excellent road links – so you avoid all the hassle of getting through an airport and you can carry as much on board as, well, as you can carry.

In many cases, cruise lines like P&O (and big cruise agents Page & Moy) also have a well-organised coach transport system that picks up regionally, with the added bonus you put your cases on the coach at your starting point and pick them up again outside your cabin – it is all done for you. Saga Cruises, with their highly specific one-ship operation, go even further with private car and limousine transfers. There are no airport lounges to fester in, no long flights and no tedious airport-to-port transfers. Your cruise experience begins the moment you arrive at the port and, for anyone nervous of flying, it is a heaven-sent opportunity to travel without that particular worry. The down-side of ex-UK cruises is twofold – it takes longer to get to the areas you really want to see (with often the added drawback of losing out on a couple of days of good weather), and all Mediterranean-bound cruises have to negotiate the Bay of Biscay, which can be a mean stretch of water. There is also the option of mixing both varieties, by cruising out of Britain and then flying back either at the mid-point of the cruise or its final destination somewhere further on, or the other way round by flying out and cruising back. Somehow this option lacks the appeal of either, but P&O are still adept at matching you up with your car back in Britain either way.

SHORT v LONG

The question of how long to cruise for is probably the final all-important consideration at this stage, especially for first-timers to the cruise world. With this in mind, many cruise lines (notably Carnival, Louis Cruise

Lines, NCL, Premier, Royal Olympic, Disney, Royal Caribbean and, to a certain extent, P&O and Cunard) offer a selection of three- and four-day cruises specifically designed to attract the younger, new element interested in cruising, and much of the hardware used on these routes has been significantly up-graded by many lines from the rather tired, older ships that used to concentrate on this part of the business. The basic product is a rather more intense version of longer cruises, with more crammed into the available time, but is still a fairly accurate reflection of what it is all about and can make for a thoroughly worthwhile introduction, especially as an add-on to a land-based holiday. The main markets for the three- and four-day cruise are Cyprus and the Greek Islands, the Bahamas and Mexico (out of Miami, Fort Lauderdale, Tampa or Port Canaveral) and the Mexican Riviera (out of Los Angeles). My personal feeling is three days is not really long enough to appreciate fully the delights of being at sea, and, as most of the shorter options are fly-cruises only, it is quite an effort for such a limited experience (although if you are holidaying in Florida anyway they make a great add-on). But there is no denying the short-cruise option has gained significantly in popularity in the last five years, so I am probably in the minority here.

Having said all that, a week's cruise is generally regarded as the mass-market standard these days and is the area that has experienced most growth in the modern era. Seven days is obviously the ideal length of time to fit in with most holidays, especially as a cruise-and-stay option; and, if you pick the right cruise, you can enjoy the perfect cruise balance of days at sea and ports of call. It is still primarily a fly-cruise experience (there are few seven-day cruises out of Britain simply because you cannot get far enough in that time for a worthwhile, interesting round-trip cruise), and so, with the exception of Airtours and Thomson, Brits are more likely to be in the minority. Also, several of the American-designed week-long varieties in the Caribbean and even the Mediterranean are pretty port-intensive, which does not necessarily make for a relaxing experience. In addition, at the end of a week you will just be getting the hang of it – and it's time to get off!

Once you look beyond the fairly standard three-, four- and seven-day products, you find a much more eye-catching array of longer cruises which are designed in particular to appeal to the repeat passenger. They can be anything from 10 days up to the marathon world cruises of three months or more and will usually boast more exotic itineraries. As a general rule, they will also offer more days at sea (which is of direct interest to British cruisers I find) and a slight increase in the formality of the experience that goes with it (more dinners that demand a jacket and tie or DJ).

CRUISING FOR SINGLES

The attractions of cruising should, by now, be absolutely clear, but its viability does have limitations, and this is especially true for people travelling alone. Even though cruise figures show a good 10 per cent of cruisers are going solo, singles at sea consistently get the worst deals in terms of price with surcharges of up to 100 per cent on standard double-occupancy cabin rates. This is palpably unfair, but the majority of cruise lines argue they have to include a surcharge simply because their figures are all worked out on the basis of two sharing a cabin. There are, however, two ways around this for those who object to paying the extra.

Firstly, there ARE a few ships that offer genuine single cabins, although these tend to be the cabins that are most difficult to sell or are otherwise the least popular on board, such as the smallest inside ones. Several older liners (notably Fred Olsen's *Black Prince,* Thomson's *Topaz* and Saga's *Saga Rose*) plus an occasional new one (P&O lead the way here, plus Fred Olsen's *Black Watch* and Italian line Costa) offer single cabins, but they tend to be extremely limited in number and still work out slightly more expensive than double cabin rates.

TRAVEL TIP

Sadly, as single cabins are usually at a premium, you are not likely to find them discounted in the same way as many others. The key is to book as early as possible and take advantage of any early-booking incentives that many lines offer.

The second alternative to paying the single-occupancy surcharge is to take advantage of the quite common offers of a guaranteed share cabin, whereby the cruise line will attempt to find you a fellow passenger of the same sex and smoking preference. This way you pay only the normal double occupancy rate, and, if the company fails to find you a match, you get the whole cabin to yourself. Even if a cruise line does not show cabin-sharing in its brochure, it often pays to ask as they may well feel it necessary to compromise if that cruise is selling slowly.

TRAVEL TIP

Obviously, sharing a cabin with someone you have never met can have its drawbacks. Try making a guaranteed share booking out of season or on a repositioning cruise (see page 67) to increase your chance of getting offered the cabin to yourself.

If you can't avail yourself of either of these, you will find the alternative of a **guaranteed single rate**, where the cruise line guarantees the standard of your cabin (or possibly higher) but assigns the actual cabin to you only when you board, or a straightforward **single supplement**, which can be as low as 10 per cent the double occupancy fare (notably some Seabourn, Silversea and Holland America cruises); however, you can pay as much as twice the standard rate if it is a popular cruise or a larger cabin such as a suite. Once you are on board, there are obviously no limitations on singles enjoying the full range of facilities and activities, while there are several lines who go out of their way to make singles feel welcome with special parties, notably Carnival, Celebrity, Costa, Holland America, NCL, Orient, P&O, Princess and Seabourn. The romantic implications of travelling on your own have already been detailed in Chapter Three.

THE DISABLED AT SEA

It remains an awkward facet of holiday life that people with disabilities are regularly discriminated against, often thoughtlessly, but always to the point of their being excluded or their enjoyment of a particular activity being drastically reduced. This is especially true, as a general rule, at sea. Until the modern build of cruise ships, little or no thought was given to passengers with disabilities, either in providing specially adapted cabins or in making the ship generally accessible. So, if someone tries to tell you a ship built in the 1960s or 70s will happily accommodate anyone who relies on a wheelchair for their mobility, take your custom somewhere else. The very nature of sea-life makes the use of wheelchairs extremely difficult unless special provision is made or design factors are built in, as they are in newer ships. Smaller ships (under 20,000 tons) also generally have narrower aisles and companionways which make access awkward (Silversea are a notable exception here), while the older liners tend to have corridors within corridors on the main accommodation decks that again make negotiating them in a wheelchair almost impossible.

Having said all that, there is no reason why the physically challenged shouldn't enjoy a cruise as much as, or even more, than anyone else. Every new cruise ship now contains at least a handful of cabins designed for wheelchair users, with extra-wide doorways (most cabin doors are only two feet wide and hence completely inaccessible to most wheelchairs), conveniently-placed lights and shelves and bathrooms with stool-showers or grip bars.

Modern-build ships will also have plenty of lifts (the Americans call them elevators) and ramps rather than stairs into the public rooms and

TRAVEL TIP

If there is no available disabled-adapted cabin, opt for the largest-grade cabin you can afford and check the deck plan to pick one close to a lift and as near to the middle of the ship as possible to reduce any movement caused by the sea.

out on to the decks, with electric-eye doors. You MUST be sure to let the cruise line know of your disability in advance, and once again the specially adapted cabins do tend to be at a premium, so try to book early. Most lines will insist that a disabled person should bring their own wheelchair along (some ships do have them, but they are few and far between) and should be accompanied by an assistant or companion to help out in case of an emergency. However, it is always wise to double-check the exact arrangements if a ship claims to have special facilities for the disabled. Ask particularly about whether the ship docks or uses tenders at each port of call. The latter may well be completely impossible for wheelchair users.

TRAVEL TIP

Even if a cabin is specifically labelled in the brochure as for wheelchair access, get your travel agent to double-check the extent of the cabin design. It is no good if it has extra-wide doors but there is still a storm-seal (a raised lip of several inches in height) on the bathroom door.

Not every cruise line will accept guide dogs for the visually impaired, and so it is even more important to be able to take along an able-bodied companion. In addition, it is wise to let your cabin steward or stewardess know of any disability you may have, especially in case of hearing impairment, as they may have to make arrangements to enter your cabin in an emergency.

Common sense should be your guide to enjoying the full cruise experience – don't try to do anything you wouldn't normally attempt at home, and don't feel you have to try everything just because it is there! For more information or advice on this subject, you can contact the Royal Association for Disability and Rehabilitation (RADAR) in London, who publish several brochures on cruising; tel. 020 7250 3222.

TRAVEL AGENTS v
CRUISE CONSULTANTS

Now, once you have a good idea of what type of cruise you fancy, the next thing you will want to know is where to go to book it. Once again, your choice is quite varied, although, unlike the majority of holidays of the package variety, cruising does not readily conform to the type of standard retailing you encounter in your average high-street travel agent. It is more complicated, booking information is not usually accessible on their main computer terminals (although Royal Caribbean in particular are changing this aspect of the business for travel agents), it requires more specialist knowledge, and it is initially more expensive than a two-week package to the Mediterranean. The latter is crucial for two reasons. One, because the customer is spending more, they will demand a much higher level of service from the travel agent to ensure the booking is done correctly. And two, because the big multiple travel agents realise there is a boom in the British cruise business, they don't want to miss out on their slice of the pie and so are training up their sales agents to be more knowledgeable about cruising holidays in general and about selling cruises in particular. This in turn means the service does vary from each branch according to their level of training. Lunn Poly are the most recent to implement a Cruise Club for their existing cruise customers and have a number of key staff trained to offer a higher level of knowledge and service, as well as producing specialised literature in all their travel shops aimed at explaining all the advantages of cruising and highlighting its attractions (ask for the Cruise Welcome Aboard Directory which contains some useful at-a-glance information on the main lines as well as general cruise advice). Going Places have a well-organised cruise agent network, while Thomas Cook also have cruise consultants in some branches and a central cruise information service accessible from any branch. But it remains true, for all their efforts, the average high street holiday sales agent is still on the young side (average age early 20s) and there is a high turnover of staff, so some of the main misconceptions on cruising can still be perpetuated and you will not necessarily get the most comprehensive advice in this specialist area.

Thankfully, there is an organisation called PSARA that has helped to make the business of selling cruises more reliable, and there is also an alternative to the big retail outlets through specialist cruise consultants.

An important qualification to look out for when booking your cruise is if your travel agent is a member of PSARA, or the **Passenger Shipping Association Retail Agents** scheme. This body effectively tests and 'approves' all the responsible agents who sell cruises and runs training programmes and ship visits to try to ensure they really know their stuff. The trained agents will have a certificate from PSARA indicating their level of training and you can be reasonably confident they will be well clued up on recent developments as well as having a much better grasp of the complexities and varying aspects of cruising generally. In addition, if your cruise package is registered with the PSA (of which PSARA is the training arm), you can be sure your holiday will be fully protected against the possibility of the line cancelling your cruise, going bankrupt or otherwise ruining your holiday (although a full ABTA bonding is still the best protection for you and your holiday). Look up their website – www.cruiseinformationservice.co.uk – for more details or your nearest PSARA agent.

In addition to the PSARA qualification, the business of cruising is also unique in having its own specialist travel agents, or cruise consultants, who have grown up in response to the traditionally poor level of service provided by the high-street multiples. One of the prime movers in the development of cruise consultants in Britain is London-based Mundy Cruising, established back in 1970. As well as being the Harrods of cruise selling, **Mundy Cruising** produces its own brochures and newsletters with plenty of up-to-date information on the cruise world (look up www.mundycruising.com). Retired owner/director Paul Mundy was also instrumental in setting up the **Guild of Professional Cruise Agents**, who go even further than PSARA in their cruise training and the up-market service they offer as a result, and who are now becoming a far more active organisation and source of vital consumer info. The other benefit of a PSARA or GPCA travel shop is they work closely with the main cruise lines to produce their own special deals, discounts and other incentives which are not always available at the multiples, and the chances are their sales agents will have sailed on many of the ships they are dealing with and so will have first-hand knowledge of the product.

TRAVEL TIP

A quick perusal of Teletext should give you a choice of several PSARA-qualified cruise consultants and their latest offers (ITV, page 228, the last time I looked). But, always check their ABTA or PSARA qualifications for your peace of mind. It is a fast-changing section and some offers come and go suspiciously quickly. If in doubt, a cruise line will always be able to recommend a list of reputable agents.

The largest British cruise consultants are Page & Moy who frequently charter whole ships or block-book large numbers of cabins and then sell them at their own, usually discounted, rates. They publish their own Cruise Hot List (call 0116 250 7722 for a copy) with the latest deals and special offers, and arrange notable extras like coach transfers on many ex-UK sailings.

What the travel agent said

Page & Moy director David Short – another cruise addict like myself – once told me: 'Very often when I meet people after they have just come off their first cruise, the first thing they say to me is "If only I had discovered cruising when I was younger!" That is the single biggest message the industry needs to get across, how enjoyable it is for people of ALL ages. This is especially true for people with families. It is an ideal kind of holiday. From the age of three or so upwards, it just gets better and better for kids as they get older. And, if you create a happy child, you create happy parents.' So, you see, you don't have to take just my word for it.

Another GPCA cruise agent worth knowing about for their expertise are **The Cruise Line Ltd**, especially as they also publish their own informative magazine, *World of Cruising*, which contains a wealth of information for both the first-timer and experienced cruiser (but then I would say that – I edit it). Call 01273 835252 or look up www.cruiseline.co.uk for more details.

The essential advice here is to shop around before taking the plunge. A cruise still represents a significant outlay of money and it makes sense to have a good idea of all your options. Don't be afraid to ask questions, no matter how basic they may seem to you; don't be forced into accepting something which is not totally to your taste just because there is a bigger discount; and, if the advice on offer does not seem quite up to the mark, go elsewhere. Beware in particular of an agent who insists that so and so is 'The best cruise line in the world', or such and such a ship is 'The ultimate in luxury'. There are no such definitive designations and these claims are usually a sign of a major discount on an unpopular cruise. While cruising does genuinely represent great holiday excitement and value, you will NOT enjoy being put on the wrong ship for your tastes. Equally, if you are paying budget-level prices, you shouldn't expect the luxury treatment.

TRAVEL TIP

It is still possible (and I stress the 'possible' as it is gradually being eliminated by the cruise lines) to reduce your cruise cost further by flying out to Miami or Fort Lauderdale and ringing the lines direct to see if they have any last-minute availability (called 'distressed stock' in the trade), usually at knock-down prices. These walk-up cruises are not something the lines like to advertise, but you can pick up some bargains. However, it should be stressed there are no guarantees and many sailings are now fully booked well in advance. But, if you are flexible enough to give it a try, here are the local numbers to call: Carnival, 1-800 CARNIVAL; Celebrity, 305 262 6677; Costa, 1-800 462 6782; Premier, 305 358 5122; Norwegian Cruise Line, 305 436 0866 (in Miami) or 1-800 327 7030 elsewhere in Florida; and Royal Caribbean, 305 379 4731 (in Miami) or 1-800 432 6559 elsewhere in Florida. Alternatively, in the Miami area try South Beach Cruises on 305 538 3020 for any last-minute deals. Nearly all cruises depart on Saturday or Sunday and, obviously, you are taking a chance, but there are savings to be had and you are handily placed for a pleasant holiday even if you don't get on.

There are more than 1,200 PSARA travel agents, all identifiable by the white red and blue window sticker which announces them as an 'Official Travel Agent for the Cruise Industry'. For more help and advice on these matters, and for the nearest PSARA cruise agent to you, contact PSARA on 020 7436 2449 (or on their website, see page 90). For more information on the Guild of Professional Cruise Agents, call chairman Kevin Griffin at The Cruise People on 020 7723 2450 or look them up on www.leadingcruiseagents.com. And, for examples of the independent cruise consultants for whom I can personally vouch, try Cruise Club International in Bromley, Kent on 020 8466 7000 or the Cruise Advisory Service in Salisbury, Wiltshire, on 01722 335505.

THE CRUISE EXPERIENCE

Now, once you have booked your cruise, what sort of experience should you expect (apart from one that's fun, relaxing, exciting, family-orientated and value for money)?

Here, especially for cruise newcomers, is a typical example of what cruising is all about, from start to finish.

Embarkation

Your anticipation should be at its highest for the moment of boarding your chosen vessel. In most main ports, embarkation is now a process similar to an airport check-in. On American ships you will have to

Don't mention the 'D' word!

When it comes to booking a cruise, the price you see in the brochure often bears little relation to what you finally pay, except as a starting point from which to work down. It is an unfortunate fact of life for the cruise lines (but something of their own creating) passengers have grown to expect some form of discount whenever they are booking. These discounts come in various forms (and sometimes are called anything but a discount simply because the industry has become so averse to the term), but are always worth checking on. The most common incentives are the last-minute bookings where a cruise is likely to sail less than full and so the line advertises significant late discounts or two-for-one offers to try to fill the spare capacity. You may have limited choice of cabins, but, if you can travel at short notice, you can snap up some real bargains, especially in the Caribbean out of the main holiday periods. However, the industry as a whole has become a little wary of this practice and so now often tries to do things in reverse by offering significant savings for *early* bookings. In the case of Royal Caribbean and Celebrity, they offer a Breakthrough price system, with up to 30 per cent savings for early bookers. Carnival have a Today's Price offer, which is a discount which generally decreases as sailing date approaches, but most lines now highlight early booking savings (see Chapter 5 on the individual cruise lines) if you book more than 60 days in advance. On top of early-booking discounts, look out for additional discount rates with some of the Cruise Consultants (which the cruise lines pass on as an incentive for good business or for taking out block-bookings) which come *on top* of the early booking savings. Finally, you can also make substantial savings where a third or fourth person shares a cabin with two full-fare-paying adults, although you need to be very good friends as this can make for a crowded cabin in most cases.

surrender your passport (you're a foreigner, remember) and in return you will receive your Boarding Card, which in most cases you will keep with you at all times, especially when re-boarding the ship at its ports of call. It will also be your on-board credit card and ID.

TRAVEL TIP

I always try to embark at the earliest possible opportunity. The queues may well be long, but you will still be on board before the majority and will have the chance to explore the ship before it starts to get busy, which is a wonderful experience.

If you still have your cases at this point, they will be taken away from you for delivery to your cabin, so make sure they are properly marked with your deck and cabin number. On fly-cruises, the chances are your luggage will be carried from the baggage hall by the cruise line's local ground agents to the ship and aboard without you having to reclaim it.

≋ TRAVEL TIP ≋

As you are standing in the queue at the embarkation desk, try to get one of your party to make sure you have received, and filled in, the necessary paperwork which will usually consist of an embarkation form and a customs declaration. It is so annoying to get to the front of the queue and find out there is another form to fill in.

Once checked in, you will often meet the Maître D' who will show you the dining room's seating plan and your choice of First or Second Sitting. Check if your dining arrangements are as per your booking, as this will be your best chance to change them. Before you are allowed aboard, you will have to endure the obligatory Welcome Aboard photo session with the ship's photographers. You are *not* obliged to buy anything (you may not be at your best if you've just had a long flight, after all), so it is churlish to be uncooperative. This will be the first of many official photo opportunities that can be a bit irksome after a while, but they will always be on display at the ship's photo shop for you to examine before you decide whether to buy.

≋ TRAVEL TIP ≋

Your luggage should be waiting for you outside your cabin, or arrive soon after you do. If it has not arrived shortly before you are due to sail, contact the Purser's Desk urgently.

Boarding

Again, this is a moment to savour as you make your way up the gangway and into (usually) the ship's main reception area or foyer. If you are lucky enough to be walking into the *Sun Princess* for the first time (or another of the super-liners which specialize in impressive atrium lobbies), prepare to have your breath taken away by the awe-inspiring splendor of the initial view. This will be your first confirmation you have made the Right Choice. You should immediately be met by one of the Purser's or Hotel Director's staff who will ask for your cabin number and assign a steward to show you the way.

Your cabin

The steward will usually leave you at your cabin to allow your full-time steward to welcome you officially and show you how everything works (if it isn't immediately obvious – I still have nightmares about trying to use the pen in one particular cabin, only for the steward to demonstrate with great tact I was trying to open the wrong end!). Check straight away the cabin's facilities are exactly as you ordered, especially whether those twin beds do really convert into a double. Any queries or errors should be reported immediately to your steward or the Purser's Desk and, while it may take a little more time on the busiest day of the cruise, you should receive relatively prompt attention. Whether you unpack straight away is obviously up to you. First, however, cast an eye over your Cruise News, as this is the single most important piece of literature you will receive. The Cruise News (or other variation on that name) is your daily shipboard newspaper which lists all the various activities, their times and locations, dining times, opening hours of the bars, health centre and beauty salon, and the entertainment programme for the evening. It will be delivered to your cabin every evening so you can study the next day's schedule of events and plan your campaign accordingly.

Exploring your ship

If, like me, you have been studying the brochure layout of the ship avidly in advance of the cruise, you will now find it bears little or no relation to the reality. This is because, no matter how well versed you are or how many other ships you have been on, you can never get your bearings straight away, even to the point sometimes of not knowing which deck you are on. Stop just for a second and make sure of two key points: one, whether you are facing forward or aft, and two, if you are on the left or right hand side (port or starboard, see below). Try to establish some key landmarks that will enable you to orientate yourself along these two lines and you will be half-way to being able to tell your fellow passengers smugly: 'The Crow's Nest Bar? Ah yes, that's forward and up three decks'. Obviously, the way you progress after that is up to you, but I find it best to work my way systematically up through the decks before taking a turn around the topmost deck (this is usually the Sun Deck) and then retiring to the nearest bar to congratulate myself on my choice. You can also visit the Purser's Desk to arrange your on-board credit, but you will not be hassled to do this straight away as you can still start signing things to your cabin provided you have your boarding card handy. This is also your opportunity to get ahead of the rest by booking your visit to the hair salon for the optimum time for you and, if the ship has an alternative dining room, to book a visit there while you have the most choice.

TRAVEL TIP

The best advice for booking any alternative dining arrangement is to avoid the formal nights as these are best enjoyed in the main dining room. A port day may be a better choice, especially as you can probably leave the time a little later than normal to allow yourself maximum time ashore.

In most cases, before you sail (and certainly within 24 hours of being underway) there will be the Lifeboat Drill, which you are required to attend, with your life-jacket. These days it is little more than the type of safety advice everyone ignores before a plane takes off, but it is compulsory and it doesn't take too long. It is also important, especially with children, to know such details as your Muster Station and how your life-jacket does up. And, please, don't walk along with your life-jacket tapes undone and trailing behind you – the number of people who trip over them is just amazing.

The first evening

This will probably be a fairly casual affair with people boarding at different times, and it is possible you may not meet all your dinner table companions straight away. The dining room staff should be at their keenest to welcome you aboard, however, and you will be introduced in quick succession to your wine waiter/waitress, the head waiter for your section of the dining room and the Maître D', if you have not already met. The rest of the evening will be relatively low key as the entertainments staff keep their powder dry to impress you later in the cruise and the majority will opt for an early-ish night in preparation for the first full day (unless you are on a three- or four-day cruise, in which case it is party time from the moment you step aboard).

The first day

If you have chosen your itinerary carefully, you will have the enjoyment of a full day at sea to start with, thus giving you a proper and leisurely introduction to the ship. You can enjoy an early taste of the daytime events and facilities, like the deck games, and get a feel for which areas of the deck are most likely to be crowded, and where those quiet little spots are. There may also be a 'Question and Answer' session in the morning for any queries about ship-board life you may have at this stage. Watch out in your Cruise News for the Shore Excursions presentation (mentioned in Chapter Three) as this may be your first chance to book those organised shore-side visits (although many lines now provide information before you travel with the chance to book excursions in advance).

TRAVEL TIP

If you are one of those people who hate doing Christmas shopping for fear of finding everything you buy reduced in the New Year sales, don't use the first day aboard as an opportunity to do all your souvenir shopping in the ship's boutiques. Apart from the fact you may want to avoid looking like several hundred others in your MS *Whatever* T-shirt, you will probably find the shop has various special offers during the cruise, especially on the last few days, when standard items are seriously reduced in price.

The evening is likely to be a formal one, with a Welcome Aboard reception for each sitting, hosted by the Captain, which offers you the chance to sip a complimentary glass of sparkling wine and meet the rest of the ship's crew in a brief 'Who's Who' parade of the officers and entertainments staff.

The first port of call

This gives the ship a chance to slip into a different gear as the majority of events are orientated towards going ashore rather than staying on board (although there's nothing to stop you just putting your feet up by the pool all day – it's a good time to enjoy a larger amount of deck space to yourself). If you have never sailed into a new port before, it is worth being up early to enjoy that unique, heady experience as the ship takes on board the local pilot and almost imperceptibly drifts into the harbour ready for the start of a new adventure. Quite often, there will be something of an undignified stampede for the disembarkation station (which may well be lower down in the ship than the reception area where you came on) as everyone tries to get off at the same time in order to take full advantage of their port time (Princess are a notable exception for their efficient embarkation/disembarkation procedures, even on the 2,600-passenger *Grand* and *Golden Princess*). This is one of the few areas where the larger ships struggle to cope with their passenger volume, and it can take a little while to get everyone sorted out and off the ship. People booked on the first shore excursions will have right of way as they are running to a timetable and need to be first off, then it is every man (and woman) for themselves. If you are just wandering ashore under your own steam, make a good note of where the ship is docked (get the address written down if you take a local taxi) and how long it takes to walk into the main town area. Sometimes the harbour is not immediately adjacent to the town and the ship will lay on shuttle buses to do the round trip. Again, make a careful mental note of where they pick you up and drop you off. Finally, the ship will ask you to be back on board half an hour before sailing again, so try to leave 30 minutes on top of that to be on the safe side. There is no more doomed feeling than racing back to the ship thinking you might miss it – I speak from personal experience! It's not like missing a plane, either. There *won't* be another one along soon.

The final evening

Cries of 'Where did the last week/ten days/two weeks go?' abound as you realise you have arrived at the penultimate day of your cruise and have to prepare on the final evening for disembarkation the next morning (cruise ships invariably dock at the most inhospitable times, around 6-7am, in order to be able to get one load off and the next load on, the same day). There is something of an art form to preparing your cases, hand luggage and what to wear as most cruise lines will insist on having your suitcases loaded and outside your cabin door before midnight (some insist on 8pm which is patently absurd when you have not even been to dinner by that time. It pays to be 'forgetful' in that instance – as long as your cases are ready to go by midnight there should be ample time for the crew to sort them out). You will probably be given a series of colour-coded tags to put on all your luggage so it can be readily identified on the quayside. If you are on a fly-cruise and have a flight to catch that day, you shouldn't need to do any toting of your own cases, you simply identify them as yours and they will be put on the coach to the airport for you. The colour-coding

Food and Drink

Here's a typical shopping-list for a 14-day cruise aboard P&O's *Oriana* – more than a few trips to Sainsbury's!

On an average 14-day voyage, the 1,975 passengers and 760 crew will eat no less than 116,550 meals, prepared from:

Bacon, ham and gammon	3.4 tons	Fresh fruit and vegetables	28.0 tons
Beer	33,000 bottles/cans	Gin, rum and vodka	1,200 litres
Butter, fats and cheese	4.5 tons	Ice cream	1,050 gallons
Champagne, sparkling and white wine	2,600 bottles	Meat	14.4 tons
		Milk and cream	2,775 gallons
		Minerals	28,000 bottles
Coffee	0.6 tons	Potatoes	17.7 tons
Cognac	400 litres	Poultry and game	6.8 tons
Fish	3.6 tons	Red wine	1,200 bottles
Flour	8.4 tons	Shellfish	1.7 tons
Fresh eggs	51,000	Sugar	1.9 tons
		Whisky	1,600 litres

system also allows for passengers to be disembarked by flights, so, if you have an earlier plane to catch, you will be among the first off.

Other disembarkation details will include a final statement of your ship-board credit account which you should always check to make sure it tallies with your recollections of your own spending (this can be a frightening moment when the awful truth of enjoying those daily rounds of cocktails finally catches up with you!). In most cases, if you have left a credit card imprint with the Purser's Desk and the account adds up correctly, you need do nothing else. If you are paying by cheque or cash, you must obviously visit the Desk in person to pay up. The other last-evening ritual is tipping, and you will find at least three empty envelopes have mysteriously appeared in your cabin, usually marked 'Steward', 'Waiter' and 'Busboy' (if none have appeared, you can usually collect them from the main reception desk). At this stage, you have to work out the recommended daily tipping rate (every line should make this clear either in their brochure or in the Cruise News). It generally works out at $3–$3.50 (or £2–£2.30) per person per day for your cabin steward and waiter, and half that for the busboy and any assistant steward. If the head waiter or maître d' has been of particular help, $10–$15 (£7–£10) is the going rate for tipping them. The end of the last evening's meal then usually sees a mass exchange of envelopes like some secret society! Once the dining room staff have received their gratuities, it is a rare but not totally unknown occurrence for them to be less than their fully co-operative and friendly selves on the next morning. Should you run into this attitude, you should report it to the Hotel Director.

Disembarkation

Remember all those queues to get off at the ports of call? Well, this is as bad. The final ritual of disembarking is an unavoidable pain in most cases simply because the vast majority of passengers have little alternative but to hang around in the main lounges with their hand luggage, waiting to be called off. The effects can be lessened by breakfasting as late as possible (there should still be a buffet choice to avoid having to suffer first sitting in the main dining room at 6am or some similarly ridiculous hour) and taking a final stroll around deck (a surprising number of people seem to neglect this), but you will not be able to wait in your cabin as the steward will be wanting to get it ready for the next passengers, and they are on a strict timetable. Make sure you know your luggage tag colour code and try to be patient. Even allowing for a full passenger load, disembarkation rarely takes more than two hours and the whole process is pretty well organised to minimise any hassle once you are off the ship.

Returning to a UK port is still the most civilised way to conclude a cruise, and the smooth disembarkation procedures at Southampton and Dover help to minimise the 'After the Lord Mayor's Show' kind of feeling. P&O's frighteningly efficient process at the Mayflower terminal in Southampton is guaranteed to get you back in your car or coach and on the road as painlessly as possible. You just have to collect your luggage from the main holding area, load it on the trolleys provided and check in with the car parking kiosk immediately outside the terminal entrance. The main disadvantage is you are distanced from your recent maritime home with alarming rapidity and find yourself back in the real world all too quickly.

I'm afraid there is no known antidote for that sad, end-of-cruise feeling, but you can console yourself with the thought of planning your next cruise. You see, I *told* you it was addictive!

If I can add another anecdote here to further illustrate the captivating nature of cruising for all ages, we took a short family cruise on P&O's *Arcadia* in summer 1999 with our two boys Anthony (then 3½) and Mark (just 15 months), both of whom are now near-veteran cruisers themselves little more than two years later. At that time, Anthony was old enough to go into the kids' club on his own for the first time and was in child heaven as he split his time between Peter Pan's and the ship's pools. It was truly amazing to see how quickly and thoroughly he adapted to such a different environment – and how well the children's set-up suited him and his brother (although one of us always had to stay and supervise Mark as he was too young to be left on his own). The combination of organised activities, free time in the pool and two engaging ports of call (Guernsey and Amsterdam); there was, actually, a third, Zeebrugge, but the weather was so balmy we opted to stay aboard and take advantage of a near-empty Lido Deck) made for an extremely happy family for four days as we all had time to ourselves at various stages (the feature P&O Night Nursery is perfectly operated to allow parents their evening-time freedom) and made the most of our time together. However, as we pulled back into Southampton early on the final day, Anthony surveyed the

LEARNING SHIP-SPEAK

No explanation of the world of cruising would be complete at this stage without an explanation of what all those nautical terms really mean. And here, to help you be able to speak like an old salt, is my unique guide to that wonderful world of marine language.

SHIP-SPEAK	WHAT IT REALLY MEANS
Aft	Toward the stern or blunt end of the ship
Amidships	In the middle
Astern (as in, to go astern)	Reverse gear (or, a very serious look)
Avast there!	There's something rather large over there
Beam	Width of the ship (or, what you do to the ship's photographer)
Bow	The pointy bit at the front
Bridge	Where the Captain watches the computers running the ship
Bulkhead	The main 'walls' that divide the ship into compartments (see, a sensible one!)
Companionway	The ship's narrow corridor where people can't avoid being friendly
Course	Where you play golf (Eh? – Ed.)
Crew	The ship's staff (Cue the question: 'Do the crew sleep aboard?' I kid you not)
Crow's nest	A hair-do in rough seas
Disembark	Everybody Off!
Embark	Everybody On!
First sitting	The chance to digest your evening meal in time for the Midnight Buffet
Fly-cruise	A really fast cruise
Forward	Towards the pointy bit (or, the right attitude at the Singles' Party)
Funnel	A yellow-flowered aniseed-flavoured herb (Er... – Ed.)
Galley	The cause of every cruise passenger putting on about 1lb a day
Gangway	What you shout when disembarking
Gross registered tonnage	The opposite of civilised registered tonnage
Hull	A shortened greeting

Inside cabin	An obscure tailoring measurement
Knot	A nautical mile per hour that frequently gets land-lubbers in a tangle (see below)
Maître d'	The person in the dining room you will see only on the first night (to ingratiate himself) and the last (to hope for a tip)
Nautical mile	A 60th of one degree of the earth's circumference, equal to 6,080 feet, and 800 feet longer than a land mile (so there!)
Open seating	The cruise version of Open Sesame
Port	1) The left-hand side; port = left because it has the same number of letters in 2) Where the ship visits; hence, 'We left the port well alone'
Port tax	1) Left-handed drawing pins 2) A sneaky add-on charge that is gradually being phased out
Quay	What you use to unlock the door
Rudder	An alternative; as in, 'I'd rudder be on anudder cruise'
Ship	Never, *never* a Boat
Space Ratio	The bigger the ship, the more space it takes up in port
Stabiliser	The first drink of the next day
Starboard	1) An uninspired guest star 2) The right-hand side; right = starboard because it has, er, more letters in
Stateroom	Cabin, as in, look at the state of this room
Stern	The blunt end
Tender	The boats which the ship carries to get you ashore where the ship can't dock (or, what you are without a stabiliser)
Tips	'Look both ways before crossing the road' 'Neither a borrower nor a lender be', etc.
'Weigh anchor!'	'23lb 4oz!' (My mum's favourite nautical joke)

embarkation scene from the cabin window and asked quite plaintively: 'But Daddy, why do we have to get off?' There was just no answer to that.

Suffice it to say here, we have found cruising to be the ideal family holiday on a number of occasions, from Northern Europe to the Mediterranean and Caribbean, and I know I will have no trouble persuading my brood to set sail again in future, sure in the knowledge we will all have a thoroughly enjoyable – and quite magical – time together.

To complete this rather irreverent finale, I'm going to borrow a few famous cruise 'quotes', as asked by some of the (American, I hope) passengers of Celebrity, and a few others.

'Does the elevator go to the front of the ship?'

'Why does the ship rock only when we are at sea?'

'Does the ship generate its own electricity?' (You can just imagine the answer: 'No madam, can't you see the cable we're running all way back to Miami?')

'Will I get wet if I go snorkelling?'

'Which stairs go up?'

'What do you do with the ice carvings after they melt?' (Have you ever heard of water carvings?)

'Does the crew sleep on board?' (No, they swim ashore every night.)

'Is there water all around the island?'

'What time is the midnight buffet?' (This one is the oldest and most often-repeated saying.)

'Will the trap-shooting be held outside?' ('No sir, we thought we'd use your cabin.')

'How will we know which photos are ours?'

And my current favourite – to one of the deck staff: 'Is that sea water in the pool?' 'Yes sir, it is.' 'Ah, that would explain why there are so many waves in it.'

All additions gratefully received.

Now, it is time to delve deeper into the specifics and ask the vitally important question, 'What line should I choose?' ...

CHAPTER FIVE

THE CRUISE LINES AND THEIR SHIPS

Having discussed the generalities of cruising and then tried to put them into perspective with Chapter Four's look at how and why to make your booking, it now seems logical to make a more in-depth examination of the cruise lines themselves, how they differ, the ships they offer and what to expect of the different cruise experiences.

At the last count, there were 40 major cruise lines all selling directly to the great British public. With the aid of the Brit's Guide categories, you should be able to draw a comprehensive picture of the style and appeal of each one and decide which is the one for you. It should also be fairly evident where a cruise line deals more heavily in the UK market (like the predominantly British-orientated ships of P&O, Airtours, Thomson, Swan Hellenic and Fred Olsen), and I make no apologies for concentrating more of my attention and therefore more of this book's space on them for obvious reasons. No other travel guide attempts to do this, but I am convinced it is a worthwhile exercise and you can be sure, therefore, of the best possible attention to detail in the *British* area of the market.

To that end, several of the ships have been marked out as *Brit's Guide Favourites* due to their innate Brit appeal. Some are obvious (where they cater specifically for UK passengers), others not so obvious (where they have yet to be 'discovered'), but all possess an extra element that makes them a bit special for the domestic market.

Look out at the end of the book for the **Daily Express** **British Cruise Awards**, a celebrated new feature in the cruise world created by the Brit's Guide and put together by an eminent panel of experts, which has really given the industry a new dimension.

When it comes to the technical terminology, the Space Ratio figure, remember, is the rather arbitrary figure derived by dividing the ship's gross registered tonnage by its full passenger load to give you a general idea of spaciousness. Anything 20 or less is poor, 30 is average, 40 very good and 50 or above is excellent. The five Rating categories, remember, are Standard, Superior, Premier, Deluxe and Ultra-Deluxe, where **Standard** means older ships and value for money rather than finesse; **Superior** covers better quality older ships or newer ones that don't quite reach the super-liner level of style; **Premier** is the large, new mass-market range; **Deluxe** introduces a touch of class to all levels of hardware and

103

service; and **Ultra-Deluxe** means true luxury.

The Passenger/Crew figures provide a quick guide to the service levels aboard, with a ratio of 2.3:1 being the industry average while anything approaching 1.5:1 is outstanding.

AFRICAN SAFARI CLUB

Ship	Tonnage	Passengers/ Crew	Space Ratio	Built/ Refurbished	Cruise Area	Rating
Royal Star	5,600	222/120	25.2	1956/94	Indian Ocean	Standard

Cruise line notes

African Safari Club is a Swiss-owned hotel group offering specialist tours to Kenya and running its one-ship operation in conjunction with land-based holidays and safaris. It flies British customers from Gatwick to Mombasa via Frankfurt or Basel in its own aircraft and offers a combination stay at one of its resorts with a cruise varying in duration from nine to 18 nights.

Ship notes

Charming small-ship style is allied with some wonderful itineraries, taking in the Seychelles, Zanzibar, Madagascar, the Maldives, Mauritius, the Comores and even India and Sri Lanka. Limited facilities and daytime events, plus smallish cabins (and even smaller 'bathrooms') add up to a Standard rating, but service comes with a ready smile and the atmosphere is always relaxed and friendly. International cuisine style reflects fully European passenger profile, mainly couples of 40-plus. Not recommended for children or the disabled, though.

Extras

A minimum of two nights' full board at one of ASC's Kenya coast hotels is included with most packages, along with your port taxes. Single supplement is only 30 per cent on the majority of cabins and ship-board currency is, unusually, the German mark. Excellent value for money at these prices, plus there are optional safari tours. ASC also guarantee that any price reductions after booking will automatically be passed on to their customers.

For brochures, phone 020 8466 0014.

AIRTOURS
www.airtours.co.uk

Ships	Tonnage	Passengers/ Crew	Space Ratio	Built/ Refurbished	Cruise Area	Rating
Carousel	23,200	1,062/434	21.8	1971/95	Mediterranean, Caribbean, Transatlantic	Standard
Seawing	16,607	752/320	22	1971/95	Mediterranean, Canaries	Standard
Sundream	22,945	1,146/425	20	1971/94	Med, N Europe, Caribbean, Transatlantic	Standard
Sunbird	37,584	1,432/540	26.2	1982/99	Mediterranean, Caribbean	Superior

Cruise line notes

One of Britain's Big Three tour operators, Airtours effectively broke the mould of budget-level cruising when they bought two ships to enter the market in 1995. Suddenly, here was cruising offered to the British package holiday market at a hugely tempting price and without too much compromising on quality. Airtours were so successful, they sold out their summer seasons in both 1995 and 96 in double-quick time and effectively opened up the cruise world to a whole new clientele, adding a third ship in 1997 and a fourth for 1999 which significantly increased the appeal and level of their hardware. Airtours' existing tour infra-structure means they can cut down on traditional cruise overheads like flights, ground agents and shore excursions and pass on the savings to their passengers, hence terrific value for money in the Standard level of cruising and excellent shoreside organisation, too (notably on their Caribbean cruises from Barbados, with their airport-ship transfers and all shore excursions). Airtours' Scandinavian, US and Canadian travel company links mean you will find Norwegian and Danish passengers on many of their Mediterranean sailings and Americans and Canadians on the Caribbean ones, but this is essentially a British operation from top to bottom, appealing to anyone who has enjoyed a land-based Airtours holiday as well as cruisers on a budget.

A full age profile is highlighted by large numbers of families during the holiday periods and busy kids' programmes, but the ships are not well suited for disabled passengers. Initially, you just booked one of the six grades of cabin rather than a cabin in particular, and were then assigned your cabin on arrival, but they now offer a pre-booking facility (although at £50/cabin). In 2001, they opened up a new range of options to allow passengers to add on particular features, like all-inclusive drinks. The Economy holidays represent the basic level of package, while the Holiday Plus choice adds free pre-bookable flight seating, a free drink voucher, cheaper flight upgrades, a bigger luggage allowance and a pre-departure pack. The All Inclusive package adds unlimited brand name alcohol for £149 per person, per week (served between 10am and 2am; £49 for unlimited soft drinks per child), and the Prestige Option allows you to pre-book your cabin, check in later for your flight (with an increased baggage allowance), and provides free headphones and a drink voucher.

TRAVEL TIP

Airtours' standard product is seven- and 14-day fly-cruising in both the Mediterranean and Caribbean, but they also offer several cruises up to 23 days long as *Sunbird, Sundream* and *Carousel* position across the Atlantic twice a year.

Lack of some of the usual cruise formality is another Airtours policy, and they also feature an increased range of cruises throughout the Med (based in Palma or Cyprus) and the Caribbean (using Jamaica and Barbados as their home ports), including Cuba, Limon on Costa Rica, Colombia, the San Blas Islands and the Panama Canal. Regular 14-night cruises are another recent feature and indicate the company's growing sophistication. New in 2000 were a series of 14-night cruises out of Southampton and Harwich to the western Mediterranean and Canaries, the Baltic and Norwegian fjords, bringing the Airtours cruise style to Britain's front door for the first time.

Ship notes

Airtours started by buying the *Southward* from Norwegian Cruise Line (now the *Seawing,* which has been sold to Royal Olympic and chartered back) and quickly found they needed another after selling out, so they immediately added Royal Caribbean's *Nordic Prince* (now the *Carousel*) to their stable. A further Royal Caribbean vessel, *Song of Norway*, sister ship to *Nordic Prince,* soon followed. All three are 1970s vintage, and so, despite being thoroughly refurbished before sailing under the colours of Airtours' cruise arm Sun Cruises, they lack some of the sophisticated touches of modern ships. Standard cabins are a little on the cramped side (especially for wardrobe and drawer space), but they all make good use of some pleasant artwork and tasteful soft furnishings. Good and usually plentiful food is served by friendly waiters, and the eager-to-please entertainments staff run a busy programme of daily events, albeit of the more predictable kind.

The original three ships can feel a little crowded when full and deck space is then at a premium (these are originally American-market vessels, and hence open deck space was not a priority), and you may not find the overall experience relaxing if you are looking for a quiet holiday. The virtually identical *Carousel* and *Sundream* are the slightly better equipped of the trio, with a choice of three lounges to *Seawing*'s two, but the latter has the snazzier Crow's Nest Nightclub. The gyms are all rather small and could be better equipped.

New ship *Sunbird,* formerly Royal Caribbean's *Song of America,* added a new dimension in 1999, a more up-market, modern vessel packed with extra choice, facilities and glamour – including the novelty of butler service in the handful of extremely spacious and well-fitted suites. *Sunbird* comes complete with two pools (both with splash areas for the kids) on the pretty, multi-level lido deck, a fully-equipped gym and sauna, two showlounges, another four bars (two outside) and an impressive nightclub, as well as a library, glitzy casino and an enhanced range of shops and beauty salon options. All cabins have colour TV and pleasant, modern furnishings, while the 11 suites come with balconies as well as butlers in their own exclusive little enclave on the ship. Food quality is very good for this level of cruise, and the open-air Lido Buffet, quite refreshingly, offers alternative, casual dining in the evening. The deck layout is a touch awkward and confusing in places (finding the gym or beauty salon can be a challenge), but overall *Sunbird* offers the next step up for Airtours passengers. Although there are five categories of cabin, there are no real differences between the lower five, so the standard inside and outside cabins are our tip for best value. All in all, the ship is a well-polished and quite stylish offering, and her Caribbean itineraries in particular represent some of the best value to be had in this area of the cruise market.

Extras

Airtours offer excellent value for money, on-board drink prices are very reasonable and shore excursions well-organised, as you would expect from a package-holiday outfit. No frills or glitz, and the overall product could do with a bit of polish (*Sunbird* excepted), but staff help to make it a fun experience and the appeal is quite broad-based. No special provision for disabled passengers, but huge choice in the number of UK airports (from Gatwick to Glasgow) that link up with the cruises – plus dedicated check-in desks – and good number of reduced-price offers for children and one of the best charter flight operations. Their flights also come with a pre-bookable service (for a charge) and a well-worthwhile cabin up-grade, Premiair Gold, which adds exclusive, late check-in, improved entertainment and more spacious seating. Children's clubs (3-6 and 7-12s) operate on all sailings but are scaled down slightly out of the main holiday periods. There is a small charge for room service but, happily, all tips are now included. Airtours' Caribbean itineraries are particularly imaginative and come with some enticing cruise-and-stay possibilities in Majorca, Cyprus, Barbados and Jamaica. Their ease of transfer from arriving at the airport in Barbados to the ship is another notable feature of their organisation.

For a free Airtours video or brochure, call 0870 900 8639.

CARNIVAL

www.carnival.com/international

Ships	Tonnage	Passengers/ Crew	Space Ratio	Built/ Refurbished	Cruise Area	Rating
Holiday	46,052	1,452/660	31.7	1985/98	Caribbean	Superior
Jubilee	47,262	1,486/670	31.8	1986	Caribbean	Superior
Celebration	47,262	1,486/670	31.8	1987	Caribbean	Superior
Fantasy	70,367	2,056/920	34.2	1990	Bahamas	Premier
Ecstasy	70,367	2,052/920	34.2	1992	Mexican Riviera	Premier
Sensation	70,367	2,052/920	34.2	1993	Caribbean	Premier
Fascination	70,367	2,052/920	34.2	1994	Caribbean, Bahamas	Premier
Imagination	70,367	2,052/920	34.2	1995	Caribbean	Premier
Inspiration	70,367	2,052/920	34.2	1996	Caribbean	Premier
Elation	70,367	2,052/920	34.2	1997	Mexican Riviera	Premier
Paradise	70,367	2,052/920	34.2	1998	Caribbean	Premier
Carnival Destiny	101,353	2,642/1,050	38.3	1996	Caribbean	Premier
Carnival Triump	101,509	2,758/1,100	36.8	1999	Caribbean,	Premier
Carnival Victory	101,509	2,758/1,100	36.8	2000	Caribbean, Canada	Premier
Carnival Spirit	86,000	2,124/900	40.4	2001	Caribbean, Alaska	Premier
Carnival Pride	86,000	2,124/900	40.4	2002	Caribbean	Premier

Cruise line notes

Carnival is the mass-market arm of the giant American Carnival Corporation, the largest cruise operation in the world, incorporating the traditional style of Holland America, the majestic sailing ships of Windstar, a recent buy-out of big Italian line Costa and, more recently, the takeover of Cunard, which now incorporates the Ultra-Deluxe Seabourn Line as well. Carnival broke the mould of mass market cruising through the 1980s and 90s and not for nothing are their vessels dubbed the Fun Ships. They typically feature the youngest age profile anywhere at sea, with large numbers of children and college-age teens during the main holidays. That is only a small part of the story, however, as Carnival have revolutionised the US cruise industry, opening it up to a much wider audience, from the teeny-boppers right through to their parents and even their grandparents. There is an overwhelming sense of glitz and glitter about all the ships, but the one drawback with their wild neon colour schemes and fun-style decor is that it tends to date rather quickly, hence the older ships in the line are starting to look in need of a new image. It is very much a package cruise experience in modern surroundings, with the bonus of above-average food, fabulous evening shows and almost non-stop entertainment. You don't take a Carnival cruise for a rest cure! The ship names alone tell you they are a long way removed from the cruise formality of yesteryear. The itineraries are all standard fare and the shore excursions pretty ordinary since the ships are as much a destination in themselves as the ports of call. You'll find every possible amenity and facility aboard, especially when it comes to activities for the kids. Carnival has not been a big player in the British cruise market in the past, but they are now far more visible and attractive as a result of a marketing link with Airtours, who offer some great cruise-and-stay Florida and Caribbean packages or even a Mexican Riviera cruise combined with a Las Vegas stay. All in all, it represents some of the best value in the whole of the cruise world, provided you are comfortable with the unreserved American style.

Ship notes

Almost the ultimate in slab-sided, floating hotel-block appearance, Carnival ships are subdivided into four different classes: the mid-size but still high-density Holiday ships (*Holiday, Jubilee and Celebration*); the eight super-liner Fantasy vessels (*Fantasy, Ecstasy, Sensation, Inspiration, Fascination, Imagination, Elation* and *Paradise*), which introduced an amazing level of modern styling and facilities; the three mega-liner Destiny ships (*Carnival Destiny, Triumph* and *Victory*), the first to top the 100,000-ton mark; and the two new Spirit class (*Carnival Spirit* and *Pride*). The three mega-liners saw designer Joe Farcus really let his imagination run riot, with a huge retractable glass dome over one of the three outdoor pools, the world's longest waterslide at sea (all of 200ft long and adding visually to the line's trademark winged funnel), a glass-domed nine-storey atrium, a three-level, 1,000-seater showlounge, 418 cabins with balconies (more than half of them outside ones), a massive spa and gymnasium and a pair of two-storey dining rooms. The eight *Fantasy*-class ships all feature individual design themes running throughout the vessel, such as a Metropolis theme on *Ecstasy*, with some quite outrageous use of bold, in-your-face architecture on the first four. Farcus rather toned this down a touch on the *Imagination*, while the *Inspiration* shows some almost elegant features, such as the classically-themed Chopin Bar, the French-accented principal promenade and the art nouveau decor throughout, notably in the Grand Atrium. The Shakespeare Library is a bit tacky for anyone acquainted with genuine period style, but the Rock and Roll Dance Club, the ship's disco, is a positive riot of lights, TV screens and pulsating imagery that goes down well with the younger set. The 1998 duo *Elation* and *Paradise* feature some of the most elaborate kids' facilities in Children's World, a three-section interactive play area, as well as more activities for teenagers. Virtual World adds the latest in high-tech video and arcade games, but all vessels cater extremely well for the 2–15 age group with their facilities and organised activities.

The new Carnival Spirit added still more refinement to the company's style in 2001, exhibiting a more airy and sophisticated touch in many areas. While not as big as the mega-liner trio, *Spirit* still offers a terrific range of on-board choice, with three pools (one covered by a retractable dome) and a kids' pool, a two-level spa and gymnasium, a wedding chapel (Carnival's first), massive children's facilities, a casual buffet-style Seaview Bistro and a reservations-only alternative restaurant, the Nouveau Supper Club, high up on the sports deck and affording great views as well as an imaginative new dining choice. The arrival of *Carnival Pride* in January 2002 should further enhance the line's impressive credentials for mass appeal in the mass market.

TRAVEL TIP

Carnival's three- and four-day cruises aboard *Fantasy* and seven-dayers on new ship *Carnival Pride,* both out of Port Canaveral, only an hour's drive from Orlando, are an excellent add-on to a holiday in the world's theme park capital city.

Extras

Cabins are surprisingly spacious and well-equipped for this sector of the market, while the public rooms are all imaginatively themed and styled, if your senses can get past the vivid neon lights and the bright, clashing colours of the decor. Indoor promenades promote the image of being in a typical American shopping mall, but, while the emphasis is on the non-stop glitter of places like the garish Diamonds Are Forever disco (on *Fascination),* there are quieter, more subtle retreats on each ship, as in the classy Chinatown Lounge (on *Ecstasy).* On-board entertainment is high-energy, glamorous and quite diverse, from Country and Western duos to magicians, jugglers and full-scale Las Vegas revues, while the Camp Carnival kids' programme is one of the best in the business. Health and spa facilities on all ships are excellent, and Carnival also offers a well-organised and competitively priced wedding service. There are tried and tested shore excursions in Alaska due to the company tie-up with Holland America. Their Caribbean product features a range of departure points with Miami *(Paradise, Imagination* and *Fascination, Carnival Triumph* and *Victory* and *Carnival Spirit),* Tampa *(Sensation* and *Jubilee),* New Orleans *(Inspiration),* Port Canaveral *(Fantasy* and *Carnival Pride),* Galveston in Texas *(Celebration)* and San Juan *(Holiday* and *Carnival Destiny)* all being used. Paradise is also the first cruise ship to be completely non-smoking. Reasonable wheelchair access features on all ships, too.
For Carnival's UK office, phone 020 7940 4466.

CELEBRITY
www.celebrity-cruises.com

Ships	Tonnage	Passengers/ Crew	Space Ratio	Built/ Refurbished	Cruise Area	Rating
Horizon	46,811	1,354/652	34.5	1990/99	Caribbean, Bermuda	Deluxe *Brit's Guide* Favourite
Zenith	47,255	1,374/670	34.3	1992/99	Caribbean, Bermuda	Deluxe *Brit's Guide* Favourite
Century	70,606	1,778/843	39.7	1995	Caribbean	Deluxe *Brit's Guide* Favourite
Galaxy	77,713	1,870/900	41.5	1996	Caribbean, N Europe, Trans-Atlantic	Deluxe *Brit's Guide* Favourite
Mercury	77,713	1,870/900	41.5	1997	Alaska, Hawaii, S America	Deluxe *Brit's Guide* Favourite
Millennium	91,000	2,049/999	44.4	2000	Caribbean, Alaska	Deluxe
Infinity	91,000	2,049/999	44.4	2001	Caribbean, Alaska, Panama Canal	Deluxe
Summit	91,000	2,049/999	44.4	2001	Caribbean	Deluxe

Cruise line notes

Now owned by Royal Caribbean after a 1997 takeover, Celebrity continue to operate as a distinct, contrasting product in much the same way as Holland American remain separate from Carnival. Their style remains an up-market version of the mass Caribbean experience, with strong European overtones, especially as they now offer a more widespread choice, including Hawaii and South America. Touches of the traditional cruise atmosphere and style mix with ultra-modern design but in a more refined way. The trio of *Century, Galaxy* and *Mercury,* incorporate some of the most sophisticated yet chic marine design, like state-of-the-art theatres, wonderfully inviting central atriums and virtual reality gymnasiums, and also offer more open deck space than is common in the American market. The latest threesome of *Millennium, Infinity* and *Summit* add an even more sumptuous touch in many areas, notably their speciality alternative restaurant with its demonstration kitchen (on

Millennium, this is the Olympic Restaurant, complete with original wood panelling from the White Star ship *Olympic,* sister of the ill-fated but magnificent *Titanic*), and superb children's facilities (although I also feel there is a touch of Royal Caribbean glitz here and there, as witnessed by the nine-storey atrium, complete with glass-sided, outside-facing lifts). The passenger profile tends to be slightly older (and so more formal) than some of the Caribbean competition, but Celebrity still run some busy and popular children's programmes in the holiday periods, including their trademark Slumber Parties, where youngsters eat and play games from 8pm until as late as 2am under the supervision of the children's counsellors, while their children's menus are also above average. Daytime activities are fairly routine, as are the shore excursions, but they are paying more attention to the evening entertainment these days so there are some quite high-powered show offerings.

TRAVEL TIP

The best value aboard Celebrity ships, as on most of the up-market lines, is with the standard range of cabins and especially the inside ones (although you might want to avoid those aft on *Zenith*'s Europa Deck on prime holiday sailings as the children's playroom is situated there).

Ship notes

Horizon and *Zenith* were the vanguard of the Celebrity style in the early 1990s and have been beautifully maintained in keeping with the line's up-market touch. They lack a proper, wrap-around promenade deck but feature some classic, elegant decor that is easy on the eye. *Century, Galaxy* and *Mercury* really took Celebrity's appeal into the big league with a huge range of lavish public rooms and imaginative design, all with a high-tech edge. They boast acres of open deck space, superb beauty and fitness facilities in their AquaSpa centres (and these really are some of the best you will find anywhere), as well as an increased range of children's activities, including junior discos and video games rooms.

TRAVEL TIP

For a true romantic touch, treat yourself and partner to a Rasul mud treatment in the AquaSpa. It's novel, it's fun and it's potentially seriously sensual.

Galaxy, in particular, highlighted this breakthrough in classy modern design, with her two-storey restaurant, eye-catching theatre and startling Savoy Nightclub all outstanding features in the cruise world. It adds up to a ship overflowing with the 'wow' factor and one that is even quite sexy. The Millennium trio added to this process of grand-scale cruising with a three-tier theatre, an AquaDome-covered pool, vast children's Fun

Factory and astounding range of lounges and bars. They still manage to come up with a rather bewildering array of 20 cabin types, including four balconied versions, but the category 3 (Large Ocean View with Veranda) and category 7 (Ocean View with Panoramic Window) look to be the best value. Elsewhere, the *Summit* boasts a speciality restaurant with theming from the classic 1930s French liner *Normandie*, while the *Infinity* takes her design and decor from the famous *United States,* launched in 1952. All three boast another three full-scale restaurants or cafés, plus one of the prettiest pool decks of any of the new build of cruise ships.

Extras

The cuisine has been Celebrity's watchword from the start and is among the best at sea, comparing even with some of the Ultra-Deluxe range. It is designed by famous French chef Michel Roux, who remains a consultant on all things food-orientated and ensures a consistently high standard. A special 'elegant' high tea is a feature of every cruise, while the service is just the right blend of friendly and efficient. Cabins throughout the line are above average in space terms and are all elegantly finished. Butler service is also available with all suites and *Galaxy, Mercury* and *Century* boast some of the largest suites at sea, a massive 1,100sq ft of space. Celebrity also offer an excellent range of land-based add-ons, plus a tailor-made service to increase their overall appeal. Some elaborate AquaSpa packages can be pre-purchased from £159-£359. Port taxes are all included and there are some nice extras with all suites, like complimentary thalassotherapy and in-room afternoon tea service.

TRAVEL TIP

The Fleet Bar (*Zenith*) and America's Cup Club (*Horizon*) are two of the most inviting and relaxing places at sea to sit and enjoy a drink and watch the world sail by.

For Celebrity's UK brochure phoneline, call 0800 018 7070.

COSTA CRUISES
www.costacruises.co.uk

Ships	Tonnage	Passengers/ Crew	Space Ratio	Built/ Refurbished	Cruise Area	Rating
Costa Riviera	31,500	958/470	32.3	1963/96	Mediterranean, Canaries	Standard
Costa Tropicale	36,674	1,022/550	35.8	1982/01	Mediterranean, Canaries	Superior
Costa Marina	25,441	760/391	33	1990	Mediterranean, N Europe, S America, Transatlantic	Superior
Costa Allegra	29,500	806/418	36.6	1992	Mediterranean, Canaries, S America, Transatlantic	Superior
Costa Classica	53,000	1,304/610	40.6	1992	Caribbean, Mediterranean, Transatlantic	Premier
Costa Romantica	53,000	1,346/610	39.3	1993	N Europe, Mediterranean, Transatlantic S America	Premier, *Brit's Guide* Favourite
Costa Victoria	75,000	1,928/800	38.9	1996	Caribbean, Mediterranean, Transatlantic	Premier, *Brit's Guide* Favourite
Costa Atlantica	84,000	2,112/906	39.7	2000	Mediterranean, Caribbean, Transatlantic	Premier

Cruise line notes

Despite being the subject of another of the cruise world's takeovers in 1997, Costa continue to go about their own business, slowly increasing their UK profile. The Italian nature of their operation is very much part of their style and they attract large numbers of European passengers on their Mediterranean sailings. In fact, Costa can largely sell out their July and August cruises out of Genoa from the Italian market alone (with a high percentage of honeymooners).

The difference between the European and Caribbean sailings is quite marked, though, with the American market providing the bulk of the passengers in the 45-plus age profile in the latter. Unusually, the *CostaClassica* operates a series of sailings out of the French island of Guadeloupe, which adds to their European flavour. On the European routes, the atmosphere and ambience are distinctly Italian – lively, fun and a little noisy – and Brits sailing aboard need to be open-minded and good Europeans. The style is quite informal, and don't expect the queues to be as nice and orderly as on American or British vessels, either! Costa have also increased their seven-day offerings, to the extent of introducing some week-long fly-cruises to northern Europe, thus attracting a younger crowd on those sailings than the 10-day and longer itineraries. Cuisine is typically Italian (great for pasta-lovers), while service is friendly without being memorable. Their winter South American voyages, out of Rio de Janeiro and Buenos Aires, were another attractive new feature in 2000, and there are no less than 12 transatlantic sailings to enjoy as well. As part of the Carnival operation, Costa has benefited from two additional ships, with the *Costa Tropicale* being moved over from the Carnival fleet in 2001 and the *Westerdam* due to transfer from Holland America in 2002 (to be renamed *Costa Europa*), while there are more dramatic new-builds lined up for 2003 and 2004.

TRAVEL TIP

Unless you are a real fan of all things Italian, Costa's summer sailings are not recommended for Brits as you will be among a small minority of non-Italian-speaking passengers. Beware, also, of the rather tedious long announcements in all the different languages on most ships.

Ship notes

There is quite a difference through the fleet, with the older vessels veering towards the more traditional ocean-going liner style, with unusual itineraries, while the newer ones have all the latest in the way of modern facilities and a more up-market feel to attract the American market. The

TRAVEL TIP

Costa's sailings out of Venice are most popular with the British market, especially in May, June, September and October. Brits make up a good 15 per cent of the passenger profile at these times.

newer ships are invariably more spacious, too, offering bigger standard cabins and with quite an inviting, airy feel to all the public rooms. The interior styling is where they score heavily for the European market as they veer drastically away from the American preference for glitz and concentrate instead on an understated chic that is more relaxing and comfortable, especially for British tastes. The *Costa Classica* and *Costa Romantica* are both fine examples of this bold difference in emphasis (making them *Brit's Guide* Favourites), while the *Costa Victoria* delivers an even greater level of quality while sticking with this style. Indeed, the *Victoria* possibly sets new benchmarks for this contemporary European design, with a four-storey forward observation lounge area, complete with waterfall, a state-of-the-art shopping gallery, an indoor pool and jogging track, a tennis court and a proper wrap-around promenade deck. All the ships, new and old, feature generous amounts of open deck space.

The new *Costa Atlantica* goes slightly against the European grain as she shows more of the Carnival line glitz and, while she has some breathtaking features, like the alternative dining Café Florian, the three-storey Caruso Theatre and balconies with 70 per cent of her cabins, there is a distinct American feel to many of the public rooms.

Extras

The line has its own private island off the coast of the Dominican Republic which makes for a relaxing day's visit on eastern Caribbean routes, while shore excursions generally are quite sporty and active-minded, as well as being hugely varied on the European routes. The ships feature the extra culinary delight of a 24-hour pizzeria, which goes down especially well with youngsters. Excellent year-round kids' clubs (3–6, 7–12 and 13–17) in the Caribbean (high season only in the Med), but only *Atlantica* and *Victoria* offer group baby-sitting for under-3s (for a nominal charge). In the Caribbean, Costa offers couples the chance to renew their wedding vows in a special ship-board ceremony. The six newest ships all feature wheelchair-accessible cabins. *Atlantica* and *Victoria*'s back-to-back seven-day itineraries around the east and west Caribbean are a popular choice with British passengers looking for a two-week cruise.

For their UK office, phone 020 7940 4499.

CRYSTAL CRUISES
www.crystalcruises.com

Ships	Tonnage	Passengers/ Crew	Space Ratio	Built/ Refurbished	Cruise Area	Rating
Crystal Harmony	49,400	940/545	52.5	1990/97	Worldwide	Ultra-deluxe
Crystal Symphony	51,000	940/545	54.2	1995	Worldwide	Ultra-deluxe

Cruise line notes

How do you start to describe arguably the most lavish large-ship experience in the world? It isn't easy as there is so much to recommend on these two ships which have set new standards for the Ultra-Deluxe end of the market. The smaller ships in this category may do things to a slightly higher degree of service and opulence, but this Japanese-owned and American-marketed line has carved out its own niche in terms of providing big-ship variety and facilities with small-ship quality of service, cuisine and elegance. For large, modern cruise ships they even look classy, which is no mean feat these days. A Crystal cruise is characterised by an atmosphere of friendly, personal charm that is never too formal but never too familiar. From the moment you step on board to the last morning, you are looked after with a wonderfully eager-to-please yet efficient manner which befits a line that includes butler service throughout its Penthouse Decks, a high percentage of balconied cabins, two additional restaurants, high-powered guest lecturers and a breathtaking range of quality entertainments, from paddle-tennis tournaments to classical concerts and ballet. It should go without saying the cuisine is on a par with many fine restaurants. Crystal also sets great store by its big-production shows, and they can be very elaborate indeed with staging worthy of any top West End theatre. Staff are all highly motivated and extremely personable, daytime activities diverse and extremely sociable and shore excursions wide-ranging and always excellently escorted and presented. Indeed, for the up-scale expense of a Crystal cruise, their excursions are remarkably well-priced and offer some of the best value of any in the cruise world. The passenger profile tends to be 40-plus and children are a rarity (although Crystal does provide children's counsellors on sailings where there will be a number of families), while the style is distinctly formal, with more days at sea than most of the American cruise lines. The two ships alternate through various sectors of the world; in 2002, after *Symphony* completes her 100-day Grand Pacific Circle world cruise (33 ports in 20 countries), she will cruise western Europe before heading to the Caribbean, while *Harmony* visits South America (including the Falklands) and then cruises the Pacific (including China and Japan) and Alaska before returning to the Caribbean via the Panama Canal. Crystal devotees (and lovers of the finer things in life) will also want to start saving for June 2003 when Crystal's third ship is due, a 68,000-ton vessel which promises to deliver even more of their distinctive maritime luxury, with more penthouse accommodation, fitness facilities, dining options and a new computer learning facility.

Ship notes

Both Crystal vessels feature a huge range of choice in whatever you want to do aboard. Lounges and bars abound, there are two swimming pools, a proper promenade deck and no less than six alternatives outside the main restaurant for meals and snacks (in addition to free 24-hour room

TRAVEL TIP

Both ships feature a full-size paddle-tennis court which is among the best sporting facilities at sea and is a great way to meet some of your fellow passengers.

service), including an ice cream bar and a wonderful bistro for mid-morning speciality coffees and pastries. The two small speciality restaurants – Prego (Italian) and Kyoto (Japanese) on the *Harmony,* and Prego (Italian) and Jade Garden (Asian) on *Symphony* – are both extremely popular so it is advisable to book early in the cruise. Naturally enough, both ships are wonderfully spacious, and the public rooms are all done out in individual but elegant fashion. The newer *Symphony* is virtually a sister ship of the *Harmony,* but with even more balconies and enhanced cabin space in the lower grades, a bigger casino and central Plaza, and a bigger Lido Café, which provides buffet breakfast and lunch, as well as a video games room. Club 2100, *Harmony*'s second evening lounge, is a stunning venue, while *Symphony*'s standout location is the Starlite Club. Even the standard cabins are beautifully appointed and fitted out, with queen-sized beds, proper baths, bathrobes, hairdryers, personal safes, sitting areas, VCR as well as TV and mini-fridges. Their Computer University@Sea programme has been extended to all sailings due to popular demand.

Extras

All this luxury obviously comes at a price, and Crystal are not cheap. But, by taking a basic grade cabin, you could be on to some of the best value anywhere at sea. The Gentleman Host programme is a much-appreciated touch for ladies travelling alone, while dinner can be served in your cabin, course by course, as it would in the restaurant. Indeed, eating breakfast on your own balcony in the morning must be one of life's great extravagances. Both ships are fully prepared for disabled passengers and possess extensive book and video libraries. In fact, the only flaw in the up-market nature of the Crystal operation is their two-sitting dining policy, which is impossible to get round on a 940-passenger ship. However, the alternative dining options easily counteract that one small defect, and, particularly if you choose the second sitting, you are likely to have a dining experience as exclusive as on any of the smaller ships. Happily, all port taxes and tips are now included for the UK market. *Choosing a Cruise* researcher Carolyn Voce puts Crystal top of her cruise hit parade, most notably after her honeymoon on Harmony in 1999 ("We could not have started our married life on a more enjoyable note," she says) and a Far East leg of *Symphony*'s world cruise in 2001 ("There can be no better holiday afloat, in my opinion") in conjunction with the Leading Hotels of the World group, a marketing alliance which sees Crystal able to extend their ocean-going excellence to their land-based options, too.

Call 020 7287 9040 for brochures.

CUNARD
www.cunard.com

Ships	Tonnage	Passengers/ Crew	Space Ratio	Built/ Refurbished	Cruise Area	Rating
Caronia	23,492	736/390	33.4	1973/99	S America, Med, N Europe, S Atlantic	Deluxe, *Brit's* *Guide* *Favourite*
QE2	70,327	1,750/1,015	40.1	1969/99	Wordwide, inc Transatlantic	Deluxe *Brit's* *Guide* *Favourite*

Cruise line notes

After a huge amount of company re-organisation after its takeover by the Carnival Corporation in 1998, Cunard has now emerged as a streamlined, classic two-ship operation, with the prospect of the world's most dramatic new ship – *Queen Mary 2* – joining them in 2003. They specialise in a mix of line voyages and extended journeys around parts of the world like northern Europe and South America, while the grand QE2 continues to be the only ship in the world offering regular transatlantic sailings. Her annual world cruise, spanning some 120 days, remains another trademark feature, although it is now also offered in a series of much smaller, but very tempting, slices, from seven to 99 days. The completely refurbished *Caronia*, formerly the *Vistafjord*, is now one of the most genteel and stylish small liners left in service. Both ships also feature a fair amount of ex-UK voyages in the summer months as Carnival have brought Cunard more in line with her traditional roots, which remain a hit on both sides of the Atlantic (hence there are likely to be as many Americans as UK passengers on board at any time). All the early plans for QM2 suggest something like QE2 built along the lines of *Voyager of the Seas,* with a high proportion of balconied cabins, numerous dining options (including Grill Rooms for the higher category cabins), an 1100-seat lounge, a ballroom, an education centre and even a maritime museum. She will measure up as the largest (150,000 tons), longest (1,132ft), tallest (236ft) and widest (135ft) passenger ship ever built, carrying 2,620 guests (considerably fewer than *Voyager*) and 1,254 crew. Truly, she will be a sea-going phenomenon.

Ship notes

Both current vessels are one-offs, QE2 being the last liner of her type and *Caronia* another fine ship for the discerning passenger. Indeed, while she harks back to the beginning of the modern cruise era, *Caronia* remains firmly rooted in the past, with her beautifully tasteful and original decor throughout (notably in the cabins), unusual itineraries with longer sea-time and a distinctly friendly and relaxed ambience provided by her Scandinavian and German crew. The ageless QE2 will continue providing a source of great cruise tradition for many years yet after extensive refits in 1994, 1996 and 2000. Better bathroom facilities and in-cabin TV (including satellite and video channels) serve to keep her up to date yet aloof from the rest of the cruise world. Her deluxe range of cabins display a magnificent spaciousness that goes hand in hand with the subdued elegance of the fittings. As a result of her heritage, QE2 is the last ship still operating a type of class system, with four standards of restaurant (one, the Queen's Grill, having its own exclusive lounge) that reflect the grade of cabin you select. This harks back to the days of First, Second and Third Class bookings, and the modern version is much cherished by those who can afford it. It does leave the ship open to different ratings (from Deluxe to Ultra-Deluxe) according to cabin type and where you dine, while the lowest 'class', which consists of the inside cabins and the two most basic outside categories plus dining in the two-seating Mauretania Restaurant, can be rather the poor relation, with a distinct difference in the quality of the food, too. She still tends to draw a more elderly crowd, although the shorter cruises attract their fair share of families and even honeymooners.

TRAVEL TIP

For those who find the glitz and glitter of the new breed of ship just too ghastly, the QE2 is the perfect antidote. She is also well suited to first-timers and families on her short-range cruises of three to six days.

QE2 remains, however, almost a museum to the age of classic liners, with her labyrinthine corridors and seemingly endless companionways, huge expanses of open decks, elegant furnishing and subdued decor – a world apart from the new breed of mega-ships. She is still effortlessly spacious, has superb sailing characteristics and boasts the two single most spectacular suites at sea, the *Queen Mary* and *Queen Elizabeth* (complete with butler service), which are split-level, and have their own private deck space as well as conservatories, lounges, walk-in closets and marbled bathrooms. Ultimately, a QE2 cruise is as much an experience in British heritage as it is a sea voyage.

Extras

Gentlemen Hosts are available on both ships, while QE2 also possesses a massive range of health facilities and spa treatments, along with the only Harrods at sea.

For a brochure, call 023 8071 6500.

DISNEY CRUISE LINE

www.disneycruise.com

Ships	Tonnage	Passengers/Crew	Space Ratio	Built/Refurbished	Cruise Area	Rating
Disney Magic	83,000	1,750/950	35.4	1998	Caribbean	Premier
Disney Wonder	83,000	1,750/950	35.4	1999	Bahamas	Premier

Cruise line notes

Disney's first ship set sail in July 1998 with some stunning hardware, an innovative approach to cruising and a sprinkling of the company's 'pixie dust' that makes their product so, well, magical. This especially appeals to families, although couples without children and singles are by no means left out. Chairman Michael Eisner told his designers 'I want you to out-tradition tradition', and they have obliged handsomely, even if the finished article still owes as much to their seamless theme park philosophy as to cruising's heritage. The line's other proud claim is for an all-encompassing package. From the moment you land at Orlando Airport you are met by Disney Cruise Line coaches, transferred directly to your resort hotel for three or four days, then taken straight to the purpose-built cruise terminal at Port Canaveral (50 minutes away), where the credit card 'Key to the Kingdom' that opened your hotel room also unlocks your cabin. The one bugbear for British guests, being 'foreigners', is we must go through passport control at check-in and need to be up ultra-early (like at 6am) for immigration when the ship returns. *Disney Wonder*'s three-day trip takes in Nassau, the Bahamas' capital, and Disney's own private island beach paradise, Castaway Cay. The four-day version adds a day at sea to sample the ship's almost overwhelming array of facilities. New in 2000 was the eagerly-awaited 7-day cruise on *Disney Magic*, which visits St Maarten and St Thomas in the Caribbean as well as Castaway Cay, and provides three sea-days to enjoy fully all the on-board amenities. In 2002, the *Magic* will start to offer alternating 7-day cruises, with a new weekly itinerary that takes in Key West, Cozumel, Cayman Islands and Castaway Cay (from May 11). The extra days mean a more relaxed voyage from the short-haul hustle-bustle, and there are some standout additional features, like the adults-only champagne brunch (for just $10 extra), the amazing artistic illusion show C'Est Magique and a character breakfast featuring a host of Disney favourites (just as much fun for mum and dad as the kids!). On top of their state-of-the-art hardware, service is impeccably smooth, from their eager-to-please resort style, while entertainment and dining are also a cut above, with the company anxious to provide more than just the usual experiences. My only reservations are the Disney-orientated theatre extravaganzas are a bit twee for a late-evening audience (although they work superbly in a matinee setting on the 7-day voyage), and prices for drinks, excursions, etc, are in keeping with the up-scale nature of it all, i.e. a tad expensive.

Ship notes

Just listing all the facilities on the virtually identical sisters is a lengthy task and makes you realise the three-day cruise is inadequate to appreciate everything on offer. Spacious, airy cabins, even at standard levels (going up to some huge suites, again with families in mind), a vast array of public rooms (including a whole deck of the most elaborate kids' facilities at sea, supervised from 9am to 1am), three pools (one for adults, another for families and a third, with waterslide, for 'kids only'), four restaurants (with the refined Italian-themed Palo for adults only) and a wonderful, three-storey entrance atrium that underlines the graceful Art Deco styling which Michael Eisner demanded and is also seen in the classical, two-funnel profile. What you won't find is a casino (not for Disney's family image) or, more surprisingly, a proper observation lounge to watch the sea go by. Other highlights are the amazing 'rotation' dining system, where guests take turns at the family options of elegant Lumiere's/Triton's, tropical Parrot Cay and the mind-boggling Animator's Palate; the sports-themed ESPN Skybox bar; and Beat Street, the lively adults-only entertainment district consisting of a stylish piano bar, live music hall and disco and a novel comedy club. The 975-seat Walt Disney Theater features original musical productions which are a strong family favourite. Finally, there is a full-service health spa and a gym which overlooks the bridge so you can keep an eye on the Captain! Inevitably, on-board shopping is fully Disney-orientated, but also offers another useful diversion for children.

Extras

Children's activities are superbly organised and supervised, both on the ship and Castaway Cay, which also boasts a sensational array of facilities for kids and adults, including cycling, snorkelling, shopping, eating and drinking, beach sports and even massage (on the adults-only beach). Parents leaving their children in the kids' club programme even get a pager to stay in touch. Most packages are sold as a cruise-and-stay with a week or more in Orlando first, but it is possible to book a cruise-only package separately (and with great rates) through www.dreamsunlimitedtravel.com, a Disney specialist. And, of course, if you have got a stay at Walt Disney World first, you will experience the best family entertainment resort in the world (read my book *A Brit's Guide to Orlando* [Foulsham, £11.99] if you don't believe me!).

For a Walt Disney Travel Company brochure (which includes all their cruises), call 0870 2424 910.

FESTIVAL

www.festivalcruises.com

Ships	Tonnage	Passengers/ Crew	Space Ratio	Built/ Refurbished	Cruise Area	Rating
Bolero	15,781	900/338	17.5	1968/95	Mediterranean	Standard
Azur	15,000	665/340	19.6	1971/94	Mediterranean, Canaries	Standard
Flamenco	17,270	720/270	23.8	1972/95	Mediterranean, N Europe, Canaries	Standard
Mistral	47,900	1,196/470	40.0	1999	Mediterranean, Caribbean, Transatlantic	Superior
European Vision	58,600	1,560/711	37.5	2001	Mediterranean, Caribbean, Transatlantic	Premier

Cruise line notes

Festival are relatively new on the Mediterranean scene and added their second ship the *Bolero* (formerly NCL's *Starward*) only in 1996 with a third, *Flamenco* (formerly *Southern Cross*), a year later, but they continue to make great strides in terms of product delivery and popularity. Indeed, they moved on to a different level altogether with the delivery of the exceedingly smart *Mistral* in 1999, marking Festival out as one of the most forward-thinking of the smaller lines. They will build on that sound base with new ships in both 2001 and 2002, with the new *European Vision* creating a new brand signature, with the older ships forming the Discovery fleet (with more unusual itineraries) and the newest ones being the Premium fleet (more standard itineraries but in grander on-board style). The ambience is Mediterranean once again, but all ships attract a high percentage of British passengers with their keenly-priced operation, offering a good-value product, friendly service and plenty of well-organised activities. Cruise style on board is fairly informal and there are some imaginative itineraries, including many of the Greek islands and the Corinth Canal. Courteous staff help to mask a lack of finesse in places, which is especially revealed when the older trio are full, but the food is sound and plentiful (there's even a post-midnight buffet snack). Most itineraries are quite port-intensive, so there are few at-sea days. The daily programmes are geared mainly towards active couples, although there is a children's playroom on all but *Bolero* and organised kids' activities during the main holiday periods. *European Vision* adds a real element of sophistication to the cuisine, with a 24-hour café and enhanced buffet dining, while Festival have also introduced designated hosts for each of the four main languages on board and made the daily entertainments comprehensively themed. In fact, the innovative thinking behind *Vision* (and her 2002 sister, *European Stars*) promise to take the company well into the Premier class for the first time.

Ship notes

Both *Azur* and *Bolero* are quite smart and stylish in appearance (albeit showing signs of their age, high-density and, in peak season, quite raucous) and will appeal to young, first-timers as very different from what they might have believed the cruise experience to be like. The constant multi-language announcements are a bit tedious, but they are well maintained and the decor is quite bright and stylish, if a little plain in the cabins. Cabins on *Bolero* are only adequate for two in many cases and a real squeeze where they take three or four, but two cabins are now adapted for disabled passengers. *Azur* continues to be Festival's workhorse, with 10, 11 and 12-day trips round the Greek islands and eastern Med, and she can be a crowded proposition when full, even in the bright and airy Riviera Restaurant. Deck space is at a premium (and rather noisy by the twin funnels on Sun Deck), but the excellent attitude of the entertainment staff helps smooth over the rough edges and provide an excellent introduction to European mass-market cruising. *Flamenco,* formerly the popular *Southern Cross* of defunct CTC Lines, adds a greater range of on-board facilities, more generous cabin and deck space and rather more finesse for her sailings into northern Europe as well as the eastern Med before wintering in the Canaries. *Mistral* adds a classy, up-market quality to Festival's range. Though she is not a mega-ship, she has all the amenities of her larger brethren yet a touch more personality and charm, with a noticeably chic, European styling that comes as a welcome change from the large-scale American offerings. She boasts a high Space Ratio figure (40) for her Superior (borderline Premier) rating, well-fitted, pleasant cabins (plus 80 balconied suites), and an excellent array of lounges and bars. The pool deck is pretty and inviting, with a unique open-air thalassotherapy pool, and there is a magnificent gym, beauty salon and treatment centre, including a range of thermal suites the equal of anything at sea. There are children's and teens' clubs, a sophisticated nightclub, an airy main dining room and even first-class medical facilities should they be necessary. My only reservations are the £15 charge per non-suite passenger to dine at the alternative Rialto Grill and the rather bland nature of the European-styled entertainment in the glitzy Carousel Lounge. Given that her prices are not much above the rest of the fleet, even on her imaginative winter Caribbean itineraries out of Guadeloupe, *Mistral* represents one of the bargains of the modern cruise world. *Vision* and *Stars* add more balconied cabins, an Internet café, rock-climbing wall and mini-golf course, i.e. super-liner facilities but on a more personal, mid-size scale.

Extras

Excellent pricing remains Festival's watchword, along with their sense of European chic and a more personal experience than is often the case on larger ships. They represent no-nonsense good value, with flights from Edinburgh, Manchester, Dublin and Birmingham, in addition to London, and children's rates that cover up to 17-year-olds. There are also big savings on back-to-back cruises, and, happily, port taxes are now included, too. *Mistral* and *European Vision* have some well-equipped cabins for passengers with disabilities.

For their UK office, phone 020 7436 0827.

FIRST CHOICE

www.firstchoice.co.uk

Ships	Tonnage	Passengers/ Crew	Space Ratio	Built/ Refurbished	Cruise Area	Rating
Ausonia	12,609	506/210	24.9	1957/1999	Mediterranean	Standard

Cruise line notes

Another of the big tour operators to start their own-brand cruise operations, First Choice made their debut in 1999 with a mixture of offerings, but have now refined that to just two ships, the fully-chartered *Ausonia* and the *Island Escape* of sister company Island (see below). After flirting briefly with ex-UK cruises to Cyprus and back, they have now refined matters to purely Mediterranean voyages (plus the Caribbean in winter with Island). And, like Airtours and Thomson, First Choice offer a well-grooved cruise-and-stay operation based on either Majorca or Cyprus. The *Ausonia* is home-ported (March to October) in Limassol, and hence concentrates on two eastern Med itineraries which can be combined into a 14-day voyage. There is also a wide choice of accommodation for a week's stay on Cyprus, including Family Choice and all-inclusive hotels. Flights are with their own in-house airline Air 2000, with no less than 14 UK airports from which to choose (and the chance to pre-book seats for £7 a head), and the shoreside operation is slick and well-organised. *Ausonia* has few children's facilities, but both ships have a full programme of organised activities for youngsters.

Ship notes

Ausonia is an aging but well-preserved veteran cruiser, who has served for various Italian and Greek lines over the years. Currently owned by Cypriot Louis Cruise Line, she offers a taste of the cruise style of yesteryear with modern on-board services. Although she shows her age in places, much of the décor is new and is pleasantly bright and inviting. Public rooms and facilities are limited to a couple of lounges, one main restaurant, a buffet alternative, a library, two shops, a small casino and tiny swimming pool. Cabins are also on the small side – with the exception of the four suites – and there are only four basic grades, of which you choose the type and deck but not the specific cabin (unless you want to pay a £20/week pre-booking supplement), while there are a handful of single cabins but nothing that is well-adapted for disabled passengers. Entertainment sticks to the tried and trusted formula of evening cabaret, dancing and talent nights (including karaoke), plus a few novel touches like murder mystery nights, themed deck parties and plays. Although you will find families aboard in holiday periods, she is still best-suited to the 50-plus age range, offering a good introduction to the cruise world at an affordable price.

Extras

As one of the big, reliable tour operators, First Choice provide a consistent level of service in areas such as entertainments, food and shore excursions. There are special cruise check-in desks at Gatwick and Manchester airports to minimise queuing in the (increasingly crowded) Majorcan port of Palma, while you can book an Air 2000 Premium service up-grade (extra leg-room, in-flight service and baggage allowance) for £29 a person. Port taxes are included as, in theory, are the 'basic daily tips', but the brochure says you will 'probably' still want to tip. Hmmm.

For a brochure, call 0870 750 0001.

HEBRIDEAN ISLAND CRUISES
www.hebridean.co.uk

Ship	Tonnage	Passengers/Crew	Space Ratio	Built/Refurbished	Cruise Area	Rating
Hebridean Princess	2,112	50/35	38.4	1964/1989	Scotland, Ireland	Deluxe
Hebridean Spirit	4,200	79/70	53.1	1991/2001	N Europe, Mediterranean, Indian Ocean	Ultra-Deluxe

Cruise line notes

Far away from the world of the package holiday is Hebridean Island Cruises. This all-British operation is a real gem for lovers of the outdoor life with plenty of comfort, especially as, in 2001, they acquired a second ship to take their operations much further afield than their traditional areas of the Scottish coastal waterways and Ireland. These cruises are for people who just want to relax, enjoy the wonderful social ambience and be carried away into a world that is several light years removed from the normal hustle and bustle. Specialist guides accompany all cruises and give informal talks and lectures. While the classic little *Hebridean Princess* operates just from March to October, the new *Spirit* follows the sun year-round, from July in Norway and up to the Arctic Circle, to winter in the Indian Ocean, visiting the Red Sea and the Maldives. The personal level of service, outstanding cuisine, single-seating dining and superb quality of the fixtures and fittings – with every cabin individually designed and decorated, using exquisite fabrics and furnishings – all add up to a unique and quite exclusive cruise experience light years removed from the norm.

Ship notes

Princess is not so much a cruise ship as a luxurious, floating country hotel that delivers a charming level of service as you travel through and around some breathtaking scenery. It is the elegance of your own private yacht, the quaint atmosphere of a nineteenth-century inn and the sheer beauty of high quality decor. The experience is mainly about the places you cruise, getting well off the beaten track and stopping to visit some splendidly remote town or village, but there are also a few on-board facilities like a mini-gym, deck quoits, clay pigeon shooting and an excellent library. The use of the ship's bikes, speedboats and fishing gear is included. The Tiree Lounge, complete with a real stone fireplace, has to be one of the most sumptuous public rooms of any ship at sea. The bar carries (as you'd expect) a magnificent range of whiskies. The new *Hebridean Spirit* is a more modern prospect, although still with relatively few on-board facilities and an atmosphere more of relaxed charm than cruising sophistication. Uniquely for such a small ship, she does have a spa and a small pool. There is also a well-stocked library, three lounges, a wonderful restaurant and a sheltered sun deck. All flights to join the ship are by an exclusive charter with the use of a private lounge at London's Stansted airport. As with her sister, the use of rich woods, deep-pile carpets, soft sofas and large armchairs abound. And, while her first season had only just got under way at the time of writing, her itinerary alone – notably the cruises along the coast of India and Sri Lanka – makes her an outstanding prospect.

In fact, the multi-million pound refit looks to be money extremely well spent as the finished product comes over as first class, with the warmth and cosiness of all the public rooms, added to some stylish, individual and well-fitted cabins (the C grade look the best value here), making for a genuine Ultra-Deluxe feel.

Extras

There are no single supplements as both ships feature single cabins, and single travellers are made to feel especially welcome. Tips are not so much included as actively discouraged, and the only other on-board spend is for alcoholic drinks, phone calls and anything purchased in the ship shop. Both vessels usually anchor at night so you don't miss any of the scenery. It can also cost as much as £220 on top of your cruise fare to get to and from Oban by rail to pick up the *Princess*. But, ultimately, it is the uniqueness of exclusivity of the package that is the essence of its appeal, and that is hard to put a price on. There is no provision for the disabled, and it goes without saying this is not a cruise for children.

TRAVEL TIP

The Columba Restaurant on *Princess* can accommodate all 50 passengers in one sitting and boasts fresh, local produce served with great style.

For one of their splendid brochures, call 01756 701338.

HOLLAND AMERICA LINE
www.hollandamerica.com

Ships	Tonnage	Passengers/ Crew	Space Ratio	Built/ Refurbished	Cruise Area	Rating
Noordam	33,930	1,210/540	28	1984	Caribbean, Transatlantic, Mediterranean, N Europe	Premier
Westerdam (moving to Costa Cruises in May 2002)	53,872	1,494/642	36	1986/90	Caribbean, Panama Canal	Premier
Statendam	55,451	1,264/588	36	1993	Mexico, Hawaii, Alaska	Deluxe
Maasdam	55,451	1,264/588	36	1993	Caribbean	Deluxe
Ryndam	55,451	1,264/588	36	1994	S America, Antarctica, Mexico, Hawaii, Alaska	Deluxe
Veendam	55,541	1,264/588	36	1996	Caribbean, Panama Canal, Alaska	Deluxe
Rotterdam	62,000	1,320/644	46.9	1997	Caribbean, Panama Canal, Canada, New England, Transatlantic	Deluxe
Volendam	63,000	1,440/670	43.7	1999	Caribbean, Panama Canal, Alaska	Deluxe
Zaandam	63,000	1,440/570	43.7	2000	Caribbean, Panama Canal, Alaska	Deluxe
Amsterdam	61,000	1,380/670	44.2	2000	Caribbean, Mediterranean, N Europe Transatlantic, World Cruise	Deluxe

Cruise line notes

This originally Dutch line can give P&O and Cunard a run for their money in the longevity stakes since they have been carrying passengers since 1871, and even their 1989 acquisition by the Carnival Corporation failed to alter their chosen commitment to 'A Tradition of Excellence'. Even allowing for their recent ships being some of the most modern in the world, HAL remain as one of the dwindling band of traditional cruise exponents and tend to attract a more knowledgeable, mature passenger, primarily American, but with a growing following in Europe. They are even starting to attract a slightly younger crowd, couples in their 30s on some of their Caribbean and European routes, but one of their undoubted strengths is the Alaskan routes they offer with great precision and style, and these still attract an older clientele. HAL's attention to detail and polished style more than make up for food that doesn't quite live up to its Deluxe rating (with the exception of some spectacular buffets), while their activities are increasingly varied and lively and the range of entertainment is good if not startling. Service is a HAL watchword – it tends to be formal but personal, efficient but relaxed, helping to create that refined, elegant atmosphere that was the key to the cruising of yesteryear. Decor tends to be a little garish in places as for some reason the interior designers are keen on lots of oranges and reds, but otherwise they manage contemporary design with a more cultured appearance that provides a warm feel, if a little over-rich for my personal taste. While they have been something of a well-kept secret in Europe, that is changing as they now feature at least two ships in the Med or northern Europe each year. HAL have been expanding their itineraries in recent years to South America, with Antarctica featuring for the first time in 2002, and they will have another high-quality offering in the fleet when the *Seabourn Sun* transfers from sister line Seabourn late in 2001 (to be renamed *Prinsendam*). There is also a new class of ship due to debut with them next year, with the 84,000-ton *Zuiderdam* the first of five new-builds that will take their style to even grander proportions.

Ship notes

Just about the only thing you won't find aboard a HAL cruise ship is extensive facilities for children, but even this detail is changing (see Extras, below). Otherwise, they have the lot, including some of the best fitness facilities at sea, great deck sports, two large pools – one covered by a sliding glass roof (on all but *Noordam* and *Westerdam*) – multi-storey atriums, fountains and elaborate showlounges. The newest ships (starting with the four Statendam-class) are striving to attract a younger clientele while still appealing to their traditional passengers, and it isn't at all a bad compromise. Entertainment varies from high-energy stage shows to classical concerts, and the public rooms are never less than elegant and occasionally, in the case of the trademark piano bars, real romantic little hideaways. HAL also score heavily with their cabins, which offer a level of spaciousness way beyond most expectations, even among the lower grades. Once again, the message is to choose the lowest grade possible for the best value, although the high proportion of cabins with balconies (not on the older duo) is also quite tempting, and they are all complemented by some extremely smart fittings and furnishings. Another HAL trademark is the use of millions of dollars-worth of antiques throughout their ships, providing additional focal points. Brilliant passenger flow is aided by the clever use of lots of smaller rooms to break the ship up well, although the split-level dining room, complete with grand staircase and musicians' gallery, goes against this trend and is equally impressive. In 1997, new flagship *Rotterdam* took HAL's traditional appeal in the modern idiom to a new level, with more use of woods and darker colours for that true liner feel. However, she is still bang up to date in her choice and range of facilities, which include the first dedicated children's playroom on a HAL ship and a two-tier showlounge. *Volendam* and *Zaandam* combined some of the best features of *Rotterdam* and the *Statendam* series in a new package, with bold, art deco styling, a revamped pool deck and no less than 197 suites or mini-suites with balconies, plus the alternative restaurant that is such a striking addition on the *Rotterdam. Amsterdam* assumed joint-flagship status when she arrived in late 2000 and takes over the signature world cruise duties in 2002. She also features a state-of-the-art Internet café (plus data ports in every cabin) and an all-suite deck with concierge service – a throwback to the more class-conscious days of cruising – with its own private lounge and additional exclusive services. Internet facilities were subsequently retro-fitted to all HAL ships by the end of 2001. The newest quartet have also succeeded in pushing the line towards the top of the Deluxe class, alongside accomplished exponents Celebrity.

Extras

A recent addition is Half Moon Cay in the Bahamas, HAL's own private island, with a shopping plaza, food pavilion, white sand beach and an array of water sports on offer. Classic afternoon tea is given a Dutch twist at least once every voyage, while top-of-the-range suites all feature an in-cabin dining alternative. HAL's Dutch officers and Filipino crew make for a warm and friendly service combination. The company's shore excursions in Alaska are some of the best in the market due to their long-standing expertise in this area. Check out the top level observation lounge on each ship – always called the Crow's Nest – for a wonderful place to sip cocktails. Good provision for disabled passengers, especially with the generous-width wheelchair-friendly cabins. HAL is making a big effort to win over 'junior cruisers' with a dramatically enhanced activity programme for children, Club HAL (for the 5–8s, 9–12s and teens), aboard its Caribbean and even Alaska sailings. A full-time youth co-ordinator is on every ship, with assistants to maintain a ratio of one adult to every 30 children, and their Alaskan programme will even offer special shore excursions for 6–12-year-olds and teenagers. The *Maasdam*, with her year-round Caribbean voyages, had brand new kids and teens rooms built in 2001, complete with computers, games and large-screen TVs. Less formal Lido dining on some evenings is a new feature, and other 'extras' include a free ice-cream parlour, pre-dinner hors d'oeuvres in the lounges, fresh fruit in cabins daily, fresh popcorn at the cinema and even gentleman social hosts on sailings of 14 days or more.

For Holland America's UK office, ring 020 7940 4477.

TRAVEL TIP

The 'No tips' policy should be a bonus, but most American passengers still tip their restaurant and cabin staff at the end of the cruise, so beware the all-inclusive tag on this count unless you are happy to be the odd one out. Annoyingly, tipping guidelines are not given out.

ISLAND
www.myislandcruise.com

Ships	Tonnage	Passengers/ Crew	Space Ratio	Built/ Refurbished	Cruise Area	Rating
Island Escape	40,132	1,700/610	23.6	1982/01	Mediterranean, Caribbean, Transatlantic	Superior (expected)

Cruise line notes

Due to start operations in March 2002 is a cruise newcomer – a joint venture between Royal Caribbean and First Choice – who promise to introduce a different, more relaxed and informal style of cruising, aimed primarily at the 30-40 age group, especially families, that is 'fresh, contemporary and more up-beat'. Their watchwords are 'Relaxotherapy' (ugh!), ad-lib dining (no set times or allocated places), no jacket required (keeping things casual at all times) and Friends on Board (a partnership with names like Costa Coffee, Oddbins and Holmes Place spas to provide some of the essential services). They aim to challenge preconceptions of cruising being about shuffleboard and sequins (which we have already seen that it isn't in many places, but that's a minor quibble), and plan to bring things right up to date with modern Internet facilities, three children's clubs and more dynamic evening entertainment, from deck parties to retro nights and adult games to cabarets. Their pricing structure is distinctly of the tour operator variety (and most flights are with First Choice carrier Air 2000) so it will be interesting to see how they deliver this relaxed, more youthful and image-conscious style ('that lazy Sunday feeling … every day') without compromising on the quality of an expected Superior level cruise.

Ship notes

The newly-renamed *Island Escape* was formerly the plodding *Viking Serenade* of Royal Caribbean, a high-density converted ferry designed for short-haul cruising to the likes of the Mexican Riviera, where the aim was to get people off the ship rather than have them fill the limited public rooms and deck space. She is due for a complete overhaul and refurbishment before she sails under Island colours which, frankly, she needs. Awkward passenger flow, tiny cabins (apart from one genuine suite, a handful with balconies and three configured for disabled guests), narrow, claustrophobic corridors and a haphazard scattering of cabin types make for a number of challenges for the new operation to deliver the necessary 'relaxotherapy.' On the plus side, there are three good lounges (including the nightclub situated high around the funnel), a casino, decent gymnasium and three restaurants for their open-seating dining policy. She will sail two western Mediterranean routes out of Palma, which can be combined for a two-week cruise, while there are also a good range of cruise-and-stay options around Majorca. In the winter, she is expected to move across to the Caribbean.

Extras

With First Choice's tour operator expertise behind the project, there ought to be a sound level of shoreside expertise with ship transfers and excursions. Tips are included and the big-name on-board partnerships should ensure a much higher level of service than you would otherwise expect. Their prices are also an eye-catcher – from just £499 for a standard inside cabin. But you hope they will attract passengers for their avowed intent to be youthful, unstructured and carefree rather than at the budget end of the range.

For a brochure, call 0870 600 1160

LOUIS CRUISE LINES
www.louiscruises.com

Ships	Tonnage	Passengers/ Crew	Space Ratio	Built/ Refurbished	Cruise Area	Rating
Princesa Victoria	14,538	566/230	26.5	1936/93	Eastern Mediterranean	Standard
Serenade	14,173	672/200	21.0	1957/85	Eastern Mediterranean	Standard
Princesa Marissa	10,487	855/185	12.2	1966/95	Eastern Mediterranean	Standard
Calypso	11,162	618/190	18.0	1967/00	Eastern Mediterranean	Standard
Princesa Cypria	9,984	621/180	16.0	1968/90	Eastern Mediterranean	Standard

Cruise line notes

This Greek-Cypriot line – which acquired a 70 per cent interest in Royal Olympic in 2000 – has proved popular with the British holiday market on Cyprus and now has a London office to encourage more direct bookings from the UK. Their stock-in-trade is a two- or three-day tour to Egypt and the Holy Land, where the transport is largely incidental to the itineraries. The ships, all aging liners, are pretty crowded when full, and functional rather than remarkable, but, at the prices they charge, a lot can be overlooked. Also on the plus-side, the food is good and plentiful and you are not likely to spend too long on board with their port-intensive schedules. You can choose from two-day trips to Egypt, Rhodes, the Lebanon or Israel, three-day Egypt-Israel combinations, five-day Greek Island adventures (mainly for the local Cypriot market) or a seven-day Greek Islands cruise. The passenger profile is likely to be a fair European mix, with a good percentage of Brits, hence the irritation of public announcements in several different languages. Evening entertainment is limited to non-language-specific acts and the staff are eager to please without having any great finesse.

Ship notes

While all the ships (apart from three on long-term charter) are of veteran status, Louis maintain them well and they are ideally suited to the short runs they do, although *Princesa Amorosa* is a touch spartan for a full week's cruise. The *Marissa* possesses a few cabins without private facilities, which is unusual these days, and there is not a great range of facilities. *Cypria* is geared up more for the local market, while the venerable *Victoria* remains a minor classic of old-world style, with generous open deck space and some larger-than-average cabins. Recent acquisitions *Serenade* and *Calypso* provide more contrast, with the former another classic 1950s liner while the latter has a more modern feel due to recent duty for the German Transocean company.

Extras

At these prices it is churlish to quibble about the relative lack of facilities aboard Louis vessels, especially as their main focus is providing an excellent-value trip to the sights of Israel (with all-inclusive tours to Jerusalem) and Egypt (all-inclusive tours to Cairo and the Pyramids of Giza). They also have a flair for the friendly if you are a fan of Greek hospitality.

For details in the UK, phone 020 7383 2882.

MEDITERRANEAN SHIPPING CRUISES

www.msccruise.com

Ships	Tonnage	Passengers/ Crew	Space Ratio	Built/ Refurbished	Cruise Area	Rating
Monterey	21,051	600/280	35	1952/98	Mediterranean, Canaries, Indian Ocean	Standard
Rhapsody	17,495	804/350	21.7	1977/98	Mediterranean, South America, Transatlantic	Standard
Melody	36,500	1,200/535	30.4	1982/99	Mediterranean, Caribbean, Transatlantic	Superior

Cruise line notes

This wholly Italian company is proving ever more popular in the British market for its combination of traditional cruise ship style with modern appeal at a budget price. MSC has also gone into the new-build business, with an order for a 1,600-passenger ship for 2003. The majority of passengers on board (around 65 per cent) are Italian and the age range tends to be not much more than 40-45, making for a boisterous and lively cruise profile, but there are rarely fewer than 50 Brits aboard and up to 100 on many sailings. This does make for the bugbear of constant lengthy multi-lingual announcements, and the entertainment has to be of more universal appeal (jugglers, singers and dancers) than on British- or American-dominated cruises, but the whole style of the cruise is genuinely friendly and warm, with lashings of Italian verve (not least in the food, with great pasta in particular) and service. It is broad-based, cosmopolitan and informal, and it is a style that goes down well with seasoned travellers and repeat cruisers, as well as anyone devoted to Italian holidays generally. Like Costa, mid-July through to the end of August is MSC's peak European period, and the number of Brits aboard drops off.

TRAVEL TIP

In typical Italian fashion, MSC ships make much more of mealtimes, particularly dinner, than their American counterparts. There is no hustle to get first-sitting diners out, and so there is more emphasis here on the service, food and ambience than on the typical evening showtimes.

A broad range of itineraries feature good programmes in the eastern Mediterranean in particular, while their three longer voyages (down East Africa to Durban, transatlantic to Florida and to Rio de Janeiro) are especially popular as they offer more sea days and exotic ports of call. Their series of seven-night cruises from Rio on *Rhapsody* offer another exciting cruise alternative.

Ship notes

Monterey is a classic ocean liner given a thorough modern overhaul to provide facilities such as fitness centre, jacuzzis, nightclub and beauty salon. She sails well (in keeping with ships of this vintage), and the cabin varieties tend to be less uniform and more individualistic, compact but comfortable (although she possesses some extremely spacious suites). There is also an excellent prom deck and plenty of open deck space, while there are some lovely authentic touches with the decor, like wood panelling and brass railings, that hark back to their original lives. *Monterey*'s split-level dining room, with original engraved glass from its early days, is another eye-catcher. *Rhapsody* is more of a purpose-built modern cruiser, and her 1970s build means cabins tend to be a bit more cramped and not so well insulated, but she still has a good amount of deck space for the sun-worshippers and some outstanding public rooms, like the Top Sail Lounge and indoor-outdoor 8 Bells Nightclub. Most recent acquisition *Melody* is another of the more modern build of cruise ship that started to provide more spacious cabins and be more generous with deck space. She also has MSC's first children's programme and is a good prospect for families.

Extras

The on-board currency is the lire (although, like all other lines, you just sign for drinks and other purchases as you go along), so you may want to take a calculator along to work out how much money you are really spending! None of the ships have any disabled passenger facilities. *Rhapsody* and *Melody* offer two attractive transatlantic repositioning cruises in autumn and spring, with *Melody* going on to a series of 11-night Caribbean sailings out of Fort Lauderdale that offer some more imaginative itineraries plus the option of a completely European cruise atmosphere which is a real rarity in this American-dominated segment of the market. The ship's sailing time of 8pm also allows for same-day flights to Miami, which cuts out the need for an overnight stay and helps to fit more comfortably with a two-week holiday schedule. For those with more time to spare, *Melody* can combine two back-to-back cruises for one splendid 23-night Caribbean-Panama-South America spectacular.

For more details or a brochure, phone 020 7637 2525.

NORWEGIAN CRUISE LINE
www.uk.ncl.com

Ships	Tonnage	Passengers/ Crew	Space Ratio	Built/ Refurbished	Cruise Area	Rating
Norwegian Sea	42,246	1,504/630	28	1988	Caribbean, Bahamas, New England	Premier
Norwegian Majesty	38,000	1,460/550	26	1992/99	Caribbean, Bermuda	Premier
Norwegian Dream	46,000	1,748/614	26.3	1992/98	Caribbean, Mediterranean, N Europe, Transatlantic S America	Premier,
Norwegian Wind	46,000	1,748/614	26.3	1993/98	Caribbean, Pacific, Alaska	Premier
Norwegian Sky	80,000	2,002/950	39.9	1999	Caribbean, Alaska, Hawaii	Premier **Brit's Guide Favourite**
Norwegian Sun	80,000	2,002/950	39.9	2001	Caribbean, New England, Canada	Premier (expected)
Norwegian Star	91,000	2,200/1,100	41.3	2001	Hawaii	Premier (expected)

Cruise line notes

The pioneers of one-class, Caribbean fly-cruising, NCL suffered at the hands of their more go-ahead rivals through the early 1990s but have bounced back as one of the key players and continue to deliver a well-organised, consistent product. Now under the ownership of Far East-based Star Cruises (following a takeover in 2000), NCL are benefitting both from Star's fresh approach to the business and their financial muscle, which sees a host of new ships on line in the next few years. After the impressive debut of their *Norwegian Sky,* NCL have a sister ship ready to take her bow and an even more ambitious vessel due out at the end of 2001. The *Norwegian Star* was originally intended for the Star Cruises fleet, but she has been diverted to be Norwegian's new flagship and the standard-bearer for their inventive Freestyle policy, which offers a more informal, relaxed and flexible style of on-board service. All the NCL ships are being retro-fitted to allow for the principal Freestyle elements of open-seating dining, more restaurant choice, more staff, lifestyle and well-being programmes, and more guest-friendly disembarkation (with none of the hustle to get you off the ship first thing in the morning), but the *Sun* and especially the *Star* are the first to be purpose-built with these criteria in mind. Their appeal remains a touch more British-accented than many American lines and they continue to develop imaginative itineraries, such as Hawaii and the Black Sea, while adding destinations like Belize to existing tried and trusted Caribbean routes. As befits pioneers in their field, they still deliver some imaginative touches, like their alternative dining (now a real standout feature under the Freestyle programme), weekly Chocoholics Buffet, Dive-In snorkelling programme, themed sports cruises (especially for American football lovers), Sports Bars and non-smoking cabins. *Norwegian Sky* added still more features, like an Internet Café, cigar club, martini bar and butler service with its suites, and their rivals have promptly copied the Internet provision developments. They attract a younger, livelier crowd without going as far as Carnival's rather raucous image and have an excellent, well-supervised children's programme on all ships. Entertainment, both day and night, is plentiful, high energy and well-organised, as are the shore excursions, and the big showtimes are both ambitious and eye-catching.

TRAVEL TIP

Couples looking for that romantic touch on *Sky* should ask for a dining reservation in the elegant Horizons Restaurant, which specialises in tables for two. Also be sure to visit le Bistro and Gatsby's Wine Bar.

Ship notes

Their fleet has undergone some dramatic changes in recent years, with the emphasis now on a fairly new range of ships. The classic liner *Norway* has been transferred to Star Cruises, as has the old *Norwegian Star,* leaving the 1988-built *Norwegian Sea* as the oldest performer left in the NCL stable. Her standard cabins could do with being a bit bigger for a seven-day cruise, especially for cupboard space, but the finish is never less than smart. She is quite novel in the American market for possessing a full, wrap-around promenade deck, and there is an impressive range of public rooms, from the small, intimate Oscar's piano bar to the impressive, large-scale Cabaret showlounge. There is a surprisingly spacious pool and sun deck, and, overall, the *Sea* succeeds in creating a more intimate ambience at the same time as providing big-ship style, while her three and four-day winter cruises out of Miami are an attractive add-on to a Florida holiday. *Norwegian Majesty* is quite a chic, refreshing alternative to the bland, identikit ships, with outstanding features like the outdoor Piazza San Marco, serving pizza, ribs and ice cream, surprisingly spacious cabins and good attention to detail. The provision of open deck space could be better, though. A clever enlargement in 1999 added a second dining room and Le Bistro option, extra pool on the sun deck, new casino and another 200 cabins. Sister ships *Norwegian Dream* and *Wind* – a pair of bright, innovative, medium-sized cruisers with an above-average feel for the Premier market – are also practically brand new after their enlargement in 1998 and, while some of the decor is a bit bland, they both have a warm, friendly ambience that perfectly suits their cruise style. Both inside and outside cabins are reasonably spacious (although a bit short of drawer and cupboard room, and the shower/bathrooms are tiny), the outside decks are attractive, especially with the tiered stern, and they maintain a pleasant, small-ship feel while providing all the amenities of something bigger. The extra elements of their enlargement process added a glamorous casino, a revamped sun deck with two pools and a swim-up bar, a nightclub, children's room, circular central restaurant (albeit still lacking the charm of the aft dining rooms) and a series of suites with balconies (the only ones on the ships). The duo have also become the line's adventurers, with some trail-blazing itineraries to Australia, New Zealand and the Far East (*Norwegian Wind*) and South America (*Norwegian Dream*).

TRAVEL TIP

There is little real distinction in *Majesty*'s main grades of cabin (with the exception of a few suites), so the lower grades are by far the best value.

Norwegian Sky marked another major progression in NCL's re-birth, a thoroughly modern yet classy super-liner, packed with facilities and extra features like the Sky Mobile drinks cart, pool-side suntan sprays, alternative Chinese/Italian restaurant, champagne and vodka bar (serving caviar and foie gras) and Internet connections in every cabin. In fact, there are no less than seven dining options, eight lounges or bars (including the two-tier Stardust showlounge), two pools and a paddling pool, full range of kids' facilities (including teen disco and video arcade) and a huge casino and shopping gallery, while 258 of the 1,001 cabins have balconies. *Norwegian Sun* promised to build on this success story with yet more dining options (including a Sushi Bar), children's pool and play area, and even a chapel for weddings. *Norwegian Star* should be another story altogether, especially as she is destined to be their first year-round Hawaiian cruiser (and they have had to do away with an on-board casino to comply with local laws). She will have no less than 10 restaurants and 11 different menus every night (including a Pacific Rim restaurant featuring a fusion of Californian, Hawaiian and Asian cuisine), 70 per cent of outside cabins with balconies, a new category of villa accommodation in a purpose-built steel and glass construction atop the ship (and including private deck areas), and a huge range of sports and exercise facilities. The Hawaii-based Mandara Spa have also been contracted to provide an even more sophisticated level of on-board pampering. All in all, she could even push NCL into the Deluxe category for the first time, but we await the reality of the project before passing judgement.

Extras

NCL offers an especially good product for younger singles, with a Guaranteed Singles Rate, and promises to keep everyone busy and involved if they want to be. Families will also enjoy being aboard, with the different Kids' Crew programmes for 3–17-year olds. NCL runs golf clinics in Bermuda and Barbados and an excellent range of shore excursions in Alaska. All the ships offer cabins for the disabled (with 20 on *Norwegian Star*). NCL was the first line to develop the 'private island' port of call, with the uninhabited tropical island of Great Stirrup Cay in the Bahamas being acquired to provide passengers sailing out of Miami and Fort Lauderdale with their own paradise beach retreat. Six beaches, two bars, a barbecue buffet, water sports, volleyball and table tennis are all laid on and add an extra dimension to any cruise. All tips can be added to your on-board account at a rate of $10 per person per day. All port taxes are also included.

For brochures, call 0800 525483.

FRED OLSEN
www.fredolsen.co.uk

Ships	Tonnage	Passengers/ Crew	Space Ratio	Built/ Refurbished	Cruise Area	Rating
Black Prince	11,209	446/200	25.1	1966/87	Mediterranean, Canaries, N Europe, Caribbean	Standard, *Brit's Guide* Favourite
Black Watch	28,492	798/330	35.5	1972/96	Mediterranean, N Europe, Africa, Caribbean, Canaries	Superior, *Brit's Guide* Favourite
Braemar	19,089	802/320	23.8	1993/01	Mediterranean, Canaries, N Europe, Caribbean	Premier (expected)

Cruise line notes

In many ways, Fred Olsen's *Black Prince* is the epitome of traditional British cruising, with a strong and loyal following attracted to its no-frills, sensibly-priced, year-round consistent quality and its intelligent programme of well-designed itineraries, which received another boost in late summer 2001 with the addition of a third ship, the former chic mid-sized *Cunard/Crown Dynasty,* now renamed *Braemar.* They are one of the prime movers in ex-UK cruising and, to a large extent, pioneered the way for the provision of ambitious new cruise facilities at Dover, which offer an attractive new gateway to the cruise world. The line sails far and wide (including new ventures up the Amazon and around Africa) to give its predominantly 50-plus age group great value for money in a consistently smart, clean and relatively sophisticated environment. With the advantages of sailing out of a British port, Olsen passengers begin their holiday as soon as they reach Dover (although there are now a number of fly-cruises), and the line makes sure everyone is made to feel welcome and part of the family from the outset. It provides quite a formal atmosphere on the whole, accentuated by the old-fashioned charm of the decor and the informative port lectures and other talks. Cuisine is good and consistent without being spectacular and service is never less than friendly. On-board entertainment tends towards the tried and trusted, with bingo, singalongs, gardening lectures and dance classes complementing the more predictable cabaret evenings, which include old-time music hall acts, plus a series of themed cruises, from art, antiquities and even genealogy to bridge, wildlife and sports. The entertainment staff have to be quite versatile to handle a number of different activities and on the whole they do a remarkable job. Like only a handful of her fellow ex-UK operators, on-board currency is sterling for a change and drinks charges are more modest British pub prices.

TRAVEL TIP

The brochure makes choosing your grade of cabin rather confusing for newcomers. There are no less than 14 categories on *Black Prince,* but the best value are the E grade of the outside two-berths, H grade of the inner two-berths and the few B grade family cabins which are the only ones on board with double beds.

Ship notes

The *Black Prince* has an almost yacht-like feel to her and the small-ship ambience is complemented by the intimate atmosphere of most of the public rooms, even the two-tiered Neptune showlounge. She also possesses some smart touches, like a new fitness centre, complete with indoor pool and solarium, non-smoking restaurants and a remarkable outdoor marina centre which swings into action off the stern and port side in calm waters, offering an enclosed pool in the sea for swimming, and the chance to water-ski, windsurf and sail from its teak decks. Typically with a ship of this vintage, there is a vast range of cabin types, including a surprisingly high number of singles. They are generally quite spacious (although not when the fold-down beds are in place in the cabins where the second berth is of this type) with pleasant fittings and furnishings, including TV and hairdryers, but cupboard space varies from generous (E and A grades and the Junior Suites) to minuscule (F and H and the majority of Lido Deck cabins) and the bathrooms (shower-rooms in most cases) are tiny and far from high-spec. Pleasingly, though, they all have (admittedly rather small) portholes instead of the windows which are now so popular on modern ships, and these add the proper nautical flavour to your cabin. Outstanding public rooms are the elegant Aquitaine Lounge and the upper level of the showlounge, the Lido Lounge, which has a pleasant conservatory atmosphere. Outside, the pool deck has a neat wooden terrace arrangement surrounding it, but the sunning space is quite limited and the stairs are quite steep for elderly passengers (although there are lifts to all decks). The Balblom Restaurant offers indoor/outdoor buffet dining with excellent all-round sea views.

The addition of the *Black Watch* (the former *Star Odyssey* of the old Royal Cruise Line) in 1996 represented a step up in class rating as well as size for Fred Olsen. She features larger than average cabins (all with hairdryers and TV as standard), some generous suites (choose the Marquee rather than Premier Suites for better value), and an excellent range of public rooms, right down to the alternative brasserie-type restaurant, the Garden Café, which offers evening dining without the formality. Good open deck space is complemented by the top-level Observatory lounge, complete with binoculars. Extra quality touches come in the form of the Explorers Library and Dalreoch Card Room, both new and both the product of the traditional feel supplied by British ship designers McNeece. More than anything, however, *Black Watch* gives passengers a choice about almost everything (there are no less than six bars, four lounges, two pools, an attractive gym, a nightclub and a cinema/lecture room) and in a style as good as anything else in the Superior range. Her itineraries (from three nights to 69 on the round Africa journey) also add to the ship's flexibility. Again, best value is in the lower-grade cabins which are equally spacious as more expensive ones, but have portholes rather than windows. *Braemar* was a new acquisition at the time of writing, a relatively new ship but of a modest size that should suit Olsen well. A lovely range of public rooms, well appointed cabins (if slightly on the small side, especially for cupboard space), a bright, open ambience throughout and a wonderfully welcoming five-storey atrium all add up to a (probable) Premier rating, especially after a quick re-fit to give her some of the traditional Fred Olsen style. Like *Black Watch,* she will also have cabins reconfigured for single occupancy.

Extras

The high number of single cabins are a notable feature of the *Black Prince,* although she does not have cabins adapted for the disabled (there are four aboard *Black Watch*). Only the newer ship carries children's facilities (there is really not much call for them aboard the *Prince,* which employs children's hosts only for the main summer holiday sailings). Olsen have negotiated special rates with National Express coaches to get you to their ports from anywhere in the UK, which takes care of your luggage right from the start. Their series of well-written shore tour guides help you to plan your off-ship excursions in advance, which is a great idea. There are now gentlemen dance hosts for single passengers on every *Black Prince* and *Watch* cruise.

For their UK office and brochures, call 01473 292222.

ORIENT LINES
www.orientlines.com

Ship	Tonnage	Passengers/ Crew	Space Ratio	Built/ Refurbished	Cruise Area	Rating
Marco Polo	22,080	860/356	25.6	1966/93	N Europe, Mediterranean, South America, Antarctica	Premier, ***Brit's Guide* Favourite**
Crown Odyssey	34,250	1,050/470	32.6	1988/96	Mediterranean, Hawaii, Far East, South Pacific, Indian Ocean	Premier

Cruise line notes

This is a wonderfully original product in the modern-day cruise world, covering as it does some of the most exotic, exciting and innovative destinations in genuine comfort and style and yet with the feel of expedition cruising. Now owned by Star Cruises (who took over previous owners NCL in 2000) but continuing as a distinctly separate brand (and with a new ship from their parent company in 2002), Orient attract those cruisers (and well-travelled holidaymakers generally) who have been there and done just about all of it but still want something different. The rating is fairly arbitrary as there is little to compare Orient with in those terms, but suffice it to say it is a relatively formal and distinguished cruise experience with high-quality food and service, a comprehensive level of lectures and specialist talks, a high comfort level in the public rooms and a low-key level of entertainment and facilities, apart from the destination-orientated programme of lectures. Both vessels are ideal for those who enjoy relaxing days at sea, to make the most of the ship's attractions (with the exception, however, of their destination-intensive Mediterranean programme), who like a social, relaxed atmosphere in the 50-plus age range (with a healthy Anglo-American mix, plus a strong Australian contingent on the South Pacific cruises) and who take a keen, intelligent interest in the flora, fauna and culture of the more unusual areas it visits. Their Antarctica programme is possibly the best at sea, offering as it does a real close-up experience, but still in great ship-borne comfort. Orient are keen to spread their gospel to a younger audience as well (especially on the more informal summer Med itineraries), and their cruises would certainly suit couples who don't demand the non-stop party atmosphere, late-night discos and the latest in cruise gimmicks. The addition of *Crown Odyssey* (formerly the excellent *Norwegian Crown*) in 2000 more than doubled Orient's capacity and introduced new routes to Scandinavia, Hawaii, the Panama Canal and more of South America, adding to the line's appeal as a true global adventurer. Orient are also one of the lines (NCL and Silversea being two others) to hand their health and beauty programmes and facilities over to the wonderful Mandara Spa, the most renowned spa operator in the Far East.

Ship notes

The *Marco Polo* was originally built under Soviet Union ownership and spent part of her early life as a spy ship before British entrepreneur and travel addict Gerry Herrod bought her up to turn her into the sophisticated world traveller she now is. Her ice-toughened hull and helicopter facility allow her to venture deep into the Antarctic and she has gradually built up her repertoire of fascinating itineraries, with an increasing number of seven-day voyages to add to longer ones of 30-plus days. She sails well and provides an elegant cruise vehicle with a limited range of on-board facilities, including some tastefully-decorated lounges, a good-sized gym and health centre, a small pool and an alternative dining arrangement that is extremely popular. The ship also boasts Zodiac landing craft for getting to land on the frozen wastes of Antarctica. The standard range cabins are a little cramped for more than seven-day cruises, but, typically with a ship of this age, there is a wide choice of categories and the top level ones offer some superb extra amenities such as separate living rooms, queen-sized beds, marbled bathrooms, mini-bars, bathrobes and room safes. As she is an older ship, her crew have to work harder to maintain her overall appearance, but the fact she is a proper ship, as opposed to one of the new floating hotels, is worth the occasional cleaning inconvenience.

TRAVEL TIP

It is advisable to book early in the cruise for the alternative dining nights in the Raffles Lounge which can accommodate only 75 at a time. A pre-dinner drink at Le Bar is also recommended.

Crown Odyssey adds a more modern touch to the Orient style but still maintaining the classic, long-distance voyage aura. With spacious, well-fitted cabins (and some opulent suites) and a good range of elegant public rooms, she offers existing Orient passengers the chance to try something new while acting as an attractive proposition for potential newcomers, as well as freeing up *Marco Polo* to adventure into different areas like the Amazon and Chilean fjords. In summer 2002, the *Ocean Voyager* will join the fleet, formerly the *SuperStar Aries* of Star Cruise and before that the highly-rated *Europa* of German line Hapag-Lloyd. This 37,012-ton vessel, carrying 650 passengers, will be deployed year-round on a series of Grand Voyages (see below) world-wide. The ship will feature single-seating dining and her excellent range and style of facilities – notably the spacious cabins, superb Club Belvedere observation lounge and two outdoor pools (one covered by a sliding glass roof) – should push her into the Deluxe category.

Extras

Orient's great range of itineraries remain the main attraction, but they also offer an attractive programme of hotel stays and land tours with many cruises. Their Grand Voyages programme offers a wonderful array of longer cruises in the more exotic areas, including 34 nights through the Red Sea and Indian Ocean, 23 and 27-night Asia and Far East journeys and 35 and 37-night South Pacific itineraries. Single supplements are as low as 25 per cent and there is a cabin-share scheme, while there is also a Gentleman Host programme for single lady travellers. The line provides a particularly high and sophisticated level of pre-cruise information to tie in with the extensive lecture programme, which includes guests of the calibre of David Bellamy. However, *Marco Polo* has no special children's facilities and, while there are two cabins adapted for the disabled, the use of tenders and Zodiacs at many ports is rather limiting for wheelchair-bound passengers. The genuine friendliness of the largely Filipino staff is another big plus of an Orient cruise. Passenger capacity in Antarctica is also limited to barely half the usual level and no more than 100 are allowed ashore at any one time for environmental reasons.

For the UK office, call 020 959 5900.

TRAVEL TIP

Orient's Antarctic programme books up extremely quickly. It offers a high degree of flexibility, but the itineraries cannot be set in stone because of the vagaries of the ice conditions. And, because of the near 24-hour daylight, shore visits are just as likely to be 8pm as 8am. The on-board routine is consequently fairly low-key. Many cruises come complete with pre- and post-cruise stays at outstanding hotels.

P&O
www.pocruises.com

Ships	Tonnage	Passengers/ Crew	Space Ratio	Built/ Refurbished	Cruise Area	Rating
Victoria	28,891	743/417	38.8	1966/97	Mediterranean, Caribbean, Canaries	Superior
Arcadia Adults only in 2002	63,500	1,496/650 (see Extras)	42.3	1989/97	Mediterranean, Canaries, N Europe, Caribbean,	Premier, *Brit's Guide* Favourite
Oriana	69,153	1,828/760	37.8	1995	Mediterranean, Canaries, Caribbean, World Cruise	Premier, *Brit's Guide* Favourite
Aurora	76,000	1,874/850	40.5	2000	Mediterranean, N Europe, Canaries, Caribbean, World Cruise	Premier *Brit's Guide* Favourite

Cruise line notes

Along with Cunard, P&O are one of the most well-known names in the cruise world and maintain their long and distinguished tradition in the business in the best British style. Really, P&O epitomise the British mass market, catering as they do for virtually all social tastes and pockets and all ages, from toddlers to pensioners. They maintain a high element of formality and traditional cruise elegance while being able successfully to satisfy the demands of bingo and karaoke, classical music and theatre. Along with Airtours, Thomson, Fred Olsen, First Choice and Swan Hellenic, they offer an almost exclusively British product, from the currency, to the officers, to the provision of one proper pub-style bar on each ship. For those wary of committing to an American environment, P&O is the perfect answer, especially in the shape of their newest ships *Oriana* and *Aurora,* the former as wonderful an example of modern cruise design in the traditional style as there is and the latter adding a really glamorous touch to the line. There is more emphasis on days at sea and enjoying the cruise experience than trying to do a port a day. P&O also avoid the typical American-style glitz in favour of a more reserved nautical mode; however, that doesn't mean they can't be quite innovative, as with their kids' programmes, health and fitness facilities and the state-of-the-art theatres aboard both modern super-liners. Service comes with charm and a smile from the Goan waiters and stewards, even if their English is occasionally a little suspect. Cuisine is a better-than-expected mix of traditional British fare, Goan curries and a little extra continental flair, (plus a new vegetarian menu), and is improving all the time with the corporate menus that were introduced with *Oriana.* There is also a good range of moderately-priced wines. P&O will also do something of a ship swap late in 2002, with the old-timer *Victoria* leaving the fleet and the *Oceana* joining from sister company Princess Cruises (one of the *Sun Princess* class), a 77,000-ton monolith offering a wealth of facilities and modern style.

TRAVEL TIP

Try not to arrive late for shows and plays in *Oriana*'s beautifully-appointed Theatre Royal as the design makes it difficult for latecomers to find a seat, even when it is not full. P&O should really employ proper ushers here. Seats in *Arcadia*'s Palladium showlounge can also be difficult to find unless you arrive early.

Ship notes

New to the fleet in 1998 was *Arcadia,* a more than adequate replacement for the old *Canberra.* Formerly the *Star Princess* of sister company Princess Cruises, she offers a mix of large-scale American-style glamour with more traditional P&O style. Her impressive range of facilities include six bars, two pools (one with a swim-up bar), a pizzeria and ice cream parlour, an impressive, two-level show-lounge and three-storey atrium lobby. The warming P&O touches come with the Oval pub, a proper library and card room, the Conservatory buffet dining alternative and a teenagers' disco and night nursery for the under 5s. Cabins are all well fitted and quite spacious (especially the Premier grades and Suites, all with balconies), and P&O have configured 64 for singles and eight for disabled passengers. Although considerably larger than the ship she replaced, traditional aspects like deck sports and the friendly service were transferred successfully to the new arrival (along with a number of *Canberra*'s crew).

Oriana was launched with much fanfare in 1995 and soon lived up to her billing as the first ship to be tailor-made for the British cruise market. With her combination of speed to reach her main cruising areas quickly, plus good seaworthiness, *Oriana* is perfectly suited to ex-UK voyaging and offers a sophisticated level of traditional charm while also catering for modern cruise developments such as a higher degree of entertainment, activities to keep the kids amused and in health and fitness facilities. Children under 12 can also benefit from lower fares (75 per cent off rather than 60 per cent) outside the main school holidays.

TRAVEL TIP

Be warned. For those of a sporting persuasion there is enough to keep you busy all day long and you can end up quite exhausted, especially when cruising in the warmer climates, trying to fit it all in.

In keeping with *Canberra*'s appeal, *Oriana* possesses a full range of public room options, from the Lord's Tavern pub, through the classically-styled Curzon Room to the gentlemen's club atmosphere of Anderson's. There is a small casino (a bit smoky and not too inviting for non-gamblers) and cinema, an excellent library and card room, three children's areas plus an outer deck area and pools devoted especially to the youngsters, as well as a night nursery for 2–5-year olds (a master-stroke for the family market), a disco and multi-purpose nightclub, two adults' pools, excellent deck games provisions, golf nets and a general sports net that allows for paddle tennis, football and cricket. The range of cabins is quite high compared with the American identikit format as P&O try to offer something for everyone, from some generous-sized suites, larger cabins with balconies, family three- and four-berths, single rooms and eight cabins especially adapted for disabled passengers. All cabins have a fridge, TV, hairdryer and room safe, and are bright and airy, with good use of artwork and soft furnishings, although cupboard space is a bit limited. Inside cabins are also equally as spacious as those with an exterior view. The choice of two restaurants and the bright indoor/outdoor Conservatory for buffet meals is augmented by a pizzeria, which is open throughout the day.

TRAVEL TIP

Parts of *Oriana* can get quite busy, especially in holiday periods when large numbers of families are on board, but there is always a quiet corner to be found for those not wanting to indulge in the non-stop frenzy. Try Tiffany Court for a cup of tea or coffee, Anderson's or the Curzon Room during the day for a peaceful corner to read that book, the aft areas of A, B and C decks for a bit of sunbathing and the aft Terrace Bar in mid-afternoon for a cool drink.

Oldest ship *Victoria* is still wearing extremely well. New, rich decor (in 1997) gives her a classy touch way beyond most of the Superior class, and the enhancements to areas like the Lido Buffet and International Lounge are also of a higher quality than you might expect.

Aurora, although from the same stable as *Oriana*, is noticeably more dramatic as the designers have gone for a richer, more obvious high-tech feel, yet still with enough typical P&O elements (like Anderson's lounge and the Crow's Nest observation lounge) to make their regular passengers feel at home. The range of on-board choice is almost overwhelming, with a range of bars and lounges to suit just about every taste. The Curzon Theatre is another superb entertainment centre, while the alternative showlounge Carmen's is both flexible and comfortable. The Raffles coffee and chocolate bar is an excellent (and popular) addition, while the provision of a proper cinema (also used for lectures and smaller stage shows, notably for children) is another P&O characteristic. Nightclub Masquerade is a bit bland but remains well-used until the wee, small hours, while Champions Sports Bar adds another dimension. Once again, the spa provisions are excellent and the line's tradition for a host of deck sports is well maintained. The children's facilities (in four separate sections, with their own deck space, paddling pool and a video games room) and the truly outstanding nature of the childcare staff are among the very best anywhere in the world, at sea or on land, and the night nursery system (free of charge still) is a real boon for parents. Cabins are almost identical to *Oriana,* although more (in excess of 40 per cent) have balconies and there are two sumptuous, two-storey penthouse suites. Buffet dining alternative The Orangery is also used occasionally for evening meals (notably an Indian night), while the 24-hour Café Bordeaux, with its menu changing throughout the day, is an inspired touch.

Extras

For families, the three newest ships are a perfect choice, while all the ships are an attractive proposition for singles with their cabin choice and range of social activities. *Oriana, Aurora* and *Arcadia* are well adapted for the disabled, although the use of tenders in some ports can make shore visits difficult. Check the itinerary carefully for the ports to gain maximum access. A large range of themed cruises – notably Football, Antiques and Classical Music – are always popular and there is a series of Newcomers cruises. For repeat passengers, P&O offer special deals through their POSH Club (which really does stand for Port Out, Starboard Home from the traditional era of cruising). The two world cruises are another outstanding P&O feature. There is also the option of fly-cruises as well as ex-UK cruising for those with preferences and a full range of short- and long-duration choices, from three days up to the 90-day world cruise. The three- and four-day 'sampler' cruises attract a much younger party element that seems sure to become a bigger feature in future. The self-service launderettes are a real bonus, too. In fact, the only real reason to avoid a P&O cruise is if you can't stand being surrounded by fellow Brits on your holiday.

From May 24, *Arcadia* will become the first P&O ship to be designated for Adults Only. As a result of 'passenger comments and requests' (presumably from their older customers!), the ship will not carry passengers under 16, and a number of changes will be made to the facilities to reflect this switch in emphasis. It will be interesting to see how such a dramatic, first-of-its-kind change will be received by traditional P&O-goers.

Stop press: for more P&O news see page 248, Hold the Front Page.
For a brochure, call 0990 726726.

PRINCESS CRUISES
www.princesscruises.com

Ships	Tonnage	Passengers/ Crew	Space Ratio	Built/ Refurbished	Cruise Area	Rating
Pacific Princess	20,636	640/350	32.2	1971/93	Transatlantic, Africa, Bermuda	Superior
Royal Princess	44,348	1,200/520	36.9	1984/94	S America, Mediterranean, N Europe, World Voyage	Deluxe,
Crown Princess	70,000	1,590/696	44.0	1990	Panama Canal, Caribbean, Hawaii	Premier
Regal Princess	70,000	1,590/696	44.0	1991	Mediterranean, Far East, S Pacific, N Europe, Transatlantic	Premier
Sun Princess	77,000	1,950/900	39.4	1995	Panama Canal, Alaska, Caribbean	Deluxe,
Dawn Princess	77,000	1,950/900	39.4	1997	Caribbean, Alaska	Deluxe,
Grand Princess	109,000	2,600/1,100	41.9	1998	Caribbean	Deluxe
Sea Princess	77,000	1,950/900	39.4	1999	Caribbean, Alaska, Mexico	Deluxe
Ocean Princess	77,000	1,950/900	39.4	2000	Caribbean, Alaska	Deluxe
Golden Princess	109,000	2,600/1,100	41.9	2001	Caribbean, Mediterranean, Transatlantic	Deluxe

Cruise line notes

The American arm of P&O is a much bigger, glitzier and, well, more American proposition and is something of a secret to British mass-market cruising. With 80–90 per cent US passengers, there is little of the traditional style that marks out P&O's ex-UK operation, although the older ships do go some way to redressing the balance, and Princess also offers a greater level of formality than many rivals (although still less than P&O). The core business is the Caribbean, Alaska (where they and Holland America remain the foremost lines) and Europe, and they offer a well-honed, sophisticated and port-intensive programme. They do boast quite a variety of cruise durations, with those of 10 days and above attracting a significantly older passenger profile (50–plus) than the seven-day versions, which draw a lot of families, who are extremely well catered for in both facilities and children's programmes. There is a wide variety of entertainment (with the newest six offering substantially more of everything), and much of it is quite spectacular and showy. Service generally is friendly and almost unobtrusive (and notably more up-scale on *Royal Princess*), while the cuisine has undergone something of an overhaul to ensure, by and large, it is worthy of the Deluxe rating. It is also entirely a fly-cruise operation (apart from a handful of northern European voyages from the new cruise facilities at Dover). Princess will also be sending the *Ocean Princess* over to join their P&O brand at the end of 2002, which should make quite a contrast from the old-timer *Victoria* she will be replacing! In keeping with similar developments in the cruise business, Princess also rolled out their Personal Choice Dining scheme across the two largest ships in 2001, allowing for greater flexibility and choice for all passengers. One of the three main restaurants will be open seating from 5.30pm-midnight, while the other two will maintain traditional first and second-sitting arrangements, so passengers can select their preferred dining option in advance.

Ship notes

The advent in May 1998 of what was then the World's Largest Cruise Ship marked another significant step forward in the development of the hardware that has become the industry's watchword. *Grand Princess* was built up on a near tidal wave of breathless advance publicity, and she very nearly fitted the bill on all accounts. Big, yes (try mind-bogglingly vast), but not impersonal (the number of rooms and choice of facilities sees to that); impressive, undoubtedly (well, who could fail to be impressed by Skywalkers Nightclub, suspended 150 feet up at the stern of the ship, the virtual-reality games centre, wedding chapel and alternative dining options); and immediately popular. But the real triumph in a ship this big is the fact you can be at sea with 2,600 fellow passengers and scarcely know it. The wonderful range of just about every kind of amenity, including 16 bars, eight restaurants or cafés (with a 24-hour buffet service), four swimming pools, three lounges in addition to the two-storey Princess Theatre and a myriad of other opportunities (shops, sports, library, gymnasium, card room, casino, etc., etc.), means you retain an element of the small-scale in this floating city and you are hardly ever uncomfortable with the numbers involved. Even the usually vexed business of disembarkation is handled smoothly via double gangways. Yes, this truly is the future of cruising and the public wants more – hence *Golden Princess* (showcased in Southampton in May 2001) and three more of this breed before the end of 2004. *Golden* is essentially a carbon copy of *Grand,* with the addition of an Internet centre and a few other minor structural 'tweaks'. The children's centre has been redesigned to allow for separate areas for three age groups; the mini-golf has been increased (and the golf simulators moved to the Virtual Reality Centre); the Atrium shopping area has been remodelled; the Wedding Chapel has moved on Deck 7; and some of the suites have been reconfigured. However, all this remains just a cosmetic difference from the original and highly successful formula. The dining possibilities alone make these

TRAVEL TIP

Beware one transatlantic difference – in keeping with American laws, alcoholic drinks are available only to those 21 and over.

ships stand out, and the whole, vast structure is carried off in a fashion that still hints at the small-scale and intimate. There is always an element of choice, and the only awkward thing is in deciding where to go and what to do! Both offer alternative-dining Mexican and Italian restaurants which are highly recommended but usually need to be booked early in any cruise. It is just a shame the line has to confuse everything by offering 36 categories of cabin to wade through when you basically just have inside and outside twin rooms, twin rooms with balconies, mini-suites and suites. *Star Princess* joins the fleet in February 2002, with some wonderful itineraries in the Far East and Hawaii.

TRAVEL TIP

The *Royal Princess* has a surprisingly small cinema and, for the more popular films, you should arrive early to ensure a seat. Don't expect to find an array of energetic daytime events, either, as she concentrates on providing a more relaxed atmosphere for her passengers.

The relative diversity of the rest of the fleet also gives rise to a number of other differences. The *Royal* and *Pacific* are used for the more exotic itineraries, and so attract an older passenger. Although now getting on in years, *Pacific*'s small-ship style retains an element of elegance and spaciousness both in the cabins and public rooms, and the wonderfully friendly atmosphere makes for a high repeat factor among her passengers, despite the draw of so many newer ships. The *Royal* is a bit of a one-off and a real gem in the Princess range, a more notably up-market, sleek and sophisticated cruiser, having only outside cabins and a more marked degree of design elegance. Generously spacious cabins feature throughout and many public rooms (although fewer of the latter than on many ships of the same size) come with a wonderfully light, airy feel that makes for relaxing long-distance cruising which should appeal to the British market. Small touches, like fresh flowers, cutlery placed in linen napkins on the tables in the buffet Lido and overall attention to detail, mark her out as above average. She was also chosen to trail-blaze a 72-night world cruise in 2001 that was an immediate success. The *Crown* and *Regal* are Princess Cruise's hotel-type ships, still a little unimaginative and clinical in terms of the interior decor, but with a well-worked range of facilities. They both qualify in the Premier range for their more-than-ample selection of facilities and amenities, but none of them feature a proper prom deck.

Sun added an extra element of stylishness to the Princess appeal that is maintained through sister ships, *Dawn, Sea* and *Ocean Princess* and will also be more noteworthy for the British market. As well as being quite beautiful internally (if still rather of the slab-sided, floating hotel block in overall appearance) they demonstrate an almost unique ability to bridge the transatlantic taste gap. With a generous range of public rooms on a much smaller scale than hitherto seen on Princess designs, coupled with an almost overwhelming use of eye-catching architecture (check out the four-storey main lobby and pool decks) and some distinctly traditional touches (notably in the Wheelhouse Bar and full promenade deck), the series broke new ground in super-liner appeal and sophistication. There is a full, 24-hour dining option, as well as a pizzeria, to take some of the pressure off the two main dinner sittings and provide more flexibility to enjoy the evening entertainment. Their cabins are unfailingly spacious, many with balconies, and the top-of-the-range suites are truly luxurious.

Extras

There are some great honeymoon packages, the Princess pizzerias are an outstanding feature, kids will adore the range of facilities on the newer ships and there is a comprehensive scuba-diving programme for everyone, from newcomers to experienced divers. Shore excursions are carefully thought out and well executed, and their information literature is among the best in the business. All the ships feature self-service launderettes. In addition, there are some attractive land-stay add-ons on the more exotic itineraries like the Far East, plus new options to China, Vietnam, Africa and the Indian Ocean, and their Alaskan programme is one of the best for offering a Canadian Rockies tour before the cruise. For the disabled passenger, the newest six ships have a range of specially-adapted cabins, while all the others have at least four. Port taxes are included, and there are attractive Family Fun Fares (from just £345 for the first child) for four-berth cabins, as well as group babysitting ($4/child per hour) from 10pm-1am on the super-liners (but you need to book early). Newcomers' cruises are another Princess feature. The Personal Choice dining option is a valuable addition but it does mean an extra $8/person meal gratuity is added to your ship-board account each day to replace the normal end-of-cruise tipping scenario.

Stop press: for more Princess Cruises news, see page 248, Hold the Front Page.

For a brochure, call 0870 566442.

RADISSON SEVEN SEAS CRUISES

www.rssc.com

Ships	Tonnage	Passengers/ Crew	Space Ratio	Built/ Refurbished	Cruise Area	Rating
Song of Flower	8,282	180/144	46.0	1986/90	Far East, Indian Ocean, Mediterranean, N Europe	Deluxe
Radisson Diamond	20,295	354/200	57.3	1992	Caribbean, Panama Canal, Transatlantic, Mediterranean	Deluxe
Paul Gauguin	18,800	320/206	58.7	1997	French Polynesia	Deluxe
Seven Seas Navigator	30,000	490/325	61.2	1999	Mediterranean, Transatlantic, N Europe, S America, Caribbean	Ultra-deluxe
Seven Seas Mariner	50,000	700/445	71.4	2001	Mediterranean, Transatlantic, N Europe, Caribbean	Ultra-deluxe

Cruise line notes

This is a true World Traveller series and attracts a slightly older (45-plus), more discerning and well-travelled passenger who still wants to see the sights in great comfort, enjoy five-star cuisine and service and take a keen interest in the flora, fauna and culture along the way. The itineraries are exciting, exotic and, in many cases, unique, offering the chance to get off the beaten track with well-organised shore excursions and intelligent and comprehensive lectures to accompany them. It is not a chance to enjoy glitzy entertainment, non-stop activities and the latest in cruising mod cons (although the two newest ships add state-of-the-art hardware and sophistication), and the overall atmosphere is one of relaxed formality, refined charm and an almost club-like exclusivity. The big increase in capacity brought about by *Seven Seas Navigator* and *Mariner* has not diminished this rather cosy, almost chic style but has added an extra element of luxury and indulgence previously managed only by Crystal, Silversea and Seabourn.

Ship notes

All five vessels are complete individuals, with the *Diamond* the most unusual in technical terms. Her innovative design (which makes for exceptionally smooth sailing) is a real attraction for many, and internally she is quite pretty, too, with a five-storey central hotel-style atrium, split-level main lounge, and one of the most elegant dining rooms afloat.

Cabins are all outside, many with balconies, and are wonderfully spacious and beautifully appointed, and the suites all feature superb bay windows, which add to the feeling of spaciousness. Sports facilities are excellent, with a jogging track, golf putting area and driving cage, comprehensive fitness centre and a watersports marina offering water-skiing, wind-surfing, sailing and jetskiing. There is an alternative dining option, The Grill, which is extremely popular but seats only 50 at a time, so you need to book early. Passengers are 75 per cent American, with the rest a good European mix. *Song of Flower* is a 'softer' version of the adventure type of cruise ship, visiting out-of-the-way areas but providing a more luxurious level of service and, especially, cuisine. Public rooms and cabins are relatively low-key in their decor, but the dining room is a great feature and her regular passengers will tell you she provides some of the most memorable meals at sea and a level of service found usually only in the most exclusive land-based resorts. There is a well-stocked library and a small, subtle casino that is, refreshingly, a million miles removed from the usual Las Vegas glitz. There are ten no-smoking cabins, but bathroom and cupboard space in all could be better. The 30-seat alternative dining option, Angelino's, features northern Italian specialities, but again it is popular so you should book early on for this.

TRAVEL TIP

The top category A-class suite on *Song of Flower* has plenty of extra space, but, surprisingly, no balcony. The B category offers much better value with its balcony and full-size bath.

There is a small pool and quite generous deck space for such a small ship, but the fitness centre is a bit of an after-thought. The main lounge is neat without being overly pretty, while the top level Observation Lounge offers excellent views in a quite intimate setting. Maintaining the line's tradition for classy, one-off vessels is *Paul Gauguin,* a French-built and owned ship operated by Radisson out of Tahiti for seven- and 14-night cruises around French Polynesia. She is another of the small, boutique ships along the lines of Seabourn and Silversea, only less formal. Two restaurants, three lounges, a small pool, fitness centre, spa, beauty salon and casino, and that's about it for the facilities (although the finish is of the highest quality). But, once you add in the Michelin-starred cuisine, plus sumptuous cabins (all with queen-sized or twin beds, marble bathrooms, robes, hairdryers, TV and VCR, fridge and personal safe, half with balconies), it adds up to a rich Deluxe experience. The itineraries boast unforgettable cruising – with the price tag to match. But, for those who have tired of the cruise mainstream, this is the perfect antidote.

The *Seven Seas Navigator* succeeded in giving Radisson a dramatic, top-quality edge in 1999. An all-suite, nearly all-balcony ship, she offers the latest in up-market facilities, including a two-tier showlounge, grand lobby, casino, alternative Italian dining and a full-service spa. Her generous cabins feature walk-in closets and complimentary bar and the Grand suites are truly capacious at 1,238sq ft, plus balcony. Her itineraries range from seven to 25 nights, giving a good spread of possibilities from the Mediterranean, Northern Europe and Panama Canal to a more exotic South American circumnavigation. Mariner went a step further in 2001 by being the world's first all-balcony ship, and one which put her right at the top of her class. With the extra size to add a superb range of facilities, from the Internet café and excellent spa to a short-tennis court and no less than five restaurants, she maintains the true five-star service touch with some dazzling interior design. The all-suite accommodation features extremely large walk-in wardrobes, marble bathrooms (with bath and shower), hair-dryers, TV and VCR, fridge with complimentary soft drinks and an in-suite bar. The largest measures a vast 1,580sq ft, while even the smallest give you 301sq ft (and therefore great value, too). Other standout features include high tea in the beautiful Observation Lounge and dining at Signatures, the specialist Cordon Bleu-staffed restaurant.

Extras

Much (although by no means everything) is included with Radisson Seven Seas ships, from tips and port taxes to all soft drinks and wine with dinner, while single supplements are low for many grades of cabin. All meals are single, open seating, which means you dine when *you* want, not at pre-selected times. None of the ships are suitable for children, and the newest trio all have disabled-adapted cabins.

For the UK office, call 023 8068 2285

RENAISSANCE CRUISES

www.renaisancecruises.com

Ships	Tonnage	Passengers/ Crew	Space Ratio	Built	Cruise Area	Rating
R1, R2, R3, R4, R5, R6, R7, R8	30,200	684/373	44.1	1999–2001	Far East, Caribbean, S America, Mediterranean, N Europe, Indian Ocean, S Pacific, Transatlantic	Deluxe

Cruise line notes

This American line has been one of the great rapid-expansion stories in the cruise world. From a fleet of small and rather pedestrian vessels, they now have eight identical ships of mid-size offering a huge range of itineraries almost world-wide. The identikit design means a polished, consistent product on each one of the eight, all offering open-seating dining in a choice of four restaurants and a good selection of lounges and bars, and decorated in English country-house style (with top British designer John McNeece responsible for the interior design from top to bottom). They also boast a glitzy casino, state-of-the-art health spa and a range of well-appointed (mainly outside) cabins, some 70 per cent of which have balconies. The on-board style is one of relaxed informality, although the décor and ambience are distinctly elegant and refined, as evidenced by the two-deck reception hall and the wonderfully appointed library. All vessels are non-smoking and the majority of itineraries are sold as cruise-tours, with a pre or post-cruise hotel stay to allow for a more in-depth port exploration at the beginning or end of your voyage (of particular note with their South Pacific programme out of Tahiti). In fact, the (highly) unimaginative ship names are about the only dull feature of this line, which offers a more up-market experience but without the price tag.

Ship notes

With all eight vessels being from the exact same mould (with the one minor difference that R1–R5 have a few extra cabins), they manage to deliver an awful lot in the way of facilities and service. There is a 358-seat cabaret lounge, a sports bar, indoor/outdoor buffet, card room, pizzeria, gymnasium, hair and beauty salon and two shops, while the cabins, as mentioned, have a sumptuous touch in their soft furnishings and use of dark wood. The pool deck can be cramped if the majority are looking to soak up the sun, but the levels of service and food are at the very top of the Deluxe class.

Extras

The great range of itinerary duration, from seven to 30 days (and many combinations in between) offers yet more choice with this go-ahead line and, while the entertainment is nothing startling, their on-board lecture programme is guaranteed to provide good insight into every cruise. Children are not allowed at all, hence those looking for an adults-only environment need look no further. Their pricing is extremely keen, although port taxes, tips and all drinks are extra.

Renaissance are sold largely in the UK by the Cruise Collection on 0121 445 1010.

ROYAL CARIBBEAN INTERNATIONAL
www.royalcaribbean.com

Ships	Tonnage	Passengers/ Crew	Space Ratio	Built/ Refurbished	Cruise Area	Rating
Sovereign of the Seas	73,192	2,518/814	29	1988	Bahamas	Premier
Nordic Empress	45,000	2,000/625	22.5	1990	Bermuda, Caribbean	Premier
Monarch of the Seas	73,941	2,772/822	26.6	1991	Caribbean	Premier
Majesty of the Seas	73,941	2,772/822	26.6	1992	Caribbean	Premier
Legend of the Seas	69,130	2,076/720	33.2	1995	Mediterranean, N Europe, Indian Ocean, Far East, Australasia	Premier
Splendour of the Seas	69,130	2,076/720	33.2	1995	Caribbean, Mediterranean, Transatlantic	Premier
Grandeur of the Seas	74,140	2,446/760	30.3	1996	Caribbean, Mediterranean, E Coast USA, Transatlantic	Premier
Rhapsody of the Seas	78,491	2,400/765	32.7	1997	Alaska, Hawaii, Mexican Riviera	Premier
Enchantment of the Seas	74,140	2,446/760	30.3	1997	Caribbean	Premier
Vision of the Seas	78,491	2,400/765	32.7	1998	Panama Canal, Alaska, Hawaii	Premier
Voyager of the Seas	142,000	3,100/1,181	45.8	1999	Caribbean	Premier
Explorer of the Seas	142,000	3,100/1,181	45.8	2000	Caribbean	Premier
Radiance of the Seas	88,000	2,496/864	35.2	2001	Caribbean, Alaska, Panama Canal	Premier
Adventure of the Seas	142,000	3,100/1,181	45.8	2001	Caribbean	Premier

Cruise line notes

The second of the giant American cruise companies, RCI have grown steadily with some of the most impressive hardware and deliver a consistent level of service to suit both first-timers and repeat cruisers with a touch more sophistication than Carnival, their main rivals, while they are also score highly for real innovation from their latest quartet, led by the ground-breaking *Voyager of the Seas*. The passenger profile tends to vary according to the length of cruise, with the three, four and five-day cruises attracting a younger, party-minded crowd, the seven-dayers drawn from right across the board, but especially families, and the longer voyages (12-day sailings to northern Europe, the Mediterranean, Panama Canal, Alaska and down to Australia) likely to be more in the 45–60 age range. The Caribbean is their core area, but they have now branched out further afield and are particularly prominent in Europe as well as developing new itineraries to the Far East and Hawaii. They now attract around 15 per cent of British passengers aboard many of their sailings, while *Splendour of the Seas* is marketed solely to Europe in the summer. They don't claim to offer a luxurious product, but the most recent hardware certainly puts them well into the upper end of the Premier range, beyond many of their obvious competitors. Being American, the style is necessarily glitzy (although the most recent ships also demonstrate a high-quality level of finish and décor), lively and straightforward, lacking a lot of cruising's formality (although still retaining several formal nights per cruise) but the cuisine tends towards the bland, with the exception of the speciality restaurants aboard the newest quartet, for which you need to book.

All RCI vessels cater for at least 1,000 passengers, with 3,000-plus on the dramatic 142,000-tonners, and that can make for high-density cruising, although the newest series of ships are more spacious and thoughtfully designed to improve passenger flow. Kids are well catered for with their own menus and activity programmes in four age groups and RCI are keen on sports of all kinds, from deck games, to their health facilities, shore-side golf opportunities and water sports.

Cabins (except the largest suites) are of the identikit variety, with little real difference between the categories except for which deck they are on. They are always comfortable, but tend to lack cupboard and drawer space and the fixtures and fittings are rather characterless. The most recent build (from *Legend* onwards) incorporate more balconied cabins and offer rather more all-round space, although the cabins still lack hairdryers. Each RCI ship features a Viking Crown lounge, usually set into the ship's funnel or otherwise at the top of the ship, which provides a trademark visual look to the line as well as an excellent observation lounge and night-club. Finally, entertainment: RCI set great store by the quality and quantity of their shows, and there is plenty of zest, style and razzmatazz served up every night, while they also manage to find some extremely sharp comedians.

Ship notes

Prior to the advent of *Voyager of the Seas*, (almost eight times bigger than their first ship, *Song of Norway*, in 1970) Royal Caribbean's fleet has been dominated by the two new-build series, the *Sovereign*, *Majesty* and *Monarch* (1988–92) and *Legend*, *Splendour*, *Grandeur*, *Rhapsody*,

Enchantment and *Vision* (1995–98), which introduced a new level of sophistication into the mass market. A greater variety of public rooms is the key to the latter six, while all nine benefit from the impressive central multi-storey atrium lobbies, complete with glass-sided lifts, that prove a handy reference point to negotiating the many decks. The 18-hole mini-golf courses on *Legend* and *Splendour* are fun for the kids, although at $5 a time they are not cheap, and they are perhaps a bit too gimmicky, but the splendid Solarium pool and deck area, with optional sliding glass roof, is certainly a winner. The amount of glass used on these ships, and consequently the amount of natural light that streams in, provides another pleasant feature. It has real practical application in places like Alaska where it can be chilly yet you still want a good outside view, and it is more likely to appeal to European tastes. Their sheer size dictates a slight lack of ship character, however.

The Sovereign-class ships all possess, for my money, the most pleasant indoor/outdoor buffet dining options of all the super-liners, the Windjammer Café, which is a beautifully airy, split-level affair complete with plants and waterfalls. It was this sort of innovation, plus the big atrium lobbies, which convinced the mass market of the wisdom of such large-scale operations, and RCI carry it off probably better than anyone. *Nordic Empress* is the company's 'odd one out', a ship purpose-built for the short-haul market to the Bahamas but still with a great degree of sophistication, from her light, airy design to her proper promenade deck and excellent pool deck, which is a focal point day and night. Cabins are still on the small side, but the public rooms have excellent eye appeal and common-sense passenger flow attributes.

The debut in 1999 of the world's largest cruise ship, *Voyager of the Seas,* and her subsequent two sisters *Explorer* and *Adventure* (with another to come in 2003), took Royal Caribbean to a new level, with the most mind-boggling array of facilities seen to date. Her sheer size (twice as big, in tonnage terms, as *QE2* or *Oriana*) is only a start, as this is a vessel that almost doesn't need to cruise anywhere. Witness the basics – three main dining rooms, five alternatives (including a 24-hour 1950s diner, an Italian restaurant and a promenade café), a 1,347-seat, five-deck theatre based on Milan's La Scala, three more lounges (including the space-age, two-level Vault nightclub), another 15 bars (including sports, champagne, piano, aquarium and cigar bars), the largest casino at sea, three pools (one with retractable glass roof), an Internet centre and a wedding chapel. And that's before you get to the real innovations: the world's first 'horizontal atrium', a four-deck, 200-yard Royal Promenade of shops and entertainment; a 900-seat arena/broadcast centre that converts into an ice rink; a sports deck featuring mini-golf, driving range and golf simulators, rock-climbing and roller-blading, as well as basketball, volleyball and paddle-tennis; and inside cabins with a view – over the Promenade. It goes without saying there are extensive health and beauty facilities, a massive area devoted to kids, including an astronaut-based Space Theatre, teens' club, video arcade, computers and virtual-reality simulators and Adventure Beach – pools, water slide and other water-play features – and a smart library. Then there are the 1,557 cabins, including 757 with balconies, 138 with a Promenade view, 26 for disabled passengers and eight family cabins accommodating six. All come with mini-bar, hair-dryer and interactive TV, plus bigger beds, larger bathrooms and more wardrobe space than any previous RCI ship. However, with five categories of suite and 22 varieties in all, choosing your cabin is not as simple as it could be. The only other minor niggle is, because of their size, the three ships are confined to the seven-day, bread-and-butter Caribbean runs to the well-worked ports (although *Adventure,* based in San Juan, Puerto Rico, does at least travel south to Aruba and Curacao). But, as I said, with ships so crammed with facilities, who needs ports anyway? Their big-show entertainment is quite stunning, the sports opportunities are enough to satisfy even the most activity-minded passenger, and the extra element and size-impressive attributes of the Royal Promenade (which is also used for a unique parade-show twice a cruise) sets this trio so far apart from their other maritime brethren you are tempted to say: It's a ship, Jim, but not as we know it!

Never ones to stand still, RCI introduced another new class of ship in 2001 with *Radiance of the Seas,* which combine some of the best features of both the Vision and Voyager series in an all-new package. The mixture of grand spaces and more intimate corners is extremely eye-pleasing, and the addition of more alternative dining (including Chops Grill, an up-scale steakhouse), a book-and-coffee shop, a Concierge club, 3-D cinema and the first billiard club at sea (with unique, self-levelling pool tables) make for an awesome package of facilities. Cabins are all equipped with interactive TV, computer points and fridge mini-bars, while more than 50 per cent have balconies and 319 are designed for families.

Extras

The opportunity to do back-to-back seven-day cruises in the eastern and western Caribbean is another popular British choice while RCI have their own private islands, off the coast of Haiti and at CocoCay in the Bahamas, to allow for their popular beach parties. For singles, they offer a Single Guarantee cabin assignment at reasonable rates and a Share Programme, and all the newest ships offer cabins for the disabled. Port taxes are also included, while RCI offer a tempting range of cruise-and-stay options, plus wedding and anniversary packages. Tips are now an 'optional' extra at £6.45 per person per day (a touch expensive compared with British lines) but you need to specify if you *don't* want this added.

For a brochure, call 01932 834231.

Stop press: for more Royal Caribbean news, see page 248, Hold the Front Page.

ROYAL OLYMPIC CRUISES
www.royalolympiccruises.com

Ships	Tonnage	Passengers/ Crew	Space Ratio	Built/ Refurbished	Cruise Area	Rating
Stella Solaris	17,832	620/320	28.7	1953/73	Mediterranean, Panama Canal, Amazon, Transatlantic	Standard
Apollon	28,500	914/365	31.1	1955/98	Eastern Med	Standard
Odysseus	12,000	448/200	26.7	1962/99	Eastern Med	Standard
Triton	14,155	676/300	20.9	1971/92	Mediterranean	Standard
World Renaissance	12,000	474/230	25.3	1966/96	Eastern Med	Standard
Olympic Countess	18,000	814/350	21.6	1976/96	Eastern Med, S America, Panama Canal	Standard
Olympic Voyager	25,000	840/360	29.7	2000	Eastern Med, Caribbean, S America, Transatlantic	Premier
Olympic Explorer	25,000	840/360	29.7	2001	Mediterranean, Caribbean, S America, Transatlantic	Premier

Cruise line notes

The merger of the two biggest Greek cruise lines – Epirotiki and Sun Line – in late 1995 gave the Mediterranean another serious operator in the mass-market end of the business. And, while their foothold in Britain is not big, they make their product an attractive alternative. Basically, Royal Olympic has taken the personal, friendly service of Sun Lines and mixed it with Epirotiki's fun style to provide a fascinating blend of lively Greek ambience and traditional elegance. The new combination stresses a comprehensive range of itineraries in the eastern Mediterranean offering quite port-intensive tours and trying to get a little off the beaten track, thanks to their smaller ship size, visiting some of the smaller Greek Islands and places like Dubrovnik, Egypt and Israel. Recent additions are a Caribbean and South America programmes, taking in the Amazon and Orinoco Rivers. The on-board style continues to be unfailingly Greek, and so it should appeal not only to the more adventurous cruisers but also to the two million-plus Brits who holiday in Greece every year. The accent is not on a full range of daytime activities so much as on using the ships to explore the ports of call and sailing at night (a rather American concept), when the company can really turn on the Greek charm and produce a taverna-like atmosphere, complete with Greek dancing. Royal Olympic promise 'professional service, but in a fun way', with continental cuisine and more spontaneous entertainment. Of course, there are still the more traditional elements of cruise entertainers, gift shops, hairdressers and photographers, but outside those it is an entirely Greek experience. The ships are all individuals, too, and attract a more particular type of cruiser according to the area and time of year. The passenger base sees 35–40 per cent from the US, with a good European mix otherwise. The age profile tends to be in the 45–50-plus range, but July and August see all the ships welcome a younger, more boisterous holiday crowd of all nationalities – but the first language will always be English.

Ship notes

ROC have significantly changed their profile with the arrival of their first two all-new ships, the sleek, 25,000-ton pair *Olympic Voyager* and *Explorer,* which offer a clever blend of modern facilities with some of the eastern Med's most ancient ports thanks to their speed (almost 30 knots). A full and quite striking array of public rooms is complemented by well-appointed cabins that include mini-bar, hairdryer, TV and safe, while the 12 balconied sky suites come with butler service. The neat, compact design makes for a chic, intimate style, with plenty to admire on port days, too. The two seven-day itineraries are a real draw, too, with visits to three continents on *Voyager* and grand Aegean and Adriatic cruise on *Explorer,* round-trip from either Venice or Piraeus.

TRAVEL TIP

ROC is not the company for shy, retiring wallflowers. You will be expected to join in the party and there is no escaping the Greek dancing lessons!

Stella Solaris is a mature, classic liner which has aged well and continues to be elegantly fitted out to higher levels than most Standard class ships. Her passenger profile alters according to the season, with her winters spent sailing the Caribbean and Amazon on longer routes and therefore drawing an older crowd, while the summers get younger and livelier on seven-day Greek Island cruises. Despite the relatively high density when full, *Solaris* is quite a spacious vessel, both in terms of her deck capability (including a proper prom deck) and the amount of cabin space. *World Renaissance* has recently returned to the fleet and her friendly, crowded style is ideally suited to the four and five-day cruises out of Piraeus which can visit as many as six ports, hence they are not for the faint-hearted. *Odysseus* joins her on the short-cruise run, based in Crete, offering more traditional cruise ambience, bags of Greek style (notably in the Taverna, which really hums at night) and a surprisingly good range of public rooms, all tastefully decorated. Cabins are again quite generous and the sun-tan brigade are well catered for on deck. ROC has also acquired the former Cunard Caribbean favourite, now renamed *Olympic Countess,* for more Piraeus-based short voyaging, heading for a grand South America circumnavigation in winter. *Countess* remains a well-balanced, well-provisioned ship for this sort of routine and retains some pleasant public rooms, even if standard cabins are a little functional. The newer *Triton* is another quite high-density, bustling cruise ship with the benefits of a good promenade deck, lovely Greek artwork, a rather chic forward observation lounge/nightclub and more generous deck space. Cabins tend towards the small, but are all fitted out in warm, inviting fashion. She offers some imaginative seven, 10 and 11-day cruises out of Rome or Venice. The classic old-timer *Apollon,* formerly the *Empress of Canada* in her original life and the hard-working *Mardi Gras* of Carnival in the 1970s and 80s, has a good range of well-maintained facilities and generous open deck space, while her cabins range from pretty tiny to quite generous. She completes the quartet working the four and five-day routine out of Piraeus.

Extras

Their range of land-stay combinations are ideal in this part of the world, while they also offer some substantial savings for families (set rates for kids), advance bookers and longer voyages. Annoyingly, port taxes are still extra and only *Voyager* and *Explorer* are really suitable for disabled passengers. They also operate flights at no extra charge from 11 regional UK airports.

For a brochure or more information, freephone 0800 358 3535.

SAGA CRUISES
www.saga.co.uk

Ship	Tonnage	Passengers/ Crew	Space Ratio	Built/ Refurbished	Cruise Area	Rating
Saga Rose	24,474	620/350	39.4	1965/97	Mediterranean, N Europe, Canaries, Caribbean, World Cruise	Premier

Cruise line notes

Over-50s tour operator Saga opted to join the cruise world full-time in 1997 as they bought Cunard's redundant *Sagafjord* and turned her into *Saga Rose.* While still chartering with other lines, Saga now offer their own complete package, with some thoughtful European and Caribbean itineraries which build to a grand world cruise that undercuts most of the competition. Saga aim purposely at the formal element and traditional style as befits their passenger profile, and so, while modern comforts are provided (including a well-appointed gym), the accent is on pursuits for the mature passenger. Her reputation for fine cuisine under Cunard remains unchanged. Their level of service and attention to detail is excellent, and they have quickly built up a keen following for the *Rose.*

Ship notes

Sagafjord, one of the world's few classic liners, had been allowed to run to seed a little under her later days with Cunard, hence Saga sent her in for a much-needed £15-million refit and facelift in November 1997. The essence of her magnificent public rooms ensures she maintains Cunard's high-quality traditions, even if her bewildering variety of 19 (admittedly all quite spacious) cabin styles could do with being simplified. The main dining room is still one of the most timelessly gracious restaurants afloat and her wide, open deck spaces hark back to bygone days of old-fashioned elegance. Single, open-seat dining is another classic feature.

Extras

Saga offer a range of single cabins and the chance of an arranged share in a twin berth. There is also an exclusive cocktail party for singles. Tipping is another welcome inclusion, as are port taxes and travel insurance, and there is a free private car service for passengers within 75 miles of home port Dover. Four cabins were adapted for disabled passengers in the refit. The 100-day world cruise can be taken in 11 sectors, from 16 to 58 days, and there are extended tour options at some ports. Saga have also added themed cruises, with Food and Wine, Music and Art, Natural History and Gardens all featuring, while two itineraries are designated for newcomers with special Welcome Aboard features.

For brochures, call 0800 505030.

SEABOURN
www.seabourn.com

Ships	Tonnage	Passengers/Crew	Space Ratio	Built/Refurbished	Cruise Area	Rating
Seabourn Pride	9,975	204/145	48.8	1988	Caribbean, S America, N Europe, E Coast USA	Ultra-deluxe
Seabourn Spirit	9,975	204/145	48.8	1989	Far East, Indian Ocean, Mediterranean	Ultra-deluxe
Seabourn Legend	9,975	204/145	48.8	1992/95	Caribbean, Panama Canal, N Europe, Mediterranean	Ultra-deluxe
Seabourn Goddess I	4,250	116/90	36.7	1984/99	Caribbean, Mediterranean	Deluxe
Seabourn Goddess II	4,250	116/90	36.7	1985/99	Caribbean, Mediterranean	Deluxe

Cruise line notes

The small-ship fleet of this specialist has undergone several revamps since they merged with Cunard (under the Carnival Corporation banner) in 1999. Their core business (with the *Seabourn Sun* being transferred to duties with Holland America) is now a split between their three original immaculate 10,000-tonners, with the true Ultra-Deluxe touch, and the two smaller former Cunard vessels, which now offer a more laid-back, informal and unstructured approach aimed at more youthful couples looking for the Deluxe resort at sea. The itineraries are the other distinguishing feature of this utterly luxury-clad experience, circling the globe in a quest for sunshine, exotic ports of call, rich cultural experiences and beautiful scenery. The size of the ships allows them to explore areas where their larger brethren rarely venture, yet they are not small enough to feel cramped. The original trio have a more formal, country-club style and a mainly American passenger profile, while the *Goddess* duo maintain a slightly more European appeal.

Ship notes

The first three are identical sisters, yet the *Legend* was only a recent acquisition and is already in her third incarnation, having started out as the *Royal Viking Queen* and then moved to Royal Cruise Line's colours as *Queen Odyssey* before RCL folded and Seabourn moved in. The sleek trio all boast quality wherever you look, from the lower deck main restaurant, with its open-dining arrangement and Monte Carlo chic, to the top deck observation lounge, with its floor-to-ceiling windows and passenger radar screen linked to the bridge. The Veranda Café now offers an evening dining arrangement without the formality of the main restaurant. Seabourn reverted in 2001 to a policy of including all your on-board drinks, with a magnificent choice of wines in particular, while all cabins have a complimentary bar stocked with wine and spirits. The cabins feature queen-sized beds, TV and VCR, walk-in cupboards, fridge, hairdryer, sitting area and the finest in soft furnishings. Dinner can also be served in your suite. Other facilities include a marina platform that fits round the stern of the ships, offering the chance to swim in your own sea pool, go water-skiing, windsurfing or paddle-boating, or use one of the two speed-boats to go off scuba-diving or snorkelling.

TRAVEL TIP

Choosing a Cruise researcher Carolyn Voce notes the Regal Suites as best non-balcony value for money on *Pride, Legend* and *Spirit,* while she rates the trio of ships extremely highly for couples with something to celebrate, i.e. honeymoons or anniversaries.

The *Goddess* vessels deliberately go for an understated, private yacht-style approach as they strive for a younger, more informal feel and clientele. They lack some of the features of the other trio, like balconies, an observation lounge and a full alternative dining set-up but still boast the stern watersports platform and an almost unmatched crew-passenger ratio. Entertainment is low-key, with a small casino and easy-listening music in the Piano Bar, while the cuisine maintains the company's high traditions for memorable fine dining.

Extras

If all passengers can agree on one thing, it is Seabourn is the epitome of refined, flawless, unobtrusive service. The hotel manager who knows all his guests by name is just one example of the friendly, but never too familiar, approach. On top of that, NO tipping is allowed. As a result, Seabourn has a high percentage of repeat passengers. Single passengers are offered one of the lowest supplements of any cruise line, although this is still primarily the preserve of couples. There is no discounting as such (perish the thought), but there are early-booking and repeat-passenger savings to be made. Even the Norwegian officers add to the welcoming, attentive ambience that Seabourn seems to generate so effortlessly, and the experience adds up to one of the most relaxing at sea. For golfers, they offer an array of packages designed to take in some top-rated courses, with organised competitions, golf clinics and the services of a full-time professional.

For a brochure, call 0845 6011720.

SILVERSEA CRUISES
www.silversea.com

Ships	Tonnage	Passengers/ Crew	Space Ratio	Built/ Refurbished	Cruise Area	Rating
Silver Cloud	16,800	296/209	56.7	1994	Worldwide	Ultra-Deluxe
Silver Wind	16,800	296/209	56.7	1995	Worldwide	Ultra-Deluxe
Silver Shadow	25,000	388/295	64.4	2000	Worldwide	Ultra-Deluxe
Silver Whisper	25,000	388/295	64.4	2001	Worldwide	Ultra-Deluxe

Cruise line notes

If you cross the up-scale facilities of Crystal's operation with the small-scale quality of Seabourn's service, you arrive at Silversea, the fourth major player in the Ultra-Deluxe, along with Radisson's newest ships. Silversea are also the newest in the business, having started only in 1994, but they have quickly established a solid reputation for a lavish, all-inclusive experience that offers a much higher percentage of balconied cabins than Seabourn, their main competitor. They are already the most popular Ultra-Deluxe line with the British market, and that paved the way for their two newest ships, of the same overall design specifications, only bigger – 25,000 tons. Their all-inclusive package, really is just that as it includes *all* your drinks (with a choice of 50 wines at dinner) , port taxes, tips and even some shore excursions. There is also a more European feel to Silversea, hence a slight increase in formality. There is more emphasis on European destinations in their itineraries, from Istanbul to London and all the up-market ports in between, but they also seek out the exotic ports of the Far East, the South Pacific, the Arctic Circle, Sri Lanka and Africa, as well as a range of South American voyages, including the Falklands and magnificent Chilean fjords. A more recent introduction was a genuine 106-day world cruise on *Silver Wind*. Increasingly, Silversea passengers are being converted from the more exclusive land-based resorts and so they include a relatively high percentage of newcomers to cruising (although there is also a high repeat factor), but the age profile is solidly middle-aged (40-plus) and primarily couples. Once again, there is little American razzmatazz about the entertainment or décor on the original two ships, although the multi-tiered showlounge offers a touch of big-production style and is capable of putting on some quite elaborate shows and cabaret acts. Elsewhere, things are fairly restrained, with just a classical musician or two, in-cabin films and videos, a small casino, fitness classes and water sports, plus an excellent lecture programme, to while away the time. The two larger vessels have added an element of on-board glamour, with a more dramatic showlounge, additional bars and a greatly enhanced spa, run by the Far East specialists Mandara Spa.

Ship notes

Unusually for the two smaller ships, there is a wrap-around prom deck that allows for walking and jogging and a good-sized pool deck catering for a large number of sun-worshippers (there is a well-planned spread of sea days and port days on the longer itineraries, and the ship facilities will be well used). The fitness centres are state-of-the-art and the health spa offers a full range of treatments, while the Terrace Café has to be one of the most elegant buffet-style dining options at sea and the main restaurant is quite wonderfully opulent, full of warm woods, rich drapes and subtle lighting, offset by the finest china table settings. The Terrace Café is also popular for its occasional themed dinners in either Thai or Italian style. The all-suite cabins are typically spacious and lack nothing in the way of amenities, from the fully-stocked cocktail cabinets to the marbled bathrooms. *Silver Shadow* heralded an even greater wealth of features and detail, with balconies on more than 85 per cent of the cabins, an alternative pool-side dining venue, a larger spa and gym facility, a cigar lounge and a computer centre, but the same attention to service and cuisine, plus still single-seating dining. The all-suite accommodations are simply wonderful, with granite-tiled bathrooms (all with a bath and separate shower) that hint at the grandeurs of Ancient Rome, magnificent soft furnishings and seemingly acres of space (from 287sq ft up to 1,435). There is also a growing emphasis on high-quality partnerships, with the likes of Moët & Chandon, Bulgari, Davidoff and the master chef expertise of the French Relais & Chateau group heavily featured on board.

Extras

Your only extra expenditure will be for the beauty salon, boutique, casino, the occasional shore excursion and any real premium wines at dinner. Each cruise also features the Silversea Experience, a unique on-shore event for passengers that may be a beach barbecue in the Virgin Islands, wine-tasting in Bordeaux or dinner in a Victorian castle. Repeat passengers can enjoy savings on future cruises and other benefits through the Venetian Society. Two increasingly popular themed cruises are their National Geographic adventures and a superb range of golfing opportunities, called Silver Links, which guarantee access to some of the world's finest courses. Silversea even go as far as providing self-service launderettes. Children are not encouraged or well catered for, but there are wheelchair-adapted cabins on all ships. Their additional land-stay packages are designed to complement each cruise perfectly, and there are more six- and seven-day cruises to tempt newcomers.

For brochures, call 0870 333 7030.

STAR CLIPPERS
www.starclippers.com

Ships	Tonnage	Passengers/ Crew	Space Ratio	Built/ Refurbished	Cruise Area	Rating
Star Flyer	3,025	170/72	17.7	1991	Aegean, Far East	Premier
Star Clipper	3,025	170/72	17.7	1992	Caribbean, Mediterranean Transatlantic	Premier
Royal Clipper	5,000	228/100	21.9	2000	Mediterranean, Caribbean, Transatlantic	Deluxe

Cruise line notes

Star Clippers are the most relaxed, informal and authentic of the classic sailing cruise vessels. They attract an enthusiastic mix of passengers from both America and Europe, average age around 45, who may well not have cruised before but are active travellers or just love the idea of real, old-fashioned sailing. On the first two ships, the cruise experience is stripped to the bare minimum; there are no casinos, beauty parlours or showlounges, and there is only one small shop. The nearest you get to all-out entertainment is a small piano bar, so it is up to the folks on board to use the unstructured pattern to its best advantage. Swimming and windsurfing are popular, and there are lectures on navigation and sailing as well as organised aerobics and snorkelling classes. The cuisine – in single, open-seating – is hearty rather than haute cuisine (although Royal adds some extra class here), but that is not why the majority are aboard. It is to enjoy the experience of real sailing, sitting on the bowsprit safety net and watching the sea whoosh by at close hand under full sail, and delighting in the friendliness of all aboard, from the Captain down to the waiters. New vessel *Royal Clipper* adds a touch of genuine period elegance to the fleet, the largest sailing ship since the beginning of the twentieth century and one that is well worthy of a Deluxe rating. Star Clippers are marketed in Britain through the Fred Olsen line and you should find their brochure next to the *Black Prince* and *Black Watch* in most travel agents.

Ship notes

These handsome vessels do offer a sound basic level of cruise ship comfort, with clean, well-equipped (if a little cramped, in the case of the two originals) modern cabins, a couple of plunge pools and a splendid dining room. The emphasis is more on helping to raise the sails than helping to raise your on-board credit, although the varied water-sports programme is extra. The decor is classic maritime Edwardian – notably in the smart library/writing room – but the overall style is pretty casual – no jacket and tie needed here. The five-masted *Royal Clipper* goes for a distinctly opulent touch with three small pools, a three-deck atrium and a beautiful restaurant that rivals anything at sea. She boasts a marine platform right aft, which allows instant access to an array of watersports, while each of her five masts sports a unique 'lookout station' with built-in comfy settees where you can lounge, 60 feet up, with a drink! There is also a compact gym and spa, a library, an observation lounge and a shopping gallery. Add in the unique underwater views of Captain Nemo's lounge and the line's first true suites, with balconies, and *Star Clipper* represents one of the most original and rewarding experiences in the cruise world.

TRAVEL TIP

Because you are largely at the mercy of the winds, you cannot set the ship's itinerary in stone and must be prepared for last-minute alterations.

Extras

Standing by as the Captain gets the ship under sail is a wonderful experience (and there is an open bridge policy at all times), while the water sports will keep even the most energetic at full stretch. Deluxe cabins feature a whirlpool bath. However, this is definitely not the cruise for the physically disabled as there are no wheelchair provisions at all. The ships are all officially recognised scuba-dive centres and have professional courses visiting some magnificent dive areas. In addition to their main itineraries, each ship makes two long positioning cruises a year, the *Royal* and *Star Clipper* between the Med and Caribbean and the Flyer between Athens and the Far East. There are also some attractive cruise-and-stay options. There is a guaranteed single rate, but all port taxes are extra.

For a brochure or more information, call Fred Olsen on 01473 292229.

STAR CRUISES
www.starcruises.com

Ships	Tonnage	Passengers/ Crew	Space Ratio	Built/ Refurbished	Cruise Area	Rating
SuperStar Gemini	19,046	820/470	23.2	1992/95	South-east Asia	Premier
SuperStar Leo	74,500	1,974/ 1,000	37.2	1998	South-east Asia	Premier
SuperStar Virgo	74,500	1,974/ 1,100	37.2	1999	South-east Asia	Premier

Cruise line notes

This Malaysia- and Singapore-based line has entered the cruise mainstream in recent years in a major way, both with a fresh approach and a dynamic new-build policy. They went a step further in 2000 by acquiring American line NCL and gaining a true worldwide presence for the first time, and actively enhancing many areas of NCL's operations. A fleet restructuring in 2001 saw them sell off some of their older and smaller tonnage to concentrate on a series of new ships for both Star and NCL, while *SuperStar Aries,* the former Ultra-Deluxe *Europa* of German line Hapag-Lloyd, is destined to join the Orient Lines fleet in 2002. Star also has several ships purely for the local Asian market, but their newest are all geared to providing a modern, inspiring yet relaxing experience for European, American and Australian customers as well as their domestic passengers. They started marketing in Europe with the *Gemini,* formerly the *Crown Jewel* of Cunard's American-Caribbean operation of the early 90s, and quickly established a reputation as inventive thinkers who offered an alternative to the US mass market with an informal but stylish blend of up-to-date facilities and Oriental service standards. DJs are a rarity here, mealtimes are plentiful and less structured, and cruises vary from three to eight days over an increasing range of exotic Far East territory, from their core areas of Singapore, Malaysia and Thailand to Vietnam, China and Hong Kong. The Oriental influence shows through with plentiful karaoke opportunities and the private gambling clubs on all the ships (big business in this area, but not intruding on general ship activities) as well as large, glitzy casinos, but Star also offer superb and extensive children's programmes and facilities, a fine mixture of Oriental and international cuisines and a wonderfully casual ambience. Bar prices are also modest at around £1.50 for a beer and £6.50 for a reasonable bottle of wine. Be aware, however, this region of the Far East suffers from heavy seasonal weather – high humidity and rainfall and the occasional tropical storm or typhoon – between May and October.

Ship notes

The *Crown Jewel* was a fine product for the seven-day cruise market and she is well suited to short hauls around Malaysia and Thailand. The cabins could be more spacious, but they are all well furnished and quite airy and there is a generous selection of public rooms and a splendid five-storey central atrium in the best new-ship tradition. There is a full range of ship facilities, from the beauty salon (operated by the British Steiner concession) and fitness centre, to the library, casino (members only), shops, cinema, disco and smart Galaxy of the Stars showlounge. The open deck space is good for sun-worshippers (although the pool deck can get crowded) and there is also a jogging track around a proper promenade deck. New ships *Leo* and *Virgo* bring a glitzy, high-tech touch to the fleet, with the full range of modern facilities, spacious cabins, many with balconies, and an overall design ethic that takes the line near the top of the Premier category. Service standards and captivating Asian style are already an outstanding Star feature, and they hit new heights on the duo, especially with a mouth-watering array of dining opportunities – no less than six restaurants plus a round-the-clock buffet. Children's facilities are startling, with their own secure pool deck complete with slides and fountains, teens' disco, cinema and video arcade, plus Charlie's Child Care Centre, a playroom and nursery taking one to 12-year olds round the clock (although for a charge of about £2 per child per hour from 9am to midnight and £3.50 after midnight) with a full range of imaginative activities. Other novel touches include the aquaswim pool where you can swim against a current, a bridge viewing gallery, a proper pub bar and a pretty covered biergarten area overlooking the beautiful main pool deck. *Virgo* concentrates on three, four and six-night voyages from Singapore to the high spots of Malaysia and Thailand while *Leo* offers two, three and five-night cruises out of Hong Kong to Vietnam and China.

Extras

Their Asian expertise provides a good introduction to the area in a safe environment and their prices, even on short-haul cruises, represent excellent value for money. Little extras like fresh orchids and fruit in the cabins, bathrobes and slippers provided as standard, plenty of thick towels regularly changed and the helpful attitude of all the crew are additional features. There is also a refreshing 'no tipping' policy aboard all ships and port taxes are included, too. Golf packages to play three countries in five days are worth noting for sport devotees.

Star Cruises are marketed in Britain by 16 different tour operators, including Thomson and British Airways Holidays.

SWAN HELLENIC
www.swanhellenic.com

Ship	Tonnage	Passengers/ Crew	Space Ratio	Built/ Refurbished	Cruise Area	Rating
Minerva	12,500	392/157	31.8	1996	Mediterranean, N Europe, Indian Ocean, Far East	Premier, *Brit's Guide* **Favourite**

Cruise line notes

After operating on a small scale successfully for 21 years by chartering Epirotiki's little ship *Orpheus*, Swan Hellenic, the cultural cruise arm of P&O, took the plunge in 1996 with a bigger, purpose-built vessel (chartered from the Monaco-based Vlasov Group, who also operate Silversea) and have already expanded their horizons as far afield as the Indian Ocean and Far East in the winter. Their basic philosophy is 'travel broadens the mind', hence there is a strong educational content to all Swan Hellenic cruises, and they attract a well-travelled, more mature passenger who is there primarily for the itinerary rather than the style of travel. *Minerva* offers a much greater style than previously, however, incorporating as she does some up-to-the-minute features and outstanding design by British architects RPW, who are more famous for their work at the Gleneagles Hotel, Wentworth Golf Club and Claridge's in London. The line's strong suit continues to be the lecture programmes, however, with a 90-seat auditorium augmenting the main lounge for this purpose. Passengers get an insight into the art, history and archaeology of each destination from prominent guest speakers, and they now offer a greater mixture of cruise lengths, from seven to 21 days.

Ship notes

Former managing director Rupert Morley explained their strategy behind the new vessel thus: 'We set out to produce a ship that does justice to the good taste of our passengers – cultivated and traditional. Cabins are elegant and simple, while public room finishes are predominantly oak with bronze fittings rather than chrome or mirrors. The design of the ship reflects the great British traditions of travel and learning, while a strong marine element will constantly remind passengers they are at sea.' And how! *Minerva* is a little stunner in the best cruise traditions, and her cabins are all quite spacious and simply furnished, with the top-of-the-range suites offering a new level of comfort and sophistication for this line (although the bathrooms could be better). The public rooms are truly gorgeous, with good, spacious sunbathing areas, plus a health and fitness centre, beauty shop, library and self-service launderette. The dining room maintains Swan Hellenic's open-seating policy in fine style and the cuisine is a cut above many of the competitors in the Premier range.

Extras

The line maintains its 'No tipping' stance and, along with the extended itineraries, there are a series of attractive add-ons in places such as Dubai, Colombo, Singapore and Hong Kong. Many shore excursions and all port taxes and entrance fees are included, while bar prices are nearer British pub prices than the rather inflated ones aboard American ships. There are also 'cruise-and-tour' options to places like Morocco, China, Cambodia, Jordan and Sri Lanka, and 'cruise-and-beach' possibilities in the Far East. There is also a series of shorter eight and nine-day cruises designed to appeal to newcomers. Children are not really catered for, but there are four wheelchair-accessible cabins. The overall package is a bit pricey compared to many other lines in this range, but you do get a lot for your money, and no one does the educational content quite as well.

For brochures, call 020 7800 2200.

THOMSON CRUISES
www.thomson-holidays.com

Ships	Tonnage	Passengers/ Crew	Space Ratio	Built/ Refurbished	Cruise Area	Rating
Emerald	26,431	1,198/412	21.5	1958/92	Mediterranean,	Standard
Topaz	31,500	1,050/550	30	1956/98	Mediterranean, Canaries	Standard

Cruise line notes

The rapid growth of the UK cruise market through 1994 and 1995 and the startling initial success of Airtours in producing a package holiday cruise product brought the country's biggest tour operator hot-foot into the business. After several fleet variations, they have now settled on a two-ship offering, both on long-term charter but with a fully Thomson branded on-board style. Their target, therefore, is people who have enjoyed a Thomson holiday in the past and might fancy a change to what is, in theory, only an extension of the same company's product, plus previous cruisers who are looking for a good deal on their next trip. Thomson view the biggest block on more people going cruising as the perception of it as being expensive, and so they have made value for money their principal concern. They are out to attract primarily couples of 40-plus, as well as a certain element of the family market – children's prices lead in at just £199 for under 13s on a seven-night cruise, and there are kids' clubs for 3–7s and 8–12s (two to three hours a day, six days a week), plus children's menus and a teens' area on Topaz.

Thomson added a new string to their bow in 1998 with Topaz, making her all-inclusive of beer, soft drinks, cocktails and table wines, while also adding open-seating dining and a 24-hour food option, the first mass-market operator to do something which hitherto had been the preserve of the Ultra-Deluxe lines. They might have chosen a slightly better ship for the venture as *Topaz* (formerly the *Olympic* of Royal Olympic, *FiestaMarina* and *Carnivale* of Carnival and the *Empress of Britain* before that) is getting on a bit, but the all-inclusive touch is a bold one and makes Thomson's value for money here impressive. The seven- and 14-night itineraries (and consequently the shore excursions) are all well tried and trusted Mediterranean and Canary Island fare, so they have bags of Brit appeal. They use Majorca and Cyprus as their Mediterranean bases, with Corfu being added in 2002. Also new is a partnership with Festival Cruises, and notably their two newest ships *Mistral* and *European Vision*. The former features 7-day med cruises out of Naples (with cruise-and-stay options in Sorrento), while the latter features a winter Caribbean series (with a cruise-and-stay choice in the Dominican Republic).

Ship notes

Like Airtours, Thomson reduced the number of categories and initially asked their customers to book only a category rather than a specific cabin. However, they also now offer the chance to pre-book specific cabins for a £20 supplement. They also strip away some of cruising's formality with some imaginative staff, many of whom are drawn from non-cruise sources and therefore have a fresh approach. The East European dining and cabin staff are all eager to please, if occasionally difficult to communicate with, and the food is also plentiful and good quality. The ships themselves vary a fair bit, which is the one real drawback with Thomson's evenly-priced operation. The extremely well-maintained *Emerald* displays a wide range of choice and some up-to-date touches with in-cabin TV, a small gym, a dedicated nightclub and a lively all-day bar/café called Monte Carlo Court. She still retains plenty of character from her early days (as in the stained glass ceiling and musicians' balcony in the dining room), but the main Show Lounge couldn't be more modern and inviting. Cabins still vary quite a bit, despite the reduction in categories, and the standard outside variety on Concerto Deck are better value than some of the superior ones, but they are all quite spacious and include hairdryers and pleasant soft furnishings. Open deck space could be better, though, and is at a premium when the ship is full.

Topaz provides a different experience, with this veteran still offering a good range of public rooms, including two pools (one for kids, plus a jacuzzi), a fitness centre, three contrasting restaurants and three lounges, plus a casino and sports bar and disco. Due to her vintage, cabins come in a greater variety than the simplified brochure categories and most inside ones are plain and small, with even smaller 'bathrooms'. The superior outside category are definitely the best bet here, while there will be five genuine suites from December 2001. Features which stand out include 24-hour buffet dining in The Yacht Club and the amazing Le Cabaret Restaurant, a dinner-show entertainment extravaganza where even the waiters and waitresses are choreographed in step with the stage show, which takes you Around the World in 80 Minutes with great pizzazz. The main dining room, The Topaz Room, is a classic venue from this era of genuine, ocean-going liners, while there is also a good shopping arcade and a beauty salon with massage treatments. *Topaz* boasts a great amount of open deck space, which allows the sun-worshippers a bit of elbow room for a change. On-board entertainment is also well above average on both ships.

Extras

Thomson was the first major Standard-level operator to include all tips, removing one of the biggest bugbears at this level. Their general holiday expertise also makes for quite a slick operation, especially for shore excursions, and their comprehensive flight programme means you can set out from as many as 20 regional airports. They also offer a number of attractive cruise-and-stay packages in Majorca, Corfu, Cyprus and the Canaries. Two cruises can be taken back-to-back to give a full two weeks' worth of Mediterranean fun. And, at these prices, you'll be hard pushed to get better value anywhere in the cruise world. *Stop press: for more Thomson news, see page 248, Hold the Front Page.*

For a brochure or more information, call Thomson Direct on 0870 550 2562.

WINDSTAR CRUISES
www.windstarcruises.com

Ships	Tonnage	Passengers/ Crew	Space Ratio	Built/ Refurbished	Cruise Area	Rating
Wind Star	5,703	148/91	38.5	1986	C America, Mediterranean, Transatlantic	Deluxe
Wind Song	5,703	148/91	38.5	1987	Costa Rica, Panama Canal, New Zealand	Deluxe
Wind Spirit	5,703	148/91	38.5	1988	Caribbean, Mediterranean, Transatlantic	Deluxe
Wind Surf	14,745	312/163	47.2	1989/98	Caribbean, Mediterranean, Transatlantic	Deluxe

Cruise line notes

Despite being owned by the giant American Carnival Corporation, Windstar maintain their own style and continue to grow with the acquisition in 1998 of the much larger Club Med I vessel, now renamed *Wind Surf*. They attract a high percentage of Americans keen to sample the sailing experience (although this one is a bit of a cheat as the sails are computer-controlled) in an elegant atmosphere that manages to retain a relatively informal manner. Passengers tend to be quite active couples in their 30s and 40s, and slightly older groups who are attracted by the line's more exclusive itineraries, like their new Pacific coast cruises from magnificent Costa Rica and seven-day sailings to Belize in central America from Cancún. On board, the main attraction is as much the open, friendly ambience as any great sophistication in the facilities, although the Windstar ships do possess the highest general comfort levels of the ships in this market. 'Casual elegance' is the theme of the dress code (jacket and tie not required) while there is no great organised schedule of events. Life is relaxed, unstructured and definitely for the hearty, outdoor type who enjoys water sports more than showlounges. The dining is open-seating and the cuisine and service are distinctly sophisticated, especially when compared to the fare on standard American cruises. All four vessels maintain an 'open bridge' policy to allow passengers to see how it is done at any time. The quartet will all sail in various parts of the Mediterranean in the summer, from Turkey and the Greek isles to the Italian and French Rivieras, Barcelona and even out to Lisbon.

Ship notes

Uniquely, there is just one class of cabin on the identical trio (with the exception of a couple of suites), and all are outside, airy and well appointed, with a queen-sized bed (that converts to a twin), teak-deck bathroom (but with shower only), TV, VCR and CD player, mini-bar, fridge and 24-hour room service. The use of wood generally throughout the ships is an admirable feature, and the few public rooms (restaurant, shop, library, casino, lounge and piano bar, plus fitness room, sauna and the Verandah open-air dining options are quite elegant in a traditional fashion. *Wind Surf* adds even more opulence and options, with 31 double-size suites, a second restaurant and a comprehensive health spa. The ships also feature a water sports platform astern that allows for windsurfing, sailing, water-skiing, snorkelling and scuba-diving.

Extras

The wonderful feeling of freedom with sail travel is never better felt than aboard a Windstar vessel with her more up-market elegance. You can arrive in some of the smaller, more exotic ports of call and really feel you are a privileged individual to be there. The friendly nature of everyone on board only accentuates this feeling and it is the ideal 'Get away from it all' type of holiday. For honeymooners it also represents one of the most romantic hide-aways possible, provided you are not looking for lots of up-scale evening entertainment (on honeymoon – come on!). There are no children's facilities, but older children should revel in the great range of watersports on offer. However, the ships are not well designed for disabled passengers. Port taxes are extra.

For a brochure, call their London office on 020 7940 4460.

BEST OF THE REST

To complete this section on the cruise lines of the world, there are a handful of others worthy of mention, albeit in more abbreviated form, for more unusual cruises or where their impact on the British market is negligible at the moment, but has scope to increase.

Abercrombie & Kent

Area: South America, Antarctic, Northern Europe.
Ships: *Explorer.*
Rating: Standard
This up-market company specialise in worldwide tours, particularly safaris and other off-the-beaten-track adventures, and their one-ship cruise operation has been running since 1990 with a high degree of expedition-type flavour. Of special interest are their spring voyages along the Amazon River, a full 2,000 miles and further than any other cruise ship. *Explorer* is a unique little adventurer (just 2,398 tons), offering the chance to get right up close with the landscape you have come to see. She is not exactly built for creature comforts, hence only a Standard rating, but she is serviceable enough, although her lack of space (and some tiny cabins) means she is definitely not for the disabled or people with children. She features a comprehensive and sophisticated lecture programme to back up her itineraries and rubber Zodiac boats for shore excursions. There are few on-board facilities as the emphasis is on shore-side activities, lectures and films. Her usual passenger complement consists of Americans and Germans, with a few other European nationalities. Age profile tends to be a healthy and adventurous 50-plus. All tips and shore excursions are included in the basic price. They also collaborate on Royal Geographical Society Tours, a special association of operators who share the Society's belief in the value and enjoyment of geography and environmental matters. For brochures, phone 020 7730 9600.

Arcalia Shipping

Area: Northern Europe, Med, Canaries.
Ships: *Funchal, Princess Danae, Arion.*
Rating: Standard
This Portuguese operator enjoys a higher profile in the UK thanks to the marketing expertise of Cruise & Maritime Services (01322 860770), Arcalia's appointed General Sales Agent, who also promote German operator Transocean (see page 181) and Club Cruise in Holland. During the summer season (May-November), Arcalia charter their vessels to several British tour operators, notably Travelsphere, Travelscope Cruises and Festive Holidays. The ships are exclusively UK passenger charters at these times, with a predominantly Portuguese crew and British cruise staff and entertainment, and the trio are renowned for their warm, friendly hospitality with attentive service and above average cuisine for their Standard rating. *Danae* is the flagship and, at 16,500 tons, usually carries

around 550 passengers. She is a classic little liner of 1955 vintage with a surprisingly wide range of facilities and sound, good-sized cabins. She was renovated in 1974 and extensively refurbished again in 1997. *Funchal* at 10,000 tons is a more intimate cruiser with a proud maritime heritage. Built in 1961 and recently up-graded to carry some 500 passengers, she provides a cosy and friendly style of cruising, still with a good choice of facilities and one-seating dining. *Arion,* at 5,000 tons, is the newest addition to the fleet, which debuted in summer 2000 (after an extensive refit from her former life as Astra I). She carries some 330 passengers and provides a more intimate style, with a high ratio of outside cabins and a one-sitting dining arrangement. She also visits some of the smaller and more infrequently-visited ports of call. **Cruise & Maritime Services** provide a range of services to charterers and ship owners alike, including shore excursion and cruise staff and entertainment packages. Their programmes consist of:

Travelsphere: their early summer programme includes a 12-night North Cape cruise from Dover on *Princess Danae,* while the late summer season offers voyages on *Funchal* to and from Toulon and Venice, including the Greek isles. Durations vary from 10 to 12 nights. Call Travelsphere on 01858 410818.

Travelscope: in late summer 2001, Travelscope offered a programme of three 5/6-night West Mediterranean and round-Italy cruises (from Nice and Venice) on *Arion.* Details for 2002 were still being finalised as we went to press. Call Travelscope on 01453 820022.

Festive: their summer 2002 programme is based on a series of three 7- to 10-night ex-Dover and Southampton cruises to Norway's fjords and also southbound sunshine options to Spain, Portugal and North Africa operated by *Princess Danae.* Festive have also featured autumn cruises to the Canaries and Madeira on *Funchal* in the past, but no details were available for 2002 as we went to press. Call Festive on 08705 758 758.

La Compagnie des Iles du Ponant

Area: Caribbean, South America, East Coast USA, Canada.
Ships: *Le Levant, Le Ponant.*
Rating: Deluxe.
This French line joined the band of small, luxury operators in late 1998 with the 90-passenger yacht-cruiser *Le Levant,* with some truly imaginative itineraries around the Caribbean, up the Amazon, America's East Coast and the Great Lakes. The small-scale, intimate atmosphere is perfectly suited to their more up-scale style but in a more relaxed manner than Silversea or Seabourn (although not quite with the same service standards). Motor-yacht *Le Ponant* plies the smaller Caribbean islands in best sailing-ship fashion, carrying just 64 passengers, again with the (French) accent on informality. For more details or a brochure, call the Cruise Portfolio on 020 7434 0089.

Clipper Cruise Line

Area: Seven- to 22-day routes around eastern USA, the Caribbean, Panama Canal, Alaska, South America, Australia, Far East, Arctic and Antarctica.
Ships: *Nantucket Clipper, Yorktown Clipper, Clipper Adventurer, Clipper Odyssey*.
Rating: Standard.
A quartet of tiny (1,471, 2,354, 5,218 and 5,750 tons respectively) small-scale vessels offer a sophisticated, unfussy version of close-in cruising, geared more toward nature studies than mainstream cruise enjoyment. They have the ability to nose into little-seen parts of the Americas in a relaxed, country-club atmosphere. *Clipper Adventurer* is a former Russian explorer with an ice-hardened hull that allows her to venture into the Arctic and Antarctica. The most recent aquisition, Clipper Odyssey, journeys into little-visited ports of Australasia, the South Pacific and Far East as far as Japan, while also taking in the Great Barrier Reef, Hong Kong and volcanic Krakatau. Facilities on all four are limited, but the accent is more on social and intellectual pursuits, with guest lecturers and destination-intensive itineraries. Clipper are marketed in Britain through Kuoni on 020 7499 8636 or 0161 832 0667.

St Helena Line Ltd

Area: 35- to 39-day routes from Cardiff to St Helena, Tristan Da Cunha, Ascension Island and South Africa.
Ship: RMS *St Helena*.
Rating: Superior.
Not so much a cruise as an experience aboard a modern 6,767-ton cargo vessel operating round trips to the South Atlantic with 128 passengers. Creature comforts include a pool, a shop, sun lounge and dining room, an excellent library, deck sports and low-key evening entertainment, as well as simple but comfortable cabins (although not all with private facilities). The voyage is not so much about cruise luxury as the chance to enjoy sailing some of the remotest waters on earth, visiting rocky outposts like St Helena, where the ship spends at least one night, affording a unique opportunity (it is accessible only by sea) to explore this fascinating seventeenth-century British colony, the quaint capital Jamestown and its extremes of countryside, from wind-eroded desert to mountainous cliffs. The ship is also now fully on-line for e-mail, etc. For more information, call Curnow Shipping on 01326 211466.

Hapag-Lloyd Tours

Area: worldwide adventures.
Ships: *Bremen, Hanseatic, Columbus, Europa*.
Rating: Superior – Ultra-Deluxe.
This diverse fleet operates in some of the most far-flung corners of the world in expedition style but great comfort. The clientèle is largely German, but all the ships are bilingual, with a highly personal, indulgent service. *Hanseatic* (9,000 tons, Ultra-Deluxe) and *Bremen* (6,752,

Superior) are the adventurers, with ice-hardened hulls to visit Antarctica and the North-West Passage, as well as northern Europe, Alaska, the Russian Far East, South America and the Falklands. *Hanseatic* is an especially classy adventurer, more like an exclusive country club than a ship, with spacious cabins, elegant public rooms and an 'open bridge' policy for guests to visit at any time. *Columbus* (14,000 tons, Premier) is their most inventive product, a mass-market ship launched in 1997 for extensive cruises of America's Great Lakes, offering one all-British autumn voyage. This chic and well-appointed ship, featuring spacious cabins, a small but inviting range of public rooms and excellent cuisine, is the ideal answer for those after the 'something new' factor. New ship *Europa* (in 2000) delivers a truly luxurious experience, a 28,600-ton vessel carrying only 408 (giving a massive Space Ratio figure of 70) in worldwide splendour. With more than 80 per cent of cabins having balconies, a full range of public rooms (including their first casino) and a true international style, *Europa* features a lengthy world cruise, also available in sectors, before she returns in April to the Mediterranean. For more information on Hapag-Lloyd, call agents The Cruise Portfolio on 020 7434 0089.

Noble Caledonia

Area: worldwide adventures.
Ships: *Caledonian Star* (and various charters).
Rating: Superior

Not so much a cruise company as 'a collection of random travel ideas', from a seven-day walk in North Cyprus to a 65-day Antarctic circumnavigation. If you want something different, this is the company to call, with their cruise operation typically wide-ranging. *Caledonian Star* is a thoroughly British product, offering an experience light years from the conventional around the likes of the Seychelles, Bali, Australia's Great Barrier Reef, Fiji and down to New Zealand, as well as northern Europe. The accent is on a warm, convivial atmosphere (maximum 110 passengers on the 3,095 ton ship) and an intelligent programme of lectures, films and shore expeditions. There is no obvious ostentation, but there is plenty of charm in a smart-casual style and with a private yacht feel. In addition, the company charters other expedition-type vessels, including the ice-breaker *Kapitan Khlebnikov*, the *Irrawaddy Princess* river cruiser in Burma, the *World Discoverer* to Antarctica, Alaska and the South Pacific, the *Bali Sea Dancer* around Indonesia, the cruise-ferry operations of Norwegian Coastal Voyages and trips to the Galapagos Islands. For a brochure, call their head office in London on 020 7409 0376.

Norwegian Coastal Voyages

Area: Norway.
Ships: various cruise-ferries.
Rating: Superior.
Not so much a cruise line as a commercial coastal service along the
Norwegian fjords, from Bergen to Kirkenes, north of the Arctic Circle.
With a variety of now fairly modern ships (they have six up-to-date
cruise-ferries, plus two new generation ultra-modern Millennium class
ships in spring 2002, which will replace the two traditional coastal
steamers on this route), NCV offer a variety of experiences in the style of
travel as well as the ports of call and, their year-round sailings mean you
can sample the Midnight Sun as well as the Northern Lights. You can also
cruise-and-stay in several cities or fjords, making for a superb package
that really gets you away from the cruise mainstream and into a genuine
close-up view of a fascinating country and its people. For more details or
a brochure, call Norwegian Coastal Voyages on 020 7559 6666.

Page & Moy

Area: Northern Europe, Med.
Ship: *Ocean Majesty* and other charters
Rating: Standard.
As well as being the biggest cruise agent in Britain, Page & Moy are
increasingly active in the charter business, with block bookings on several
lines (notably Fred Olsen's *Black Prince*) and, since 1998, 18 full sailings
of the Greek-owned *Ocean Majesty* (10,417 tons), a well-equipped, if
high-density, vessel boasting smart public rooms and friendly service. The
smallish cabins and relatively limited deck space should not be a big
drawback with the ship's destination-intensive itineraries (from seven to
14 nights) to the Baltic, Madeira, Iceland, Norwegian fjords, North Cape
(ex-UK from Harwich) and fly-cruises to the Med and Red Sea. The full-
ship charters allow Page & Moy to provide a fully British service, from the
cuisine to on-board currency and evening entertainment, with guest
celebrities on many cruises. There is also a special £5 coach offer to
Harwich or Gatwick, Stansted and Manchester airports from anywhere in
the country. All your tips are also included, as are port and airport taxes,
while several cruises feature organised bridge-playing programmes and
one is a special National Trust itinerary with guest speakers. In 2002,
Page & Moy will also have a series of cruises in the Med on Arcalia's
Princess Danae. For details or a brochure, call 0116 250 7890.

Peter Deilmann Cruises

Area: worldwide.
Ship: *Deutschland.*
Rating: Ultra-Deluxe.
This is still relatively new to the British market, but it truly is a product to make the rest of the cruise world take notice. German operator Peter Deilmann, also Europe's leading river-cruise company as well as owners of the 50-passenger sailing ship *Lili Marleen,* have lavished a small fortune on recreating a classic ship in the 22,400-ton, 580-passenger *Deutschland.* If she weren't so new, you might think you had travelled back 70 years to cruising's Golden Age and great liners like *Bremen, Europa* and *Normandie;* there are no casinos, nightclubs or theatres; instead you get a sumptuous Edwardian-style show-lounge, a saloon bar of the most exquisite finish and opulence, three magnificent restaurants and an overall attention to quality and detail which puts you in mind of a great opera house or museum rather than a cruise ship. Add in the 'modern' features of cinema, health spa, two pools, gymnasium and shopping gallery, plus beautifully appointed cabins and attentive service, and you have a startling product for the discerning, older passenger. At least 90 per cent of guests are likely to be German, and English is only the second language (albeit well spoken by most of the staff) but she is being marketed increasingly in the US as well as Britain, which means the bilingual operation will grow steadily, especially for her worldwide itinerary range which offers two-week sectors from the Mediterranean and Baltic to South America, the Far East and Africa. Given the outstanding nature of *Deutschland* herself, this should be an experience to appeal to many real cruise aficionados. For a brochure, call 020 7436 2931.

Transocean Tours

Area: worldwide cruises.
Ships: *Astor, Astoria.*
Rating: Premier.
This German line offers exciting and quality-conscious vessels with a spacious feel and real finesse that traverse large areas of the world and so can boast some wonderful itineraries, including a 120-day world cruise (available in six sectors) on the 20,150-ton *Astor.* She also travels northern Europe and the Caribbean in a fair degree of comfort, with well-equipped, spacious cabins and a generous range of tastefully decorated public rooms. The 18,591-ton *Astoria,* built in 1981 and extensively refurbished as *Arkona* in 1995, adds more delightful small-ship charm with excellent facilities and high-quality contemporary decor. For details of Transocean's British options, call Cruise & Maritime Services on 01322 860770.

Voyages of Discovery

Area: Mediterranean, Red Sea, Alaska, Russian Far East, Antarctica.
Ships: *Ocean Majesty, Funchal* and other charters.
Rating: Standard.

This British company look to provide a more relaxing but still authentic programme of discovery cruises on a whole range of ships in some of the more far-flung corners of the world with an educational and cultural theme. In the Mediterranean, they charter the *Ocean Majesty* (see Page & Moy), while the venerable 10,000-ton *Funchal* (from Arcalia Shipping) will operate a series of cruises from May to November to the Med and Black Sea, around Britain, to the Norwegian fjords and into the Baltic as far as St Petersburg. The Med cruises sail from Venice, Athens, Kusadasi and Alexandria, while the northern Europe series sails from Harwich. Neither is particularly sophisticated, but both still provide excellent value for money and the kind of small-scale cruising – with an excellent programme of guest lecturers – that makes the experience educational as well as fun. Voyages of Discovery also have bookings with adventure specialists Quark Expeditions (to little-seen corners of the Arctic and Antarctic) and Society Expeditions that add a whole range of thrilling itineraries for the audacious traveller who doesn't mind a more spartan level of cruise style. For details and brochures, call 01444 462150.

CHAPTER SIX

WHERE CAN I CRUISE?

In many cases, it is a question of saving the best until last when you come to consider your options for exactly where in the world to enjoy the cruise experience. It should now be fairly evident you have a breathtaking range of choice in the style of cruising you select, and the same is equally the case when it comes to deciding the area that most takes your fancy. The long and the short of it is simply you can sample just about anywhere in the world where it is possible for a ship to sail. As already noted, you can choose itineraries that are port-intensive or ones which offer more days at sea; where the accent is on the destinations themselves or where it is more about the style in which you travel; and you can sample extremes of temperature, from the frozen ice continents to the tropical rain forests.

There is, of course, an extra element in all this, namely the cruise season for any particular area. The Mediterranean and Alaska – two of the most popular and rapidly-expanding cruise destinations – are both primarily a spring and summer prospect, while even the Caribbean, for all that it offers year-round sunshine, has some unpredictable weather, notably in the hurricane season from July to November, which is particularly bad news for cruising (not that it means you are likely to be in danger, just that you can find ports of call cancelled at short notice and the seas a little rougher than their usual tranquil state). The two big hurricanes in the autumn of 1995 effectively took the Caribbean's two most visited destinations, the US Virgin Island of St Thomas and the Dutch/French isle of St Maarten, out of commission for several months and forced the cruise lines to reschedule hurriedly many of their itineraries. It made big news at the time, of course, because it was so extreme and such a rarity, but it does serve to indicate nothing is totally reliable when you have the weather as one of your main operating factors. For this reason, remember itineraries can change at short notice. When it comes to the cruise seasons, you will find the American lines also divide their operations into three distinct periods according to the demand. High Season marks the main holiday periods in the States, when the majority are looking to get away, and hence prices are higher, discounts are rare and ships are closest to capacity. The Shoulder, or Value, Season marks the periods either side of the peak demands where larger numbers are still in search of their holiday, but can be more flexible with their vacation time. Finally, the Low, or Economy, Season indicates the periods of least demand, for example May and September in the Alaska run, when prices are lowest and the ships are likely to be at their quietest. Quite often, only a few weeks can separate the High and Low seasons for a given area, and it stands to reason if you can be flexible with your holiday time you can make the biggest savings.

GATEWAY TO THE WORLD

Seasonality apart, of course, it remains true your choice is utterly worldwide. If you fancy exploring the North-West Passage, there is a ship (Hapag-Lloyd's *Hanseatic,* for example) to take you there; if your family is adventurous enough to want to sail around Cape Horn at the tip of South America, you have that choice open to you as well (try Silversea, Seabourn, Royal Olympic, NCL, Costa or Princess); perhaps the less-explored corners of the Mediterranean appeal to you, in which case there is now a growing band of ships eager to satisfy that demand, too (Star Clippers and Royal Olympic both boast some innovative itineraries); or, if you just want to enjoy the general cruise experience, relax and unwind in the sunshine, the Caribbean remains the perfect setting and any one of two dozen cruise lines can tempt you in that vicinity. Whale-watching in Alaska? Penguins in Antarctica? Native tribes along the Amazon? Archaeology of the Middle East? Shopping in Hong Kong? Investigating ancient cultures in the Pacific Islands? The list goes on and on, and it gets bigger every year as the lines continue to cater for the 'Something New' brigade.

But, before I get too carried away with the exotica of modern cruising, let's try to get a realistic idea of where the major cruise areas are, and where you will find the greatest numbers of British passengers.

The most obvious feature of the differences between where the British market chooses to cruise and where the rest of the world (the American section, or the other 75 per cent of the market) goes, is in the Mediterranean/Caribbean percentages. While the Caribbean makes up more than half of the US market, it represents less than a quarter of the British choice; and, while Americans in the Med number only 12.7 per cent of their total, it is a whopping 44 per cent share of the British market. Alaska is way up in American popularity, but that is largely because it is so much easier for them to get there. It is also one of the biggest growth areas, in comparative terms, for the British cruise passenger, up 19.5 per cent in 2000 against 1999, while the Far East was up seven per cent.

WHERE THE WORLD CRUISES

Destination	The British Market	The American Market
The Mediterranean	44.0%	12.7%
The Caribbean	19.0%	44.5%
The Atlantic (inc the Canaries)	8.5%	1.85%
Northern Europe	8.0%	8.1%
Others (including P Canal, Hawaii)	4.8%	11.73%
World Cruises and Line Voyages	4.5%	2.61%
Alaska	4.5%	8.0%
Far East/Australia	3.3%	3.74%
Indian Ocean	1.5%	0.24%
S America/Antarctica	1.0%	2.4%
East Coast USA (inc Bermuda)	0.9%	4.13%

So, if for British purposes the Mediterranean is Number One, let's start our study of the main cruise areas of the world there.

THE MEDITERRANEAN AND THE MIDDLE EAST
(including the Black Sea, North Africa and the Canaries)
Who goes there?

Airtours, Celebrity, Costa, Crystal, Cunard, Festival, First Choice, Hebridean Island Cruises, Holland America, Island, Louis, Mediterranean Shipping, NCL, Fred Olsen, Orient, P&O, Princess, Radisson Seven Seas, Renaissance, Royal Caribbean, Royal Olympic, Saga, Seabourn, Silversea, Star Clippers, Swan Hellenic, Thomson, Windstar

Cruise season: western Mediterranean, April–October; eastern Mediterranean (Cyprus, Middle East and Red Sea), year-round

For practical purposes in the modern cruise world, Mediterranean itineraries cover the whole spectrum from Gibraltar to the Middle East (and the Red Sea in some cases nowadays), also including the Black Sea for a handful of eastern European ports, which are now an intriguing part of many agendas. Considering the Med has been Britain's favourite foreign holiday playground since the late 1960s, it is not too surprising this is also our Number One cruise destination. A greater familiarity with European culture, the relatively short distances and the fact it is a slightly cheaper option than long-haul fly-cruises all combine to make the area more attractive to us.

It is also, however, arguably the most dynamic and sought-after cruise region in the world, hence more ships are being positioned for a summer season in the Med all the time, offering a greater variety of destination (and price) as the lines seek out more attractive itineraries to offer their repeat passengers. The big American companies Royal Caribbean and Princess are at the forefront of this development, but a number of the smaller players are equally keen to explore the possibilities and in some ways offer a more attractive product, notably the likes of Orient, Star Clippers and Radisson Seven Seas. Not to be outdone in their own backyard, so to speak, giant Italian line Costa (which also deals in the American market) is exploring new routes and bringing its newest ships into the area, while the two main Greek lines, Epirotiki and Sun Line, actually merged in order to create a better marketing opportunity for themselves (Royal Olympic). P&O and Fred Olsen, both long-established in this field, have continued to expand their repertoire, while newcomers like Airtours, Thomson and Festival have all taken advantage of the cruise boom generally, as well as the Med in particular, to establish themselves quite firmly in the area. Celebrity, First Choice and Island are the latest to seek a piece of the action here.

TRAVEL TIP

The Mediterranean (and northern Europe, for that matter) by cruise ship represents probably the most cost-effective way to visit Europe's major cities. It would be hideously expensive to try to visit, say, Florence, Rome, Athens and Istanbul on a flight-and-hotel basis in one go, whereas a cruise can do all that for you without having to unpack more than once.

As a result of all this hectic development (and much of it has taken place only in the last few years), the Mediterranean cruise passenger now gets a much better deal in terms of both price, as the competition hots up, and the hardware involved, as newer ships compete for your attention. Your choice of where to go is also being revised almost monthly. As the political situations in the former Yugoslavia, the Black Sea countries and the Middle East fluctuate, so the cruise lines will look to re-establish visits to places like Croatia, Albania, Lebanon, Syria, Georgia and the Red Sea. The cruise season has also developed apace, with the frontiers being pushed back all the time from the more obvious spring, summer and early autumn stages to encompass March and November and even the winter months in the eastern Med and Red Sea.

Taking the Mediterranean country by country, these are your choices in broad terms.

Portugal

Yes, I know it's not actually in the Mediterranean (even my geography is not that bad), but it is commonly a starting point for Mediterranean ex-UK cruises, with the capital of **Lisbon** the main port of call. It offers a spectacular entrance as you sail under the April 25th Bridge, and the city itself is well worth one of the standard half-day tours which most ships will offer as there is a lot to see in a few hours.

Don't miss: the historic city's authentic old Alfama Quarter.

Gibraltar

This British colony on the tip of southern Spain is a popular port for just about every line and offers passengers longing for a good pint of beer or a plate of fish and chips the chance to visit a home away from home. You can see all there is to see in the city itself, go shopping in Marks & Spencer, have lunch in a proper pub and ride the cable car to the top of the Rock under your own steam in less than a full day, so an excursion is somewhat unnecessary.

Don't miss: St Michael's Cave in the middle of the Rock, with its labyrinthine tunnels and massive cavern which stages regular concerts.

TRAVEL TIP

Watch out for the Barbary apes on the Rock – they will happily make off with any unsecured item you leave undefended – sunglasses, handbags, hats and even cameras. You have been warned.

Spain

The old city of Vigo, on the Atlantic Coast, is a less common port of call these days (visited on only a handful of ex-UK cruises), but is still an eye-catching place, with some spectacular views over the huge harbour from the castle-turned-hotel at Bayona. With **Barcelona** now operating as a home port for part of the year for Royal Caribbean and Princess, and **Majorca** being the centre of operations for Airtours, Thomson and Island, it is noticeable the Mediterranean focus is starting to switch away from Italy to Spain, especially for British purposes. Barcelona itself offers more authentic big-city charm, a spectacular view from Montjuic, the mountain-top venue for the 1992 Olympics, and an excellent opportunity to walk the local streets (being extra mindful not to carry your valuables carelessly as petty crime is something of a problem). Barcelona is also a fascinating port for its architecture - inspired by the unconventional Gaudi and others - shopping, culture (the fiercely proud Catalans), rambling Gothic quarter and parks.

Don't miss: the Picasso Museum for art-lovers.

Cadiz is the port city for **Seville** although several of the smaller ships can sail right up to Seville itself. Cadiz boasts an excellent old town area for keen shoppers, while the city of Seville boasts the largest Gothic cathedral in the world and some magnificent parks and gardens, which you can easily explore on your own. The Costa del Sol port of **Malaga** suffers from the summer deluge of European holidaymakers and is best visited for the chance to take a day-trip to the wonderful medieval city of **Granada**.

Don't miss: the fourteenth-century Alhambra Palace in Granada.

Ibiza offers a more authentic Spanish experience (if you can avoid the high-season sun-worshippers), plus some excellent beaches, while its sister holiday island of **Majorca** should need little introduction to British visitors. At the centre of the package holiday boom since the late 1960s, the island has some fabulous Roman ruins and charming villages (like Valldemosa and Soller, the latter with its 1920s railway still in working order), plus the inevitable beaches and a surprisingly unspoiled historic old quarter in the port of **Palma** itself. Again, shopping is a real pleasure, there are some wonderful tapas restaurants and the city's landmark cathedral is quite an awesome sight. And for a bar with a difference, check out the extraordinary Abaco.

France

The French Riviera should be an obvious attraction to anyone familiar with film-star style, designer fashions and the playgrounds of the rich and famous. It's expensive, outrageous, a bit tacky in places but otherwise still terribly chic, and those facets are all represented in the main ports of call. **Cannes** maintains its ancient heritage quite well in the face of the annual excesses of its international Film Festival and is a wonderfully relaxed port in which to shop, eat or just wander the well-kept streets. Nice (with its adjacent port town of **Villefranche** for all but the smallest ships) offers some pleasant streets to wander (notably the Promenade des Anglais where our Victorian ancestors discovered the winter package holiday) and excellent museums. **St Tropez** is the epitome of French beach culture and open-air café society, but the jewel in the crown here for sheer up-market sophistication (and outrageous prices) is **Monte Carlo**, which can also be visited from Nice (by taking the train for around £3.50 return). The famous Casino, the Hotel de Paris and the Oceanographic Museum are all complemented by some fabulous views over the Principality from its perfectly maintained gardens. And, provided you can negotiate a few hills, Monte Carlo is well suited to doing your own thing for most of the day. **Toulon** is cropping up on a few itineraries and offers a fabulous cable-car ride up Mt Faron that is easy to find on the excellent local bus system.

Don't miss: the elegant restaurants and shops of the Boulevard de la Croisette in Cannes.

The French isle of **Corsica** is a different kettle of fish altogether, a rugged, mountainous outpost famous as the birthplace of Napoleon and equally idiosyncratic. The main port of **Ajaccio** offers a pleasant, pastel-coloured town with a huge collection of Napoleonic museums, while the fortress town of **Calvi** in the north is quite breathtakingly situated (but suitable only for those who enjoy a challenging walk).

Italy

The most frequent daily port of call for many lines is **Civitavecchia** to allow for excursions to **Rome**. Much-needed extra cruise facilities are scheduled soon, as well as a new rail-link to Rome which will provide a welcome alternative to the near two-hour coach journey. Once the work is complete, Civitavecchia will be a delightful visit and Rome itself, for all the crowds and traffic congestion, is simply unmissable. The port city of **Livorno** offers trips to **Florence** to enjoy the magnificent treasures and architecture of Michelangelo, da Vinci, Donatello and Raphael. Then there is **Naples**, for a must-see chance to view the remains of Pompeii and nearby Mount Vesuvius, the picturesque, coast-hugging town of **Sorrento** (and its island of **Capri**) and the chic northern port of **Portofino** with its elegant harbour-side restaurants.

Don't miss: the Ponte Vecchio Bridge in Florence and the coastal scenery around Sorrento and Naples.

TRAVEL TIP

If you opt to go wandering on your own in most of the Italian cities – and especially in Sicily – don't carry any valuables with you, since handbag-snatching and other forms of petty crime are on the increase.

Genoa is the centre of the cruise world in Italy – and the biggest turnaround port in the Med – and is also the birthplace of Christopher Columbus, hence numerous museums and other attractions dedicated to him. If you can negotiate the traffic-choked centre, Genoa offers attractions such as the biggest aquarium in Europe and some great shopping, plus a fascinating medieval quarter and the magnificent Cathedral of San Lorenzo. New port developments are also a feature here, and the local tourist office is one of the most up-to-date in the Med. **Venice** is the other main point of embarkation for many cruises and the attractions of this quite magnificent 'floating' city should be obvious. It is a great place to visit at any time of year (you can rarely avoid the crowds) and makes for a wonderful starting and finishing point to any cruise. Finally, the islands of **Sardinia** and **Sicily** offer two more contrasting Italian experiences, with the former an increasingly up-market, quite chic development, but still with a host of authentic little villages that are best explored on a ship excursion, while Sicily ranges from its crime-hit (and rather dull) principal city of **Palermo** to the stunningly beautiful town of **Taormina**. The port of **Catania** is increasingly popular for visits to Taormina, where lovely views, attractive shopping and restaurants and the background of Mt Etna all add up to one of the Mediterranean's most visibly enjoyable ports.

Don't miss: the Greek amphitheatre perched up on the hillside above Taormina.

Malta

Rich in history and diverse cultures, Malta and its harbour town of **Valletta** is a particular personal favourite. A warm, friendly island at the 'crossroads' of the Mediterranean, its people have not forgotten their historic British ties, including the island's Second World War heroism, and so a visit here offers that extra dimension. The island itself is not outstandingly pretty and is even a little unkempt in places, but the coastline is impressively rugged and it boasts some unique sights, like the silent city of **Medina**, where no motor vehicles are allowed, some prehistoric caves and the full historical experience of the Knights of the Order of St John from the Crusades. The history of this remarkable island is fascinating, and, if you can spare half an hour, start by taking in the Malta Experience audio-visual presentation right at the end of Merchants Street in Valletta (next to Fort St Elmo) to get a full perspective of the island's significance. A new £12-million cruise terminal is in the process of taking shape along the harbour promenade.

Don't miss: St John's Cathedral in Valletta and its truly stunning internal architecture and painting.

Croatia

Croatia is another country making a tourist comeback and some cruise lines have reinstated **Dubrovnik** as a regular port of call, a welcome return for this Renaissance masterpiece of a city. Now a UNESCO world heritage site, Dubrovnik revels in its thirteenth-century traditions and is one of the Mediterranean's best-kept secrets, rivalling Venice for natural beauty.

Greece

Cruising is just the perfect way to see a lot of what this fascinating country has to offer in the best possible style. Greek accommodation can sometimes leave a lot to be desired in terms of modern creature comforts, and island-hopping by the local ferries, while fun for the young, carefree crowd, can be a frustrating and time-consuming experience. So, the cruise lines have quickly cottoned on to the attraction of offering full and varied itineraries in this area. Due to Greek cabotage laws (which may not survive EU regulations much longer), only Greek-registered vessels are allowed to offer circular cruises from a Greek home port (almost invariably Piraeus, the port for Athens), hence Royal Olympic have currently cornered the market on all the best cruise experiences in this area.

TRAVEL TIP

A lot of Greek islands are only tender ports, i.e. the ships don't dock but transfer passengers ashore by tender. This can be a concern for more elderly passengers and those whose mobility is limited. Check your cruise brochure carefully if this could be a problem for you.

However, their competitors (notably Festival, Costa and MSC) do offer a good range of Greek ports in addition to other Med destinations, and no one else is as port-intensive as Royal Olympic (which can be a drawback if you like to spend some time at sea). For a really memorable Greek cruise, the smaller ships can visit a lot of the lesser-known islands where the bigger vessels cannot get in.

Piraeus is quite often the start or finish point for many Greek cruises and, as such, can be a bit of a disappointment, to put it mildly, as it consists of some fairly mundane urban sprawl all the way into **Athens** and its congested streets. Not for nothing is this known as the TV aerial capital of the world, and it is a major feat to take any picture of the sights of Athens without it being disfigured in some way by this unfortunate background. However, if you can survive the crowds and congestion, the Acropolis is still one of the great wonders and there are numerous smaller sites which just crop up at regular intervals around the city. The many museums are a real highlight for anyone with a historical bent, while no visit is complete without seeing the traditional guards in their ceremonial uniforms, complete with pom-pom shoes and 'skirts', outside the Presidential Palace.

TRAVEL TIP

Unless you enjoy an atmosphere of almost pure carbon monoxide, Athens is not the city to wander around on foot. Apart from the fact it is a good 45-minute drive from Piraeus at most times, it is best enjoyed these days by air-conditioned coach on an official ship tour. There is also much construction in advance of the 2004 Olympics.

Once you head out from Piraeus, there are a myriad of islands vying for your attention, the main ones of which are the green (and rather British) **Corfu**, mountainous **Rhodes, Crete** (the largest of the Greek islands and therefore boasting several different ports), spectacular **Santorini**, popular **Mykonos** and the tiny uninhabited islet of **Delos**, which has some superb archaeological sites crammed into its two square miles. **Corfu** offers a graceful old town that is not too crowded with tourists in the height of summer while Rhodes has an equally fascinating old walled city as well as the brilliantly white village of **Lindos** with its picturesque Acropolis (the citadel of the old city).

The main port of **Heraklion** on Crete is less than inspiring (apart from its outstanding archaeological museum), but the island itself has two of antiquity's most famous sites, the 5,000-year-old Minoan city of **Knossos** (partly 'restored' in dubious taste by the British archaeologist Sir Arthur Evans) and the more authentic palace of Phaistos.

Don't miss: Knossos – just a short taxi ride from Heraklion and one of the great archaeological wonders for all its haphazard restoration.

Mykonos offers the more relaxed, simple charms of its beautiful main town and thatched windmills, but Santorini is simply unmissable – a craggy survivor from a huge volcanic eruption around 1500BC, its small towns and villages are all perched high atop the circular cliffs which surround the central 'lake' and small core island that is all that survives of the main volcano cone. The main town of Thera is usually full of tourists hunting around the many jewellery shops, but the views from the top are quite stunning and rightly adorn just about every Greek scenic calendar you see.

TRAVEL TIP

For visits to Santorini, you have the choice of a short (near vertical) cable car ride, or a donkey ride up the steep, hairpin-bend-littered path. Trying to walk up the path can be hazardous (for being run over by Formula One donkeys or being ankle-deep in donkey 'doings'), and if you choose to come back down by cable car, leave plenty of time as some serious queues build up in the afternoon.

The other main Greek ports are the mainland Peloponnese ones of **Nafplion** (otherwise spelt Navplion, Nauplia or Nauplion), which is the gateway to the principal archaeological sites of **Epidaurus, Corinth** and **Mycenae** and has a fine Venetian fort overlooking its harbour, and **Gythion**, the ancient port town of Sparta. Less-visited ports include **Volos**, with its precariously-perched monasteries, **Preveza**, for the up-market resort of Parga and the Byzantine churches of Arta, **Patmos**, with the spectacular monastery of St John the Divine, **Cephalonia**, the largest and most unspoilt of the Ionian islands (which include Corfu), **Katakolon** and **Patras**, both offering visits to nearby Olympia (birthplace of the modern Olympics), **Skiathos**, with its pretty town and spectacular beaches, and **Pylos**, for the chance to tour the historic town of Methone and the palace of legendary King Nestor at Englianos.

Don't miss: the incredible ancient theatre at Epidauros (otherwise spelt Epidavros) with 55 limestone rows and room for 14,000 spectators, with acoustics to match – from the topmost row, you can literally hear a coin drop on the stage.

Finally, almost without exception, the Greek ports offer some outstanding beaches to relax and unwind, as well as some of the most hospitable tavernas in the world.

Turkey

This is an area the cruise companies are only just beginning to take into account, apart from the three main ports of Istanbul, Izmir and Kusadasi. It saw a huge tourist boom in 1995 and to a large extent it is an undiscovered gem of a country. It houses some of the most complete and well-exhibited archaeological remains from the ancient world and is a history buff's paradise. If your cruise doesn't include **Istanbul** at some point, demand a refund! This is one of the most fascinating cities the Med has to offer, situated as it was in antiquity at the crossroads of Western and Eastern civilisations. Even today, it exhibits a tremendous array of co-existing cultures, not to mention some fabulous architecture, wonderful museums and a genuinely exotic atmosphere. A few ships now opt for an overnight stop in this city, which lies in both Europe and Asia because it straddles the strait of Bosporus. This just begins to give you enough time to scratch the surface, but if you can arrange a pre- or post-cruise stay, all the better.

Don't miss: the awesome Grand Bazaar for unique shopping and the Meydani precinct, boasting the wonders of the Blue Mosque, the Cathedral of St Sofia (a truly breathtaking church-turned-mosque-turned-museum) and the Topkapi Palace.

TRAVEL TIP

When visiting any mosque, you will be required to cover your legs if you are wearing shorts, in deference to the Muslim religion. Large wraps are usually provided for that purpose, and a small donation is required in exchange, so try to have some Turkish currency with you.

Izmir (or Smyrna in the ancient world) is a busy, modern city with a turbulent history and is mainly used by visiting cruise ships as a gateway to the wondrous archaeological site of **Ephesus**. However, **Kusadasi** is a closer and more suitable port of call from which to take a tour of this unmissable ruined city, so much of which has been restored to appeal to even the non-history-minded tourists. However, it requires at least two hours for a serious tour (which can be taken on your own or with a proper guide), and it can be uncomfortably hot in the height of summer. Kusadasi has also cleaned up its act considerably in the last few years to become a pretty little port in its own right.

TRAVEL TIP

If any of your ship-organised excursions includes a stop to check out Turkish carpet-making, beware. There is usually a crafty sales pitch thrown in, so try to give it a miss unless you are genuinely interested in buying (and can afford to splash out £500 or more). If you show any interest at all, you are in for the hard sell.

Of the up-and-coming ports (where you usually have to tender ashore), **Bodrum** is a young, lively, happening resort in best Med style, exceedingly busy in the summer months but also boasting a fine Crusader fortress (and some tempting and relatively inexpensive seafood restaurants overlooking the harbour), **Dikili** is the new gateway to the impressively situated ancient site of **Pergamum, Canakkale** offers its bustling waterfront cafés looking out over the narrow Dardanelles Straits, and nearby excursion to the (rather dull) site of ancient Troy (the wooden horse has long since gone) and **Antalya**, another major resort city and stopping point, affords visits to more Greek and Roman relics at **Aspendos** and **Perge**.

Don't miss: the Roman theatre of Aspendos, the finest surviving example of its kind.

Of course, all of these Mediterranean and Aegean resorts also boast excellent beaches to get away from it all for a while and perhaps sample the local alcoholic speciality, raki, the Turkish equivalent of ouzo or pernod.

The Black Sea

Another relatively recent addition to many brochures, the Black Sea offers more off-beat destinations and the chance to sample the different cultures of Bulgaria, Romania and the Ukraine. Here, at ports of call like **Nesebur** and **Varna** (Bulgaria), **Constanta** (Romania) and **Yalta** and **Odessa** (Ukraine), you can almost step backwards in time to a different century where the modern world has only just started to intrude. The relative level of poverty can be quite a surprise after Greece and Turkey and, in the Ukraine in particular, the locals seem almost desperate for foreign currency (and there is a seedy side, if you investigate too far – you don't want to get caught in need of the loo in the Ukraine, the public facilities are indescribable!). All the different ports offer similar levels of cultural experience, but, to be on the safe side, it is better to stay with an organised excursion to get the maximum out of your visit. In the Ukraine in particular you will need a separate visa, which you are required to obtain more than a month in advance, if you want to go off on your own, but don't expect too many people to speak English. The city of Odessa has its attractions with the Potemkin Steps, the neoclassical Opera House and the catacombs, but somehow both it and the fading seaside resort of Yalta (famous as the site of the Second World War peace conference between Churchill, Stalin and Roosevelt) are ultimately rather uninspiring destinations, fun to say you've been there but not on the list for an imminent return.

Cyprus

Limassol has been the principal port of call for the Greek part of this island for many years and received a boost with tour operators like Airtours and First Choice using it as a base for some of their operations, offering some attractive cruise-and-stay options. Although Greek is the language, it is a country in its own right and offers a particularly rewarding island tour lasting the best part of a day and visiting the ancient site of **Paphos**, the imposing castle at **Kolossi** and the beautiful **Troodos Mountains**, as well as the resort town itself. On the other hand, you could just grab a taxi and head for one of the many great beaches.

Middle East

Until the promised development of the ports in Syria, Jordan and Lebanon actually happens, the region tends to revolve around Egypt and Israel (although the latter is also subject to the prevailing political situation). The Syrian town of **Tartous**, although not on many itineraries, is a minor eastern Med jewel, boasting as it does access to the fabulous site of the **Krak des Chevaliers** Crusader fortress, or a trip to the capital **Damascus**, almost a scaled-down version of Istanbul. Swan Hellenic and Festival currently operate the only really extensive choice to these countries, with the extra options of **Beirut** in the Lebanon (for tours to the 5,000-year-old city of Byblos and the fascinating mountain village of Beit Eddine), **Latakia** in Syria (visiting the massive and ancient Crusader fortress of Saladin or Aleppo, which claims to be the oldest continuously inhabited city in the world) and **Aqaba** in Jordan (from where there are tours to the ancient city of Petra). Israel's ports of **Haifa** (picturesque and charming) and **Ashdod** (modern and functional) both offer tours to **Jerusalem**, which is the principal reason for visiting this region. It would be hard to see all the main sights under your own steam unless you have been here before, and the majority of ship-organised excursions will be all-day affairs, which even then can be pretty hectic. Alternative tours take in the religious stronghold of **Massada** or the **Dead Sea**, plus the ancient towns of **Nazareth** and **Bethlehem**. The city of Jerusalem itself, with its mix of Muslim, Christian and Jewish religions, is truly one of the great wonders of the Holy Land and, provided the political situation doesn't become too intense, it is an eye-opening experience.

Don't miss: the Wailing Wall, the Church of the Holy Sepulchre and the Via Dolorosa, the walk to the site of the Crucifixion.

Egypt can be something of a tourist hot-spot and it is difficult to know what to recommend as the official guidelines tend to change from month to month. Suffice it to say, the two main ports of call, **Alexandria** and **Port Said**, are both primarily gateways to (but some two hours' drive from) the city of **Cairo**, which offers an excellent museum and a chance to see the Great Pyramids and the Sphinx, and you are best advised to take an official excursion to avoid any possible problems. An alternative tour from Alexandria takes in the Second World War site of **El Alamein**, with many relics of that crucial battle. A trip through the **Suez Canal** to the Red Sea port of **Safaga** offers the opportunity to visit the ancient city of **Luxor**, which is in many ways more fulfilling and less demanding than hot, noisy Cairo, where the appearance of the massive pyramids on the outskirts of the sprawling city can be something of an anti-climax. **Aqaba** in Jordan, and **Sharm-el-Sheikh**, for visits to Mount Sinai, in Egypt, are also beginning to attract more cruise ship visits as the Red Sea features in more winter programmes.

North Africa

This vast expanse of sun-drenched coastline can boast few genuine ports of interest, especially as the levels of poverty and petty crime are not conducive to comfortable tourist visits. I have been unimpressed with Morocco more than once and heard too many unfortunate experiences from tourists in Algeria and Tunisia to be able to recommend either with any conviction. They can be intimidating countries for women in particular to visit, especially on their own. The most frequent visits are to the Tunisian capital Tunis and its port of **Sidi Bou Said**, which are notable for the chance to visit the ruins of the once-mighty city of **Carthage**, from where Hannibal set out in his attempt to conquer Rome. The Moroccan port of **Tangier** is another regular stop, offering a taste of modern French-Arab culture and the inevitable shopping experience of the casbah. The inland city of **Tetouan** makes for a fascinating day-trip and rather more authentic Arab atmosphere. **Agadir** on the Atlantic coast has become something of a favourite in recent years with cruises from and around the Canary Islands, but again it is hard to see why. Laughably dubbed 'the Miami of Morocco', it is a modern, almost purpose-built resort designed to attract the European sun-worshipper in large numbers at the beachfront hotels, but, apart from a pleasant enough expanse of beach, there is little to hold your attention. An all-day excursion to **Marrakech** is the other option from here, but that entails a good six-hour round trip by coach and is a lot of effort for the principal attraction of the huge souk or marketplace (where you may be constantly hassled by local 'guides' and it can be an unnerving experience). If you are really determined to try Marrakech, better to find a ship that puts into the port of **Casablanca**, from where the journey is less demanding, and the city itself has a real charm of its own (albeit nothing like the Humphrey Bogart film). The ancient royal capital of **Rabat** is another alternative from Casablanca. But, again, as advised above, for safety's sake it is best to stick with ship-arranged tours.

The Canary Islands

Here is another mini-cruise experience that will appeal especially to British cruisers, particularly if the Portuguese island of Madeira can be included as well. The seven islands that make up the Canaries consist of **Gran Canaria**, with its port of **Las Palmas** (a bustling, lively town on a history-rich island, boasting some impressive architecture and landscapes, including the mini-Sahara of Maspolomas); **Tenerife** served by **Santa Cruz** (a functional town with a rather congested port when full, but gateway to an island of rich contrasts, from mountainous rain-forest to wonderful beaches); the touristy **Fuerteventura**; the volcanic and treeless **Lanzarote** and its port **Arrecife** (opening up an island which boasts Fire Mountain, a still-active area of distinctly hot hills, offering a fascinating half-day tour); **La Palma** and its port **Santa Cruz de la Palma** (a tiny island that can boast the greatest altitude in the world relative to its perimeter and one of the largest volcanic craters to boot); unspoilt (and sparsely populated) **La Gomera** with its port of **San Sebastian**, and the smallest and most westerly island **El Hierro**, with the port of Valverde and some more wild, volcanic mountains. Surprisingly, the most British-feeling experience of the lot can be **Madeira**, which is some 250 miles to the north, and can be wonderfully pretty in spring with its mountain flowers in full bloom. The port and capital, **Funchal**, is a maze of winding, cobbled streets and red-roofed houses with a lively market where the majority will speak English. You can also stop off for real, traditional afternoon tea at Reid's Hotel.

Don't miss: the traditional wicker sled rides down some of the steep streets, and the chance to wander the fine gardens and call in at the Madeira cellars to sample the fine local wines, of course.

NORTHERN EUROPE
(including the British Isles)
Who goes there?

Costa, Crystal, Cunard, Festival, Hapag-Lloyd, Hebridean Island Cruises, Holland America, NCL, Fred Olsen, Orient, P&O, Princess, Radisson Seven Seas, Renaissance, Royal Caribbean, Royal Olympic, Saga, Seabourn, Silversea, Swan Hellenic

Cruise season: May-October

As with the Mediterranean, the ports of northern Europe are also very much on the cruise companies' 'hit-list' of places to expand and develop to make their itineraries increasingly attractive and a touch different. There are two distinct regions to this area's make-up, with the option of 7–15-day cruises around the Baltic Sea, taking in some of the major cities of Russia, Latvia, Germany, Denmark, Estonia, Finland, Sweden and Norway, or cruises of 9–14 days along the fjords of Norway as far as the bleak, inhospitable North Cape, Europe's most northerly point and well into the Arctic Circle. In both cases, they are very much summer-season destinations, and the attractions of the Norwegian fjords, the Midnight Sun and the forbidding northerly outcrops of our continent have much in common with those of Alaska. Once again, the cruise ship package offers the opportunity to take in the region's rich cultural diversity in the most comfortable yet still stimulating fashion. Distances between ports are relatively small, making for some more port-intensive itineraries which continue to attract quite an American following (especially those who have already 'done' Alaska and want to be able to boast the 'something different' factor). Another bonus in Scandinavia (and Holland, too) is English is widely spoken, making visits to places like Bergen, Oslo, Copenhagen and Amsterdam especially visitor-friendly. The fabulous scenery, the plentiful wildlife and the fascinating histories of the main cities are all hugely rewarding, hence the area is slowly losing its reputation for attracting only the older, 50-plus crowd. The arrival of Royal Caribbean's 12-day cruises from Harwich into the Baltic and up to the North Cape has added a glamorous edge to the hardware involved; with Costa now offering fly-cruises around the area from Copenhagen and Festival doing the same from Kiel, plus Holland America and Celebrity joining in, the competition is hotting up.

What of Britain?

When it comes to the principal British ports, it hardly seems necessary to mention they are usually only the point of embarkation for us, whereas the Americans (of whom there are still a fair number flying in for cruises with Cunard, Royal Caribbean, NCL, Holland America, Costa, Princess, Radisson Seven Seas, Seabourn and Silversea) usually see them as destinations in their own right.

Southampton remains Britain's busiest port simply in terms of passenger numbers (around 300,000) as it deals with the bulk business of Cunard and P&O, as well as occasional visits from Seabourn, Celebrity, Fred Olsen and Crystal, and, in 2000, the first ex-UK cruises of Airtours. It boasts two fine recently-refurbished passenger terminals with a total capacity (rarely reached) of 10,000 in the space of a weekend. The Mayflower Terminal (Dock Gate 10) serves the P&O ships which all sail from here almost weekly, while the QE2 Terminal (Dock Gate 4) serves, surprisingly enough, the regular visits of the QE2, plus the more infrequent visitors. Both terminals offer good seating space (as there can be a wait of an hour or more to board at peak times), plus bars, a newsagent and a currency exchange. The largest ships can call here and it is most conveniently situated for cruises out into the Atlantic and Mediterranean. Ease of access has been boosted by the completion of the M3 link to the M27 which runs through the city, and the drive from London to Southampton's dockside should not take more than an hour and a half. Rail links are also excellent. Extensive car parking is adjacent to both terminals and there is also a car collection and delivery service.

It may come as something of a surprise to people who know **Dover** only as a cross-channel ferry gateway to the hypermarkets of France, but it is the newest player in the UK cruise port stakes and has quickly established itself as the only major rival to Southampton from a standing start of no cruise ship visits as recently as 1993 to 122 in 1999. A £10-million investment in turning the derelict old Dover marine railway station into a bright, modern cruise terminal was the biggest single development in 1996, and the huge upgrade in the port's facilities (with a second purpose-built terminal added at a cost of £17.5 million for the Millennium) has quickly attracted a big increase in cruise business, with Fred Olsen switching their operations here from Southampton, and the likes of Costa, Festival, Princess, Crystal, Saga, NCL, Renaissance and Radisson Seven Seas all joining the expansion. The clever restoration of the main railway station, incorporating the listed original building itself, has allowed for ample covered parking right next to the smart new passenger facilities, which include modern check-in desks, state-of-the-art security systems for quicker baggage processing, a comfortable 450-seat lounge and a pleasant café. The second terminal offers a

700-seat lounge and even more check-in facilities and baggage-handling areas. Dover is also well served by its road links from London, especially the completed M20 route that skirts Ashford and Folkestone. The additional element of sailing out of a port that offers the White Cliffs as the backdrop is very appealing.

The port of **London** still offers a busy summer berth at Tower Bridge, especially popular with the smaller, more up-market vessels of Seabourn, Silversea, Radisson Seven Seas' *Song of Flower* and Swan Hellenic's *Minerva*. The mooring, alongside HMS *Belfast*, is not exactly a classic facility, but somehow it is typically British and sailing from there does provide the grand opportunity of seeing the beautiful Tower Bridge raised to let ships out. It is never likely to be able to take ships of any great size however, which is why a planned new terminal at Greenwich, for ships up to 50,000 tons, is an interesting prospect.

The new cruise facility at **Harwich** in Essex is another fascinating development as it has been revamped to accommodate one of the 70,000-ton super-liners of Royal Caribbean, who were joined in 1999 by Holland America Line. The dedicated terminal facility (completed in 1996) offers passenger, coach and car facilities and up-to-date baggage-handling systems. Road links are again quite good (via the M25, A12 and A120), although it is the furthest of all four from the airports of Gatwick and Heathrow. The railway service runs right into the port area as well. Page & Moy, Arcalia and Voyages of Discovery are other lines to use Harwich.

Finally, to complete the UK scene, the pretty town of St Peter Port on **Guernsey** has increasingly become a cruise stop-off in recent years as lines look to exploit shorter ex-UK journeys. The cobbled streets offer some easy-paced shopping (try Garnhams for some different gift ideas) and there are several outstanding parks (don't miss the restored Candie Gardens), while the imposing Castle Cornet offers several hours of captivating island history, including the German occupation of World War Two, all within easy walking distance of the marina (where you come in by ship's tender). Or you can just go for a stroll along the many miles of well-kept beaches.

Holland

As the northern European market has grown, so has the appeal of the ports en route, as they all seek a piece of the action, especially as umbrella organisation Cruise Europe has worked hard to increase the profile of some of its lesser lights. **Amsterdam** has seen its ship visits mushroom from a paltry 38 in 1985 to 102 In 1999 as lines like Holland America, P&O, NCL, Royal Caribbean, Celebrity and Costa discover the city's attractions. For us near neighbours, there is no real secret – just a city with a rich history (dating back to 1275), lively streets, squares and parks (especially the Artis zoo-aquarium-park for kids), a laid-back culture and a wonderfully convivial atmosphere. The 'Venice of the North' opened a new, state-of-the-art passenger terminal in 2000 as further evidence of its long-term appeal.

Don't miss: one of the many well-narrated boat tours of Amsterdam's miles of canals.

Germany

This country is usually the first stopping point for the Baltic Sea cruise, with the majority of ships now taking advantage of the 60-mile **Kiel Canal** (just 148 feet wide and mostly 46 feet deep) to avoid having to sail around Denmark. **Bremerhaven** provides access to the city of **Bremen** 37 miles inland, which is well worth a visit on any ship-organised excursion for its stunning medieval and Gothic architecture (and the oldest wine cellar/restaurant in Germany, the amazing Ratskeller). Smaller ships are also able to take in a cruise down the River Elbe to lively **Hamburg**, Germany's second-largest city, and its full range of sights and activities, including canal launch rides, museum visits, the colossal fish market and the famous red light district of St Pauli (Hamburg's answer to Soho only somehow more decadent). The ports of **Travemünde**, near Lübeck (the home of marzipan) and **Warnemünde**, in the former East Germany, are both primarily departure points for visiting **Berlin**, either by coach or train. They are much closer than Hamburg, with journey times of little more than an hour. Both Bremerhaven and Hamburg are busily investing in new cruise facilities to attract more ships in future.

Don't miss: any full-day excursion to Berlin. It is steeped in twentieth-century European history yet also possesses some very modern touches like its shops and the Berlin Zoo. The Wall, of course, no longer exists to any real extent, but famous locations like Checkpoint Charlie can still be seen (albeit now as a museum).

Estonia

The strong medieval appearance and history of **Tallinn**, the capital of this former Soviet Baltic state, which maintains its own traditions proudly in the face of centuries of foreign domination, is well worth pencilling in to your must-see list, via the port of Muuga. The so-called 'City of Colours' is an immaculately preserved fourteenth-century treasure trove of gilded churches, palaces and winding streets, and boasts the nearby lovely **Kadriorg Park** and Palace, with its State Art Museum.

Don't miss: the Town Hall Square, the focal point of Old Tallinn, and the chance to sip the local strong, black coffee while marvelling at the glorious architecture.

Latvia

Swan Hellenic, Fred Olsen and Princess were the only lines offering the Latvian capital of **Riga** in 2001 which is a shame as it is another of the Hanseatic League (a trading alliance of the thirteenth century) cities, together with Tallinn, Lubeck, Hamburg and Bremen, which means more medieval ancestry and architecture and a rich sense of history and northern European culture. The **Dome Cathedral**, dating back to 1211, and **Riga Castle**, housing three museums, can be taken in on a general walk around the city; this can be accomplished quite easily under your own steam and in relative safety (although it is still advisable to leave valuables on the ship).

Don't miss: the Old Quarter, where whole squares and terraces of seventeenth-century buildings have been preserved.

Russia

In a similar vein to Tallinn, and also still largely unscarred by modern development, is the main Russian Baltic port city of **St Petersburg**, which is a practically compulsory stop on Baltic Sea cruises. It offers a wealth of historical and architectural delights, with the world-famous **Hermitage Museum** and the **Palace of Peterhof** the jewels in the crown. The **Summer Palace** at **Petrodvorets** is another worthwhile excursion, while, as many calls now stop overnight, it is also possible to take in an evening ballet or concert performance – and come out to find it is still light thanks to Russia's summer White Nights.

TRAVEL TIP

There is increasingly a crime risk with visits to most Russian cities these days and St Petersburg is no exception. Wandering around on your own (you would need to have applied for an individual visa in the first place) is not advisable, and you are best advised to stick to ship-organised excursions. You will also be hassled by street traders who are desperate to get their hands on foreign currency.

In addition to the wonderful blend of Russian and Western European architecture (created at the demands of Peter the Great in 1703 as his 'Window on Europe'), the **Nevsky Prospektin** boulevard offers some great shopping.

Finland

The capital of **Helsinki** is another of the Baltic's elegant cultural centres, boasting wonderful fish and flower markets all well within a good walk of the docks. Its overall accent is more modern than historical (and, at the same time, superbly well kept), but the **Senate Square** is impressively old-fashioned, with its Cathedral of St Nicholas, Government Palace and Rock Church of Temppeliakuio.

Sweden

The typical cruise itinerary of Baltic capitals will also probably take in **Stockholm** and some more clean, refined Scandinavian charm. The old town of **Den Gamle Stan** is a maze of narrow streets and neat little shops, usually chock-full of amusing street performers, and is ideal for a casual wander for a couple of hours. Ship excursions also take in the Royal Palace, Old House of Parliament, the restored historic seventeenth-century warship Vasa, and its attendant museum, and occasionally the beautiful Drottningholm Palace and Theatre.

Don't miss: the early-morning cruise through the thousands of islands that choke the entrance to Stockholm's harbour.

Denmark

If it's Denmark it must be **Copenhagen**, and frequently another late-night stop to enjoy the full range of features of this lively city. Tivoli Gardens is a prime attraction with its old-world but quite thrill-based amusement park, as are Rosenborg Castle (home of the Danish crown jewels), the palaces of Christiansborg and Amalienborg, and the harbour area where Hans Christian Andersen wrote some of his fairy tales. Shop in the Stroget district, the longest traffic-free street in Europe, and tour the Carlsberg Brewery. The best port in the Baltic? Probably.

Don't miss: Tivoli Gardens at night if your ship stays late enough (many now do).

Norway

Oslo is often the final port of call on the Baltic route and will complete a fascinating tour of the Scandinavian countries in fine style. Once described to me by a Norwegian friend as 'the largest village in the world', Oslo retains the small-scale atmosphere with a clean-city culture that offers friendliness and charm in abundance (if at an outrageous price sometimes if you stop for a beer or even just a coffee). Art-lovers will want to check out the many galleries (and art shops), history buffs the twelfth-century medieval fortress of Akershus (which also houses a moving Second World War museum) and marine enthusiasts the fine collection of maritime archives, including the Viking Ship Museum and Thor Heyerdahl's Kon Tiki Museum, as well as the nearby Norwegian Folk Museum. You can also take a local train (Metro 1) to Holmenkollen for an overview of Oslofjord and a mind-boggling close-up of the ski jump. Add in the unique Vigelund Sculpture Park, the world's largest collection of outdoor sculptures, by Gustav Vigelund, and you have more than enough for any ship visit (or two).

Don't miss: Oslo.

TRAVEL TIP

While the summer weather in northern Europe is usually pleasant and warm, it makes good sense to take a sweater or two, plus a waterproof jacket for the fjords.

Norway is also popular for its utterly spectacular fjord coastline up into the Arctic Ocean, which can easily be a cruise in its own right. You start at **Bergen**, with its huge fish and flower market, quaint streets and colourful wooden houses. The Bryggen district is essential tourist fare, with its restored wooden buildings and alleyways, while the Floibanen funicular railway is another must-see attraction for a fabulous view over the whole area. You can also visit the home of the great composer Edvard

Grieg at nearby Troldhaugen, or take a flight over neighbouring Bjoernefjord and the glacier at Folgefonna. The next port of call might be the magnificent **Hardangerfjord**, with the tiny orchard village of **Ulvik** tucked in the top corner, framed by the mountainous interior. The fjord cruise then works its way steadily north taking in the increasingly picturesque sights of the mighty **Sognefjord** (Norway's largest), with its attendant picture-postcard villages of **Flaam** and **Gudvangen**, the impossibly steep **Geirangerfjord** (rated Norway's most scenic) flanked by the Seven Sisters and Bridal Veil waterfalls, **Storfjord**, offering a bus ride up the Eid River to the Mabodal Canyon and the roaring Voringfoss Waterfall, past Norway's third city of **Trondheim** (where you can see Nidaros Cathedral, the largest medieval building in Norway and the wooden church at the Trondelag Museum), and up into the Land of the Midnight Sun. Here you will find the ports of **Narvik** (from where you can catch a train into neighbouring Lapland and visit reindeer country), **Harstad** and **Tromsø** and the truly magnificent **Hollandsfjord** and **Ofotfjord** before reaching the North Cape, and the tiny fishing village of **Honnigsvåg**, from where a bus ride takes you 21 miles through the bleak Arctic tundra to the top of the 1,000-foot cliff that marks the northernmost end of mainland Europe.

Don't miss: the Flaam railway ride to Gudvangen, or the sight of the sun not setting at night in the Arctic circle.

Ireland

From the roof of Europe it is possible to sail back across the British Isles to take in arguably the newest, most surprising and eager-to-please cruise destination. The likes of Seabourn, Cunard, Silversea, Royal Caribbean, NCL, Hapag-Lloyd and Holland America have now put Ireland firmly on the cruise map, and its appeal is growing annually. **Dublin** is, unsurprisingly, the top destination for its scenic beauty and history, a great literary and cultural tradition and downright hard-to-beat hospitality, notably in the Temple Bar district.

Don't miss: the Jury's Hotel Irish cabaret or just the chance to sup a pint of real Guinness in the excellent Guinness Brewery Museum.

Cork is another historic city, with passengers able to disembark from the cruise terminal straight into the Cobh Heritage Centre. It again offers the chance to wander some ancient – as well as quite modern – streets, while Blarney Castle is only five miles away. **Waterford** is Ireland's fastest-growing port, with a new £30million development paving the way for increased cruise traffic. The quaint streets and elegant shops, two great cathedrals and the adjacent Kennedy Park are all good reasons to visit.

Don't miss: the Waterford Crystal factory and the chance to buy some of their wonderful glassware at bargain prices.

Londonderry, in Northern Ireland, is possibly the biggest surprise, with the spectacular journey along the rugged Donegal coastline into River Foyle just the precursor to a city which boasts Europe's only completely walled centre, dating back to 1618. The inner city is a wealth of shops, galleries, restaurants and museums, not to mention the occasional pub (and, again, their hospitable nature is hard to overlook), with the Tower Museum in particular winning numerous awards for its audio-visual displays.

THE CARIBBEAN

Who goes there?

Airtours, Carnival, Celebrity, Clipper Cruise Line, Costa, Crystal, Cunard, Disney, Festival, Holland America, Mediterranean Shipping, NCL, Fred Olsen, P&O, Princess, Radisson Seven Seas, Renaissance, Royal Caribbean, Royal Olympic, Saga, Seabourn, Silversea, Star Clippers, Windstar

Cruise season: year-round

The world's biggest cruise playground has been a going concern for more than 30 years and is by far the most tried and trusted product on the cruise holiday shelves. Sunshine is virtually guaranteed, the islands are the stuff of Bounty bar adverts, people are generally amiable and relaxed and the cruise ships themselves are usually the most modern and user-friendly to make sure of attracting the American market, which accounts for MILLIONS of passengers every year. As with other areas of the world, the search is on for new ports, particularly home ports, and new itineraries, like Belize and Venezuela. As a consequence, some ports like San Juan in Puerto Rico are becoming quite congested with cruise traffic, and some of the bigger islands on the main routes can be equally busy when several 70,000-ton-plus ships are in port. Airtours have tried to avoid this particular problem by basing their winter Caribbean operation on Barbados and Jamaica, with Thomson opting for the Dominican Republic. Happily, there are still plenty of alternatives to the big island congestion, and your choice has never been greater.

The cultural, scenic and geographic diversity is also huge, from the mountainous Spanish-American Puerto Rico to the flat, arid Dutch isles of Aruba and Curaçao, from the traditionally British Barbados to the Rastafarian Jamaica, and from the Bahamas off the coast of Florida right down to the Venezuelan coast of South America. In fact, the Caribbean is a huge cultural melting pot, soaking up as it has done for more than 300 years the influences of Spain, Holland, France and Denmark as well as Britain, often in quite violent fashion. The climate, of course, boasts a consistently warm, tropical nature, varying in temperature from 27°C/80°F to 38°C/100°F (so remember to take those high-factor sun creams), and gives rise to plenty of rich vegetation as well as being the perfect environment for a host of activities, from water sports to bird-watching. When it comes to food and drink, there is also an abundance of choice, from pina colada (the national drink of Puerto Rico), daiquiris (first mixed on St Thomas, claim the locals) and the ever-present rum (mixed with fresh-ground nutmeg on Grenada), to paella (Puerto Rico again), rijstaffel (an Indonesian dish popular on the Dutch Islands), curries (Trinidad) and creole cooking (with a festival every August on Guadeloupe). Fresh fruit is also universal, while the whole experience comes topped off with a diversity of music – salsa, merengue, the beguine, reggae, calypso and steel bands. The lure of the region is manifold.

For the purposes of this book (and most cruise itineraries), the Caribbean is also taken to include the Yucatan peninsula of Mexico and the Panama Canal. The region therefore stretches in an arc some 2,500 miles from the western tip of Cuba, just 90 miles off the Florida Keys, down to the last islands of Trinidad and Tobago and the coast of Venezuela. It consists of the Greater Antilles (the largest islands of Cuba, Haiti, the Dominican Republic, Jamaica, Puerto Rico and the Caymans) and the Lesser Antilles (the string of smaller islands in a rough semi-circle from the Virgin Islands to Tobago). Barbados is the eastern-most point in the area and is therefore more exposed to the Atlantic weather (hence being one of the Windward Islands), while the Leeward Islands enjoy the tranquil position of the Caribbean Sea.

Cruise capital of the world

The starting point for Caribbean cruises is likely to be either Miami or Fort Lauderdale, just to the north, which account for around five million passengers every year (and rising). **Tampa**, on Florida's Mexican Gulf coast, is actually the state's biggest port, but cruising accounts for only some 16 per cent of its business, while **Port Canaveral**, on the Atlantic coast, a short drive from Orlando, is primarily a short-haul port, although it has expanded considerably with the advent of Disney's cruise operation in 1998, for which a major new terminal was built.

Miami remains 'the cruise capital of the world' simply because of the volume it handles – some three million passengers a year and 14 large ships year-round from no less than 12 well-equipped (if rather functional) terminals. The new terminal for Royal Caribbean's massive *Voyager* and *Explorer of the Seas* is three times larger than any other anywhere else. The port is only a short taxi ride from the international airport and is also well situated to be able to enjoy the attractions of the rest of the Miami area (see below). **Port Everglades** (Fort Lauderdale) has enjoyed a massive growth in cruise business in the 1990s, almost doubling its volume to become the world's second busiest cruise port, and welcoming some of the newest, most up-market tonnage on the Caribbean runs (Princess, Celebrity and Holland America are all regulars here). Eleven modern cruise terminals, including a near-£3-million investment in Terminal Two for the arrival of the new *Sun Princess* in 1995, another £7 million on Terminal 18 in 1997 (America's largest passenger facility) plus £7 million more on improving Terminals 19, 21 and 25 by the end of 1999, and superb links with the international airport of **Fort Lauderdale** (avoiding the usual congestion and hassle at Miami) make for a slick cruise operation. Airtours also offer a direct flight here that links up with several Carnival cruises, notably the two seven-day Caribbean voyages on the new 103,000-ton *Carnival Triumph*.

In keeping with its 'cruise capital' tag, **Miami** and its surrounding beaches are a great add-on to any Caribbean cruise, offering some outstanding attractions, great shopping and nightlife and some fabulous sports opportunities. The **Art Deco district** of South Beach is Miami's main claim to fame, a series of streets surviving from the classic 1930s architecture style, and a real happening area, too. **Ocean Drive** is classic background scenery from many episodes of Miami Vice, a street of hotels, restaurants and bars that attracts all the bright young things morning, afternoon and evening (especially the evening, when it really hums with party spirit until the early hours of the morning). A 15-mile string of white-sand **beaches** – Miami's second most famous feature – sprawl northwards from here and offer plenty of opportunities for a relaxing time pre or post-cruise. The **Seaquarium** at Key Biscayne is another top-rated attraction, an exciting family day out with a fascinating array of sights, from shark-feeding to dolphin and sea-lion shows. For **shopping**, Miami boasts a superb line-up of smart malls, purpose-built tourist traps and some really up-market developments, like the **Bal Harbour** shops with designer names such as Gucci, Cartier and Chanel. When it comes to **sport,** Miami can thrill you with NBA **basketball** (Miami Heat), **American Football** (Miami Dolphins), **ice-hockey** (Florida Panthers) and the great game of **baseball** (Florida Marlins), as well as being home to some spectacular **golf** courses. Downtown Miami offers the chance to ride the Metromover overhead tramway, to go shopping in Burdines (the oldest and largest department store in Florida) and have lunch at Bayside, a lovely harbour-front collection of shops, restaurants and bars, including Miami's Hard Rock Café. You can also take a boat tour from **Bayside** around the miles of waterways that circle the city. Two other areas that should be on your must-see list are **Coconut Grove**, a lively shopping and nightlife development that has quite a chic, European feel to it, and the up-market suburb of **Coral Gables**, where you will find the beautiful Venetian Pool and the outstanding Biltmore Hotel – perfect for afternoon tea.

Don't miss: Coconut Grove at night, South Beach at any time, and the fun water-taxi rides during the day.

TRAVEL TIP

Crime is a concern in Miami, but common sense is your best defence. Don't go wandering off the beaten track at night and be aware that some fairly run-down areas of this multi-cultural city exist almost side by side with the glamorous ones.

If Miami is just too hectic and, well, American, for the land-based element of your holiday (and many lines now offer a week's stay on top of a week's cruising out of Port Everglades), **Fort Lauderdale** should suit you right down to the ground. This wonderful resort town has altogether a more relaxed air than its neighbour to the south. There are still great **beaches** to be lounged on and great **nightlife** for the younger holiday-maker, but Fort Lauderdale also boasts some sophisticated elements like the **Museum of Art, Museum of Discovery and Science** (the latter is particularly suited to children with enquiring minds), **Center for the Performing Arts** and **IMAX cinema**. **Shopping** is again first class, from the massive discount mall of **Sawgrass Mills**, to the Galleria complex. In addition, **Las Olas Boulevard** offers some smart, boutique-type shops with a dazzling array of individual arts and crafts, plus some of the most enticing restaurants in South Florida. As in Miami, you can take a wonderful water-borne tour of the area, and the **water-taxis** operate conveniently to most parts of the city. For the chance to sample some real native Florida countryside, the **Everglades** are not far inland and there are plenty of opportunities to investigate under your own steam or simply take an organised excursion that will pick you up from, and return you to, your hotel. Fort Lauderdale boasts a fine collection of Superior Small Lodgings (call the Visitors' Bureau on 954 765 4466 for details), while two of the more up-market properties are Marriott's **Harbor Beach Resort** (tel 954 525 4000) and the **Marriott Marina** (tel 954 463 4000), both with first-class facilities and convenient for the port.

Don't miss: Las Olas Boulevard at night, an Everglades airboat ride and, if you are in town in December, the glittering spectacle of the annual Winterfest Boat Parade.

Any Caribbean cruise that sails out of Miami or Fort Lauderdale will be likely to include a call at the **Bahamas** as either its opening or finishing port. This ultra-Americanised group of 700 islands (of which little more than 20 are inhabited) is a major beach holiday resort and, as such, can be incredibly busy during the main holiday periods of Christmas, Easter and summer. Visiting cruise ships are allowed to keep their casinos and gift shops open as an extra incentive to offset higher port taxes, and that gives a hint as to some of the principal attractions – duty-free shopping and gambling (which both draw the Americans like bees round a honey pot). The main resort areas tend to be high-rise and very modern, with some distinctly ordinary tourist shopping, not exactly what the Caribbean is renowned for, but the main town and harbour of **Nassau** does maintain some of its original charm and could not be more convenient to explore on foot from the docks (if you can battle through the seeming hordes of taxi drivers and tacky street vendors who throng the area). The islands boast little in the way of attractions outside the beach resorts and the towns of Nassau and Freeport (the alternative, or sometimes second, Bahamas port of call), so unless you fancy one of the raucous rum party catamaran cruises, a beach party or a fairly unnecessary town tour, save your organised excursions for elsewhere. The marine menagerie of **Coral World** on New Providence (Nassau's island – Freeport is on Grand Bahama) is worth a visit, as is the luxuriant **Garden of the Groves** and **Bahamas Museum** in Freeport. Blue Lagoon Island offers the increasingly popular chance to meet Flipper and Co, up close and personal, in their memorable **dolphin encounter**.

The **Greater Antilles** will usually be next on the agenda from the Bahamas. **Cuba** is by far the biggest island, but as it remains politically at loggerheads with the US, no American-based cruise ship will visit it. The political situation in **Haiti** tends to keep the cruise lines away from here, too, although Royal Caribbean do have a private beach set-up at **Labadee**, a tiny island off the north coast of Haiti. The **Dominican Republic**, which forms the other half of the island mass of Hispaniola with Haiti, is one of those on the list of places to be 'discovered' by the majority of cruise lines as its tourist infrastracture is still limited mainly to beach-orientated pursuits. Thomson use it as a winter base for *Emerald*, offering an attractive series of seven- and 14-day cruises that can include Venezuela, Grenada and Trinidad. There is still the charming old city of **Santo Domingo** to explore (the republic's capital, and the oldest city in the New World) with its sixteenth-century cathedral and other relics of the Christopher Columbus era, while the resort of **Casa de Campo**, with its adjacent port of **La Romanna**, is world-renowned for its full range of sports facilities.

Don't miss: shopping for amber anywhere on the island.

TRAVEL TIP

Not for nothing is El Yunque in Puerto Rico called a RAINforest so be prepared for some major precipitation – it can experience more than 60 *inches* (144 centimetres) of rain a month in the wet season from August to November! And, when walking around San Juan, keep your valuables secure as petty crime is on the increase.

The large tropical rain-forested island of **Puerto Rico** boasts just the main port of **San Juan**, which is now as much a starting point as a port of call along the way. Its heavy commercialism makes it fairly unremarkable and a bit like any other major Spanish resort you care to mention (with heavy American overtones), but the saving grace of the **Old Town**, which can easily be explored on foot, and the chance to take an excursion to the rain-forest of **El Yunque** still make San Juan worth a visit.

Don't miss: the seventeenth-century fortress of San Cristobal in the Old Town on your self-guided tour.

Jamaica has been at the centre of the Caribbean cruise business right from the word go and it remains popular, although the island has its share of crime problems, which it is attempting to deal with as an urgent tourist issue, as its increasing poverty-stricken areas do not sit easily with the wealth brought in by foreign visitors. The capital **Kingston**, an infrequent port of call, is not the place to go wandering on your own, and organised excursions generally are much the safer option. **Ocho Rios** is increasingly the main port of call to take in the spectacular **Dunn's River Falls**, the classic Jamaican postcard, where you can climb up the 600-foot falls provided you remembered to pack your swimsuit and some trainers that you don't mind getting wet. Yacht cruising, rafting and visits to the **Prospect Plantation** are the other recommended excursions, while the alternative port of **Montego Bay** offers some superb beach resorts (try Doctor's Cave Beach) and local crafts in the town, where you can expect to be pestered by the many vendors (who also wander the beaches – so keep your valuables safe or, better still, leave them on the ship). Finally, if you leave Jamaica without being offered ganja or 'waccy baccy' you haven't really seen the island!

The nearby **Cayman Islands** are almost the direct opposite of feisty Jamaica – courteous, almost reserved and quite sophisticated. Not for nothing is **Grand Cayman** known as the Switzerland of the Caribbean. It is well-organised and currency-conscious, but delivers great value for money, some wonderfully picturesque views around the main town of **George Town** and its beaches (notably **Seven Mile Beach**) and, more importantly, some of the best underwater viewing in the Caribbean. Whether you take the **Atlantis Submarine** trip or are adventurous enough to go snorkelling or scuba-diving, this is the must-see attraction of Grand Cayman. The Cayman Wall reefs are the most famous feature, along with Stingray City – an area of North Sound barely 12 feet deep where you can snorkel among the menacing (but totally harmless) rays. An unforgettable experience, but not for the faint-hearted. Grand Cayman also boasts the world's only commercial **Green Turtle Farm**, which helps to play a part in the conservation of this species, but doesn't hold back from offering a whole array of turtle dishes. No turtle products can be imported into Britain, by the way. Coach tours also stop off at the weird rock formations of **Hell** – now here's somewhere to buy the T-shirt.

Any voyage to the western Caribbean (especially popular with the four-day winter and spring cruises) is also likely to take in the part of **Mexico** which sticks out into the Caribbean, the Yucatan Peninsula. Here, the three main resort ports are all highly Americanised and can be incredibly busy, but they do offer another different cultural experience. The island of **Cozumel** is the most frequent port of call for some brilliant snorkelling and shopping (the latter of which has all but submerged the original Mexican settlement), and it is often combined with a stop at mainland **Playa del Carmen**, from where it is possible to take a tour to the Mayan Ruins of **Tulum** or **Chichen Itza**, which features some impressive towering temples. **Cancún** is a modern, purpose-built beach resort and has little in common with the rest of the region, but it is also slightly closer to Chichen Itza to avoid the six-hour round trip from Playa del Carmen.

The **Virgin Islands** are more or less at the centre of the Caribbean for cruise purposes (and also mark the beginning of the **Lesser Antilles**), and the **US Virgin Islands** (St Thomas, St John and St Croix) are an almost obligatory port of call for American ships. Up to 10 vessels at a time fill the harbour and disgorge their passengers into the streets of **Charlotte Amalie** and the biggest duty-free shopping frenzy in the Caribbean. Visit **Mountain Top** for an overview of **St Thomas** and sip a banana daiquiri at the world-famous Banana Daiquiri Bar while you look down on

Magens Bay, frequently listed among the Top Ten most beautiful beaches in the world. St Thomas and **St Croix** (the Americans pronounce it St Croy) are unfailingly American, right down to the fast-food restaurants and hotel resorts, but that does not necessarily make it a Bad Thing – the people, and taxi drivers in particular, are always polite and helpful and crime is not a problem here as it is on some islands. A visit to **St John** is also worthwhile as much of it is designated National Park, including some 5,600 acres under water. This means great, unspoilt beaches (including another Top Tenner, **Trunk Bay**) and superb snorkelling and scuba-diving. If the US Virgins still sound a bit too much for European tastes, Tortola and Virgin Gorda – the **British Virgin Islands** – will have more appeal. The lack of tourist development is quite striking in comparison to St Thomas, and the atmosphere is altogether more rustic and laid-back. **Virgin Gorda** offers the **Baths**, another stunning area for underwater exploration, while Tortola is just drop-dead tropical island pretty. The main port, **Road Town**, will keep you amused for an hour or two's gentle wander – longer if you happen to stop off at Pusser's Company Store and make the mistake of over-sampling their near-lethal rum concoctions! It has real Brit-appeal, even this far from home, and Pusser's is also a great place to stop for a bite to eat and to buy some unique souvenirs.

Don't miss: snorkelling at the Baths and a drink at Pusser's.

Running down the rest of the Lesser Antilles islands is like a trip through all the wonders of paradise, and this is the essential Caribbean that people usually think of whenever you mention the area. **St Kitt's, Montserrat, Antigua, Barbuda, Martinique, St Lucia** – the names are just as evocative as the places themselves. Here is where it is most tempting to choose an itinerary that gets you to as many of them as possible. That is fine if you have a two-week cruise and can enjoy seven or eight ports in that time, but a typical seven-day cruise that tries to fit in six or seven ports of call can be overdoing it just a bit, even in this eye-catching playground. The differences in style and appearance are not that great along this stretch, and it can all become a bit of a blur if you try to do too much, hence the frequently-heard remark that one Caribbean island looks much like another. Well, they would if you have six or seven successive island tours with little time to enjoy the distinguishing features.

Starting at the top, **St Martin/St Maarten** is split into French and Dutch portions, hence the twin name. For a tiny island (just 37 square miles) it has packed in a lot of tourist development, and the French/Dutch split makes for contrasting experiences, with the Dutch capital and port of **Phillipsburg** offering more rampant, unashamed commercialism à la St Thomas, while **Marigot** in the French area is distinctly more laid-back and authentic, with a colourful market. The French side boasts the best of some super beaches (check out Orient Bay for great sun-bathing and watersports), as well as the lovely Butterfly Farm, which always goes down well with younger children. **St Barthelémy** is a little-visited French outpost that offers the chic town of **Gustavia** and a wonderful walk up to **Les Castelets** for an overview of this uncrowded, unhurried island. **St Kitt's**, and its smaller volcanic twin neighbour of Nevis, is one of the former British colonies in the Caribbean that still has overtones of the colonial days as well as some of the most genuine Caribbean charm in the whole region. Fabulous beaches, friendly people, good shopping and lovely walks around the capital and port of **Basseterre** make this a real gem.

Don't miss: a trip to the 37-acre, seventeenth-century fortress at Brimstone Hill.

Antigua, another former British colony, is all about great beaches (the locals claim there are 365, one for every day of the year), great water sports (including a world-famous yachting festival every April) and great cricket. But you can also step back in time with a visit to the well-preserved 18th century Nelson's Dockyard, home of the British Caribbean fleet through some amazingly turbulent times. **Guadeloupe** returns to French-Caribbean style and is split into two halves, with the city of **Point-à-Pitre** dominating one half and the other boasting the unmissable lush rainforest of the **Parc Naturel**. The island features some of the best creole cooking in the world in numerous little restaurants dotted around, some of which are actually people's homes! Stop at the tourist information office at the **Place de la Victoire** for up-to-the-minute details on where to eat. Costa's *CostaClassica* and Festival's *Mistral* also use Guadeloupe as an imaginative winter home-port.

Dominica (not to be confused with the Dominican Republic in the Greater Antilles) is verdant, natural and still home to a large population of Carib Indians who were all but wiped out by the European colonists of the sixteenth and seventeenth centuries. A ship-organised tour is a good idea here as roads are poor and there are many picturesque corners to see, like **Trafalgar Falls** and its bubbling mud lake, and the glittering waterfall at **Morne Trois Pitons**. **Martinique** is more chic French-Caribbean culture, with its neat town of Fort-de-France and some elegant shopping.

Don't miss: the site of Mont Pelée, the largest volcanic eruption in the Caribbean, which killed more than 30,000 islanders in a mind-boggling explosion in 1902.

St Lucia boasts the world's only drive-in volcano (!) and sulphur springs at **Soufrière**, which is also a fascinating little town where some of the smaller cruise ships occasionally call. The big liners put in at Castries, with its smart new port facilities and inviting duty-free shops. Here you can take a catamaran trip to beautiful **Marigot Bay**, where the musical *Dr Doolittle* was filmed. **St Vincent** is the largest island of the little Grenadines, which include the exclusive **Mustique**, playground of the rich and famous. Kingstown is the vibrant capital, while the **Mesopotamia Valley** offers a long, rich tropical flora experience.

Don't miss: St Vincent Botanical Gardens, the oldest in the western hemisphere (dating back to the eighteenth century), for a fantastic collection of the weird and wonderful in the world of vegetation.

Little **Bequia** is an occasional Grenadines port of call, with its charming town of **Port Elizabeth**, and is also the gateway for boat tours to some of the many splendid beach islands that dot the vicinity. Princess Cruises (and, hence, British parent company P&O) have their own exclusive beach resort development on the private island of **Mayreau**, which makes for another pleasant diversion. Star Clippers offer scintillating seven and 14-day cruises featuring the best of the Grenadines.

TRAVEL TIP

The two coastlines of Barbados are vastly different. The east is rugged, Atlantic Ocean territory, not recommended for swimming but great for surfers, while the western shores are sandy and tranquil.

Out to the east, largely on its own, sits **Barbados**, which epitomises much of what is good about the Caribbean. Its desperately English-tinged culture, right down to Trafalgar Square and Nelson's Column in the capital **Bridgetown** (and they actually pre-date the versions in London), is still hugely appealing, and there are some great shops and restaurants (you have to try the local delicacy – flying fish, either grilled or in a sandwich) to be explored. A half-day tour isn't a bad idea here, either, as there is a lot of ground to cover, including the **Andromeda Gardens** and **Animal Flower Cave** in the north, the **Tropical Flower Forest** and **Barbados Wildlife Preserve** in the middle and some magnificent old **Plantation Houses** in the south and east, plus the memorable **Harrison's Cave**. Tours of the local distilleries are definitely overrated unless you are really into rum. The downside of Barbados is the worrying level of petty crime and the hassle of street (and beach) urchins, trying to offer you taxis or souvenirs you really wouldn't want if they were giving them away. A firm but polite 'No thanks!' is the best policy as the majority are perfectly harmless, just very poor. For shopping, the **Da Costas Mall** provides a good cross-section of what the island has to offer.

Grenada, or 'the Spice Island of the Caribbean', sits to the south of the Grenadines and boasts another of the region's most spectacular beaches, **Grande Anse**. Souvenir hunting is enjoyable and, for once, relatively hassle-free, and you will have to sample the local nutmeg-spiced rum cocktails at some point, which tend to add a picturesque haze to everything!

Don't miss: the morning arrival in the port and capital of **St George's**, one of the prettiest harbours in the Caribbean, and a wander around the town's historic warehouses and homes.

Trinidad and its smaller attendant isle of Tobago offer a different experience yet again, with quite a rich, bustling ambience that stems from its wealth as an oil producer. The main town of **Port-of-Spain** is the most highly-developed in the Caribbean and boasts an eclectic mix of architecture, bustling markets, and the wide open spaces of **Queen's Park Savannah**, ringed by the 'Magnificent Seven' mansions. Its tourism has been carefully developed along ecologically-friendly lines and offers such attractions as the **Caroni Bird Sanctuary** and **Maracas Bay**, with its 'Skyline Highway' scenic road from Port-of-Spain.

Don't miss: Asa Wright Nature Centre, an old plantation house-turned-hotel set in a forest preserve boasting some stunning birdlife.

Tobago is smaller, prettier and so sedate it is practically at a standstill compared to the rest of the world. That makes it the perfect place to 'chill out' and enjoy the great beaches, notably **Pigeon Point**.

Completing the full Caribbean sweep are the Dutch Antilles islands of **Aruba**, **Bonaire** and **Curaçao**, a trio of wind-swept, almost desert-like out-crops just north of the Venezuelan coast. The colourful port of **Oranjestad** in Aruba is handy to explore from the harbour (and offers some good shopping in the nearby malls), but the rest of the island itself is pretty arid and spartan, unless you are attracted by cacti and masses of windblown, oddly-shaped divi-divi trees. The beaches are still wonderful, though, especially **Eagle** and **Palm** on the west coast. Aruba's annual **Carnival** (in the month before Lent) is also well worth catching. Tiny Bonaire has invested in a pedestrian promenade of shops and cafés primarily for cruise visitors, while also boasting some superb scuba-diving. Curaçao is the largest and easily most impressive of the three, with the fabulous harbour of **Willemstad** boasting some picture-perfect houses along the waterfront and a floating market that sails over daily from South America, with a new state-of-the-art cruise terminal under way. Ships tie up right opposite the town centre, which is then reached by a short walk across the Queen Emma pontoon bridge that opens and closes to admit harbour traffic, a fascinating sight (have your camera ready for arrival and departure). Great shopping can be found in town, while the **Chobolobo Mansion** on the outskirts offers the chance to sample the many varieties of the sweet liqueur that takes its name from the island itself. More great snorkelling and diving is the feature of the **Underwater Marine Park**, while **Christoffel National Park**, a 4,500-acre garden and wildlife park, is the best scenic offering of all three islands, with a wonderful all-round view from the top of Mt Christoffel.

Don't miss: Curaçao Seaquarium for some well-displayed marine environments, some larger creatures like sea-lions, glass-bottomed boat rides and a small beach.

The Caribbean coast of South America also offers cruise ships some attractive ports of call and another dimension to a voyage around these parts, hence **Venezuela** and **Colombia** can expect to become featured on more itineraries in the next few years. As the tourist numbers increase, so does petty crime in the cities of **Caracas** and **Cartagena**, and here you are best advised to take a ship excursion and not to wander off on your own (especially as not all taxi drivers will speak English). Shorts, especially for women, are also frowned upon. **La Guaira** is the port for Caracas and is a busy commercial docks, so don't expect a pretty, scenic outlook. The tours into Caracas will feature the old colonial city centre, **Plaza Bolivar**, with its city hall, cathedral and statue of Simon Bolivar, and the **Boulton Museum**, housed in a restored plantation mansion with a fine collection of period paintings, documents and other artifacts.

Outside the old historic centre, the city is an exceedingly busy, modern conurbation, with a lot of high-rise development and not much thought to the overall visual impact – a bit of a mess. Alternatively, a few ships offer an (expensive) trip by plane to the spectacular **Angel Falls**, the world's highest, and the awesome **Canaima Lagoon**. The prosperous Colombian city of Cartagena is the jewel in that country's Caribbean coastline, boasting a fascinating old city, full of narrow streets, cute shops and small forts and museums, a lively, modern centre, a seventeenth-century monastery that provides a terrific overview of the city and some magnificent beaches and coastline in either direction. Tourism is gradually becoming a more recognised facet of Colombia's make-up, and the next year or two could be a good time to visit if it really takes off as a major destination for both Europe and America.

Finally, edging along the outline of South America, the last key destination in this part of the world is one of the most outstanding anywhere in the cruise ship itinerary, the **Panama Canal**. As I have already mentioned, the canal is primarily a linear cruise choice, from Fort Lauderdale, Miami or Puerto Rico through to Acapulco or Los Angeles, or vice versa, but there are a few circular options that feature a canal mini-cruise that does not go all the way through, but stops at the mid-point **Gatun Lake** and then returns to the home port. Either way you will experience one of the modern wonders of the world, a 50-mile, all-day crossing that goes 'up' over central America through a series of locks barely wide enough to admit the largest ships and 'down' again into the Pacific Ocean using a series of 'mules' (small trains) to pull the vessels into each lock. The whole process is accompanied by a running commentary over the ship's loudspeakers by a locally-supplied guide, who will astound you with the facts and figures of this awesome operation. There are no ports of call as such associated with the Canal, but a few ships now visit the coral **San Blas Islands**, just to the east of the Caribbean entrance. The San Blas are home to the Cuna Indians, who enjoy having their pictures taken in their elaborate national dress (for a price, of course – each snap will cost you about $2). It is therefore primarily a cultural experience, although there is also the chance to pick up some unique souvenirs, including the brilliantly coloured molas blouses worn by the Cuna women.

THE US WEST COAST
(including the Mexican Riviera and Alaska)
Who goes there?

Carnival, Celebrity, Clipper Cruise Line, Crystal, Holland America, NCL, Princess, Radisson Seven Seas, Royal Caribbean, Seabourn, Silversea

Cruise season: Mexican Riviera – year-round. Alaska – May-September

There are two distinct regions to the cruise world on America's West Coast, and they differ in almost every aspect of attraction, from climate and scenery to duration, passenger profile and even the hardware involved. The **Mexican Riviera** run from Los Angeles is the fast-food version of cruising: cheap, cheerful and primarily for the young crowd. The ports of call, from the Baja Peninsula (otherwise known as Baja California, but don't be fooled, this is all South of the Border) down to the big Mexican resort of Acapulco, are purely an exercise in shopping, beaches and water sports. Fun they may be, but cultural they ain't. In fact, the three- and four-day Riviera cruises are geared almost totally towards the Californian market, and the average age can be below 30 at times. Also, while the season generally is a year-long one, the busiest months are November to March, with April to October becoming the distinctly cheaper off-season.

≋ TRAVEL TIP ≋

When in Mexico, think Spanish – *don't* drink the water. In fact, unless you can be sure your drink comes out of a bottle, give it a miss altogether. Plenty of ice in a drink is also a Bad Thing – it is only frozen water after all.

Ensenada is the first stop travelling south from Los Angeles, an undistinguished town with a scruffy port. Walk in for an hour, do the shops then head back to the ship, unless you are feeling brave, in which case check out Papas & Beer, a wild, raucous bar popular with the young American crowd. You won't believe how they serve shooters (their potent liqueur mixtures), but try ordering one for your friend and stand well back – you have been warned! (See end of West Coast section for the gory details, if you must.) The purpose-built resort of **Cabo San Lucas** and its town of **San José del Cabo** offer a higher level of sophistication and some crystal-clear waters in which to take a submarine dive or the less adventurous glass-bottomed boat trip. The shopping is more presentable (especially in the markets of the town proper – the main tourist area of **Zona Dorada** is entirely predictable) while deep-sea fishing is a big draw here, too. **Mazatlan** is the biggest city on the true Mexican west coast, with good craft areas for shopping, more fishing opportunities and some good surfing beaches, while you should also watch out for the cliff divers from the main beach wall (although those in Acapulco are more spectacular). **Puerto Vallarta** is more high-rise beach development in the best Costa traditions, while **Manzanillo** is quieter, more laid-back and includes the glittering resort of Las Hadas, where the film 10 was shot. The dual resort of **Ixtapa** and **Zihuatanejo** combines a wonderful expanse of beach (check out Playa La Ropa) and genuine village charm, which comes as a welcome relief after the relentless commercialism.

Finally, **Acapulco** is the big resort centre which stirs the most mixed reaction, either adored by the lively, nightclub crowd or abhorred by those who prefer their resorts less formulaic. Whatever, it is a wonderful port to sail into, it offers some more fabulous beaches and unquestionably lively nightlife, the cliff-divers at **La Quebrada** (a short taxi-ride to the west) are a must-see if you have come all this way, and the retail opportunities are enough to keep even the most ardent shopaholics happy. The eighteenth-century fort of **El Fuerte de San Diego** is a welcome diversion away from the more obvious tourist attractions.

However, if you voyage north from Los Angeles, the cruise experience goes through a complete transformation. Through ports like San Francisco, Seattle and Vancouver and up into **Alaska**, this is one of the most dynamic (not to mention increasingly crowded) cruise areas of the world. It is easily the Number Two choice for the American market and, with the possibility of adding on a pre-cruise tour of the Canadian Rockies or a few days' stay in the wonderful city of Vancouver (both of which are big Brit attractions), it has quickly become a popular choice with us as well. As with the Norwegian fjords (and possibly even more so in the case of America's fiftieth State), the main draw is the scenery – bucketloads of it – big, raw, dramatic and, to all intents and purposes, untamed. To get up close (and I mean within a few hundred yards) of one of Alaska's many glaciers, which can be more than 20 miles long, four miles wide and 200 feet high where it slides into the fjord, and watch one of these brilliantly blue-white walls of ice losing huge chunks into the waters (the process called 'calving') is an awesome experience. Add in the lure of wonderful wildlife, from seals, sea otters, the occasional bear and the ever-present golden eagles to killer and humpback whales, and some fascinating ports, and you have a 24-carat-gold cruise experience.

The only real drawbacks with the Alaska run, apart from the big crowds it now pulls, are that the weather can be a touch unreliable early in the season (typically wet and misty along the Inside Passage) and the summer months bring on an attack of mosquitoes in many places. The other off-putting factor, that it is seen primarily for the 50-plus crowd, is steadily being eroded as the region is 'discovered' by the family market, as witnessed by the likes of the ultra-traditional Holland America line laying on children's counsellors and even special kids' shore excursions on many Alaska sailings. It truly is a magnificent mainstream cruise product and the one real worry is the market will become overloaded as the cruise lines try to get more and bigger ships working the area, with a subsequent negative effect on the delicate local eco-systems. Tourism is all very well, but there is no point in destroying the main reason for visiting in the first place, and this is an issue with which the region's various governing bodies are fully involved. The principal attraction of Glacier Bay is a current case in point, as the number of permits that allow ships to sail its breathtaking waters are limited, and the debate is about whether to increase the number of permits to meet lines' increasing demands.

The majority of ships on the Alaskan run use Vancouver as their base port for a series of circular cruises along the Inside Passage as far as Glacier Bay. Just a few (notably Princess, Crystal and Seabourn) offer the opportunity to cruise in linear fashion from Vancouver, San Francisco or Seattle right up to the main city of Anchorage (the port of Seward) and then back again on the next cruise.

TRAVEL TIP

Alaska is one of the few areas of the cruise world where it is worth splashing out on the (admittedly rather expensive) shore excursions. A helicopter flight on to one of the great glaciers is an unforgettable experience, for example.

San Francisco is a marvellous port in which to start (or finish) any cruise, and it offers a wealth of attractions in its own right, especially for visitors from our side of the Atlantic. It has long been one of my favourite US cities, and, with the dock area being surrounded by the wonderful tourist-orientated area of the **Embarcadero**, it offers one of the most scenic and enjoyable ports of call in the world. It is an easy city to negotiate on foot or by the excellent public transport system of trains, buses and the obligatory cable cars, and there is a lot to see, even given a week to try to do it all. Good shopping, museums, sights (including, of course, the Golden Gate Bridge), restaurants (especially in Chinatown) and parks all add up to a wealth of opportunities. North of California, you find the state of Washington and its capital and major port **Seattle**. Many transatlantic flights already operate into here, and then transfer cruise passengers to Vancouver by bus after an overnight stay. A few days in Seattle isn't a bad idea, either, as there is again plenty to do and see here. Historic Pioneer Square, the 74-acre urban park of Seattle Center, the 605-foot Space Needle (complete with revolving restaurant and observation deck at the top), Seattle Aquarium and the busy waterfront are the things to see, while you can also visit the Boeing Assembly Plant (the biggest aircraft-building business in the world), the Maritime and Gold Rush Museums, and tour the surrounding countryside (including the volcanic **Mount St Helens** about two hours' drive from the city) and its charming villages. Its modern, recently up-graded cruise terminal facilities can accommodate some of the biggest ships, with NCL, Holland America and Radisson Seven Seas all now regular visitors, while Royal

Caribbean operate a series of two, three and four-day cruises out of Seattle to Vancouver, Vancouver Island and its wonderfully British centre of Victoria.

Vancouver still remains the Number One port of embarkation for Alaska, and is another city where it is well worth spending some time at either end of your cruise. It is a lively, cosmopolitan city without being at all brash, and Canada's British links mean UK visitors tend to feel rather more at home here than they do in many cities in North America. An attractive downtown area (including the smart cruise facilities of Canada Place and the charming restored old city area of **Gastown**), magnificent **Stanley Park**, some great beaches, sightseeing (including Grouse Mountain by cable car, Capilano River Regional Park and the Royal Hudson steam train to the little town of Squamish), museums (don't miss **Science World** for kids and adults) and nightlife all add up to one of the world's great city experiences. Indeed, if you have both San Francisco and Vancouver on your itinerary, you will need an extra month to see it all.

Ketchikan is the first port of call on the Alaska run proper, and, if you don't need your waterproofs here it is a lucky day indeed. Average annual rainfall is close to 200 inches (480 centimetres) a year – four times that of Britain. But, despite the fact it can be wet and chilly, it gives you your first taste of the frontier country that is Alaska. It is also the totem pole capital of the world, with the opportunity to learn all about the culture of the Tlingit and Tsimshian native inhabitants of the area. Towns like Ketchikan (and virtually all the others on the Alaskan routes) have quickly adapted to the cruise business and have become adept at providing tourists with shopping and souvenir opportunities seemingly at every turn, and here the attraction is the former red light district of Creek Street, built on wooden stilts, with the original buildings converted into trendy boutique shops, while **Dolly's House** remains as a 'museum' to the street's past life. Most ships also offer an (expensive) aerial view of the neighbouring **Misty Fjords National Park** by plane or helicopter, which is another awesome sight if you can afford it.

Don't miss: Totem Bight State Historical Park, an 11-mile taxi ride to the north, with its elaborately-carved ceremonial house and focus on the Tlingit totem pole culture.

Juneau, Alaska's capital, offers a magnificent mountainside setting before you even set foot ashore. Here you can pan for gold (overrated, many find), dine out at a genuine Alaskan salmon bake (and the state is rightly famous for its salmon), raft down the **Mendenhall River** or take a canoe trip on one of the mountain lakes. The town itself offers bags of genuine frontier atmosphere (don't miss the **Red Dog Saloon** and the local Alaskan Amber beer), but the big attraction (and I mean big) is the world's only 'drive-up' glacier, the magnificent **Mendenhall Glacier**, 13 miles out of town. The setting, with its attendant Visitor Center, is one of Alaska's great sights. Once again, if your pocket can stretch to it, the most memorable excursion is a helicopter flight that actually lands you on the glacier. Back on your cruise ship, the nearby **Tracy Arm Fjord** rivals the world-famous Glacier Bay for the most awesome glacier views – this is not the time for your camera to run out of film.

Sitka harks back to Alaska's days as a Russian colony, and even boasts a genuine onion-domed **Russian Orthodox church** (rebuilt after a fire in 1966 as a beautifully restored replica which maintains its authentic atmosphere very well), while the 105-acre **Sitka National Park** is another excellent attraction, with a full historical overview of both Native American and period Russian cultures, all in a beautiful forested parkland setting. The twin towns of **Haines** and **Skagway** are pure mining country, gateway to the Klondike Gold Rushes of 1898, with cleverly re-created shop-fronts giving Skagway in particular a genuine period feel and atmosphere.

Don't miss: the White Pass and Yukon Railway trip up into the breathtakingly scenic mountains.

Wrangell is more off the beaten track of the main Inside Passage run, but was again home to more gold rush stampeders. Visit **Chief Shake's Tribal House**, surrounded by beautiful totem poles, and walk the beach at low tide to see the mysterious petroglyphs (carved ancient stones). **Glacier Bay National Park and Preserve** has no port of call but offers the chance to cruise these fabulous waters, into which pour no less than 16 lofty glaciers. Whales are also commonly sighted here, and a humpback whale breaching (leaping into the air) is one of the most unforgettable sights anywhere in the world.

Passing out of the Inside Passage brings you to the final port of **Seward**, quite often a terminus for the linear cruises, and a bit of a disappointment after all the frontier, period charm of the earlier ports, but still notable for magnificent scenery all around, like the **Kenai Fjords National Park** and **Chugach National Forest**. From here you may transfer to Anchorage for the flight back (or the flight in, if you're only just setting out). **Anchorage** itself, for the lucky few who cruise this far, provides some spectacular views over the 400-square-mile **Columbia Glacier**, the **Kenai Mountains** and inland to volcanic **Mount McKinley**. It is a big, bustling, modern city in the best American traditions where luxury hotels and great shopping are only minutes from true wilderness and historic gold trails. If you have a day or two to spare here, consider a trip to the **Denali National Park**, a semi-tamed wilderness of caribou, grizzly bears, wolves, moose, Dall sheep and other wildlife, with the chance to see sled-dog demonstrations or just hike around the nature trails with a wonderful feeling of utter freedom.

(*Papas & Beer* – the answer. Ordering a shooter is the recipe for instant mayhem to break out as the resident bartender grabs his unsuspecting 'victim' and, with whistles blowing and crowds cheering, proceeds to empty one of his lethal cocktails forcibly down the poor unfortunate's throat and then lift him or her upside down for a violent shaking to get the maximum alcoholic effect. I kid you not. Ugh!)

US EAST COAST
(including Bermuda)
Who goes there?

Carnival, Celebrity, Clipper Cruise Line, Cunard, Hapag-Lloyd, Holland America, NCL, Princess, Royal Caribbean, Seabourn, Silversea

Cruise season: May-October

Not so much a cruise area as a number of attractive destinations loosely grouped together geographically from as far afield as the Atlantic island of Bermuda (not to be confused with the Bahamas or the Caribbean as it sometimes is), some 600 miles out from New York, the coast of New England to the north (especially for the spectacular colours in the autumn), and Canada's Atlantic Maritime area, Nova Scotia, Newfoundland and the historic St Lawrence Seaway. Only a handful of lines operate here, which is a shame as it offers a fresh, uncluttered alternative to Alaska (but without the glaciers), but the big lines like Royal Caribbean, Carnival, Princess and NCL all have a growing presence which indicates it has a big future. It is very much a seasonal offering, with New York and Boston the key home ports.

Bermuda is a collection of some 150 islands, of which only 20 or so are inhabited, and the main island of **Great Bermuda** is always the principal focus and port of call – three ports in fact, as ships tend to sail out here and then spend at least a day or two around the island shuttling between the various harbours. This self-governing British colony enjoys warm summers and boasts some wonderful beaches (around 100 of them) with the attendant attractions of crystal-clear waters for scuba-diving and snorkelling. The number of ship visits is carefully controlled to prevent the small main island (just 21 square miles and with a population of some 55,000) from becoming crowded (as can be the case with the Bahamas and US Virgin Islands), hence the route is always popular and discounts are rare. However, local laws require all ships to suspend their full evening entertainment programmes, with only live music allowed so as not to compete with the island's night-time attractions. Being still typically British (down to playing cricket and having proper pubs), they take a dim view of wearing swimsuits anywhere but the beach and going without a shirt in town or wearing shorts into a restaurant are definite no-nos. For all those little idiosyncrasies, the main island has great charm and poise, with a more structured, refined atmosphere than any you would find in the Caribbean, hence it always goes down well with British visitors. The three main ports are also quite contrasting: the **Royal Dockyard** (King's Wharf) berth is at the westernmost tip and offers authentic shopping and the Bermuda Maritime Museum, which reflects the island's rich naval history; **Hamilton**, the capital, is a shopper's Mecca, especially Front Street which overlooks the harbour; and **St George's**, at the picturesque historic end of the island, is the original capital, offering colonial architecture, churches and several museums. The island also boasts an excellent bus service for getting around cheaply (or bicycle hire for the more energetic) and some spectacular coastline in addition to the beaches, with caves, grottoes and sea arches. For such a tiny land mass, Bermuda has no less than eight courses for golf fans.

Don't miss: the Crystal Caves at Harrington Sound, a bizarre collection of stalagmites and stalactites reaching out into underground sea pools.

Boston is at the centre of most of the cruise itineraries for New England and Canada, and, as such, offers another contrasting big-city experience, with a wonderful range of attractions, from walking tours of the old city (which dates back to the eighteenth century), state-of-the-art museums, opera and ballet, excellent sports, great beaches at Cape Cod, whale-watching mini-cruises and, yes, you can even visit the famous Cheers! bar (just don't expect it to look anything like the TV show internally).

Don't miss: the **Freedom Trail**, a 2½-mile walking tour of 16 of the city's most historic landmarks, including the USS *Constitution* and the Paul Revere House.

From Boston, you voyage north to the fishing villages and ports of the state of Maine. **Boothbay Harbour**, **Rockland** and **Bar Harbour** typify the quaint, almost kitsch, coastal style, with plenty of relatively unspoiled, friendly shops and restaurants (lobster is a Maine speciality), plus the opportunity to take a tour inland to see the splendour of **New England** (the collective area of the north-east states of Maine, New Hampshire, Vermont, Connecticut, Rhode Island and Massachusetts), the great rural hinterland which boasts the spectacular autumn colours in parks like **Acadia National Park**. Moving up into Canadian Nova Scotia brings the must-see port of Halifax, with the second-largest natural harbour in the world and a rich nautical history giving rise to a number of fine museums, including the **Marine Museum of the Atlantic** with its Titanic Exhibit. Check out the historic district along the waterfront and enjoy a sincere level of local hospitality and friendliness.

Don't miss: the Historic Properties, a converted nineteenth-century business district now home to an inviting range of shops, restaurants and nightclubs.

The coal-mining port of **Sydney** is another quaint old centre with the bonus of the amazing **Fortress Louisbourg**, a reconstructed eighteenth-century French fortress, peopled with real characters and featuring period atmosphere right down to the food served in the café. Mainland Labrador and the huge island of **Newfoundland** are keen to establish themselves as two of cruising's new destinations, with plenty of big, wild landscape to explore, starting from the capital city of **St John's**, with 500 years of history from the explorers to the pirates. **L'Anse Amour** offers the Labrador Straits Museum and 9,000 years of human settlement history, while the coastal waters also see an abundance of whales – and icebergs. And, if you thought the Alaskan scenery was rough and ready, check out

Labrador's north coast for some of the most rugged, daunting coastline in the world as the jagged Torngat and Kaumajet Mountains seem to soar straight out of the sea. Amazingly, there are small communities of fishermen and Inuit native inhabitants, and a flying tour along this stretch can rightly claim to be a unique experience.

Don't miss: Signal Hill National Historic Site in fascinating St John's, the old whaling capital of Red Bay, and the incredible Northern Lights in winter.

Completing the leisurely sail up this stretch of coast brings you into the St Lawrence Seaway, entrance to the great St Lawrence River and the five Great Lakes of the interior. **Prince Edward Island**, and its port of **Charlottetown**, offers more quiet scenic charm and fishing villages, the surprisingly good beaches of Prince Edward Island National Park and the shipbuilding museum. Coming into the St Lawrence brings you to the majestic French-Canadian city of **Quebec**, with its proudly preserved seventeenth-century heritage, that includes a wealth of historical detail, from battle sites to monuments and winding cobbled streets. The walled city of **Vieux Québec** is the place to wander, while **Dufferin Terrace** offers a fabulous overview of the St Lawrence.

TRAVEL TIP

Remembering a few words of your school French lessons is a good idea here as Quebec sticks fiercely to its French traditions and English is not always spoken.

Montreal, a more cosmopolitan, built-up city, is the usual cruise terminus on the St Lawrence, and visitors always marvel at how clean everywhere seems to be, and you'll hear a lot of 'Why can't they keep it like this in our city/town?' Take the Metro into the city centre (London's Underground is positively antiquated by comparison) and enjoy some fine museums (including the unmissable Canadian History Museum), restaurants (notably along Prince Arthur Mall) and shopping. Get your walking shoes on and marvel at how well-designed all cities could be if only common sense was allowed to have a say every now and then.

THE FAR EAST

Who goes there?

Crystal, Cunard, Holland America, NCL, Orient, Princess,
Radisson Seven Seas, Royal Caribbean, Seabourn, Silversea,
Star Clippers, Star Cruises, Swan Hellenic, Windstar

Cruise season: year-round (Star Cruises), October-March otherwise

In many ways, the Far East (taking this rather generalised area to stretch from Thailand, Malaysia and the island of Sumatra in the south through Singapore, Indonesia, the Philippines, Vietnam, Hong Kong, China, Korea and up to Japan) has yet to establish itself in mainstream cruising, despite the fact it has been featured in brochures for many years now. The long distances involved in flying people out to base ports in Singapore, Hong Kong and Japan, the relatively high maintenance costs for cruise ships in the region (not to mention some exorbitant port taxes for less-than-impressive facilities in some cases) and the fact it is definitely not a cheap option, all mean the Far East has been distinctly under-exploited. Despite the apparently high number of ship visits, only the Singapore/Malaysia/Hong Kong sailings of relative newcomers Star Cruises are a year-round operation, but they are extremely ambitious and are in the process of growing rapidly, anxious to attract large numbers of European passengers to this area for the first time. Star offer a mixture of two, three, five and seven-day itineraries over an increasingly wide-ranging area, from Malaysia and Thailand all the way up to China, with the bonus of some exciting new ships in *SuperStar Leo* and *Virgo*.

The other cruise lines are all short-season visitors at best, while the likes of Crystal, Cunard, Holland America, Seabourn and Silversea make only annual visits on their way round the various sectors of the world. Royal Caribbean have added a new series of cruises in this area as their *Legend of the Seas* journeys from the Med to Australia and back again during the winter.

Once again, it is the huge cultural and scenic diversity which make the Far East such a tempting destination, not to mention the sheer exotic experience of places like Bangkok, Bali and Shanghai. Mysterious (to western eyes) oriental cities, crowded markets, fabulous temples and spectacular tropical flora and fauna all add up to a wealth of tourist opportunities, and doing it all from the relative security of a ship means a lot of the possible worries of health and safety are immediately removed. And any cruise line that gives you the chance to visit Beijing and the Great Wall of China should be avidly sought out by the more discerning traveller.

Singapore is likely to become the Miami of the Far East if current developments are anything to go by, and this highly-organised city state on the tip of the Malaysian Peninsula is an excellent base from which to explore the delights of south-east Asia. Its British colony heritage still shines through (notably in the Raffles Hotel, a must for afternoon tea or an evening drink), but its modern façades, as witnessed by the thrusting city centre high-rise developments, plus its mix of Arabian, Hindu and Buddhist influences, give it a unique flavour. And, like Hong Kong, it offers some of the best shopping in the world, both for duty-free luxury items and locally-made arts and crafts, including exotic porcelain, silks and pewterware. Check out the seemingly endless arcades of Orchard Road for the best shopping, while, for devotees of Oriental cuisine, Singapore is also foodie heaven.

TRAVEL TIP

For protection against damaged or pirated goods, shop with members of Singapore's Gold Circle (look for their window stickers). Some shops also display a 'recommended' price, which means they allow bargaining.

Historic ethnic areas include Little India, Arab Street and Chinatown, and the obvious tourist attractions include the amazing **Discovery Island** of Sentosa, part theme park, part beach resort and part garden wonderland, the 'open' **Zoological Gardens, Jurong Bird Park** (the world's largest walk-in aviary), the Chinese mythological village of **Haw Par Villa** and **Empress Place**. Getting round Singapore is made easy by cheap taxi fares (tipping is not expected), an efficient bus service and the MRT (Mass Rapid Transit) rail system. Crime is also rarely a problem here as the penalties for even petty offences are swingeing. For more information, the London office of the Singapore Tourism Board (020 7437 0033) is one of the best in the business.

From Singapore, ships sail either north to Bangkok, the rest of Asia and east to the islands, or north-west to Malaysia and Thailand.

TRAVEL TIP

The Far East in general, and Singapore in particular, is not the place to have anything to do with drugs. Refuse any appeals to carry or deliver parcels for anyone, no matter how innocent they seem.

Kuala Lumpur, or KL, is the capital of Malaysia and, from its port of Port Klang, a tour of this hot, bustling city is a must. Breathtaking skyscrapers, a host of mosques and temples, bustling markets, including a lively Chinatown section, beautiful gardens and even museums (notably the **Negara Museum**) make it a history-rich destination and a fascinating place to explore, while it is also a shopper's paradise, especially for local crafts. Public transport is well-run and inexpensive.

Don't miss: the Sultan Abdul Samad Building and KL Railway Station, outstanding examples of its architectural heritage.

Penang is an island resort boasting a magnificent historical centre in

Georgetown. The seventeenth-century fortress of Fort Cornwallis is worth a visit, while Penang Museum and Art Gallery sets the island's varied history in perspective. **Kota Kinabalu** is a relatively new city of high-rise buildings, a coral-island-studded coastline and heavily wooded mountainside, topped by the imposing Mount Kinabalu. The modern mosque and museum are other attractions as are the nearby fishing villages where visitors are always afforded a generous welcome. **Kuching** is the capital of the east Malaysian state of Sarawak. Located on a riverbank, it has an eye-catching waterfront, historic buildings, beautifully landscaped parks and gardens and one of Asia's finest museums, with an excellent collection of local ethnological and archaeological material.

Thailand bills itself as 'the most exotic country in Asia' which is quite a claim considering the competition, but hard to argue against. The island of **Phuket** is a big tourist resort with fine beaches and caves, spectacular reefs and lush vegetation, with thickly forested slopes giving way to tumbling waterfalls and hidden coves. Shopping is its other principal claim to fame, especially silk and pearls.

Don't miss: the local seafood.

Pattaya is Thailand's 'Riviera', a famous beach resort of excellent water sports, especially on the offshore coral islands, and vibrant nightlife, while **Chiang Mai** is another popular tourist destination, with its slower pace of life, eye-catching temples and cottage industries, notably umbrellas, silverware, nielloware and silk. But **Bangkok**, with its port of **Laem Chabang**, is Thailand's really must-see attraction, rich in archaeological treasures, including the fabulous **Emerald Buddha Temple** and the **Grand Palace**. Take a tour along the Chao Phraya River and explore the canals of **Thonburi** for a real close-up of Thailand's modern character, and then head for some more world-class shopping, with Thai silk, rubies, sapphires, silver, ceramics and bronze all out to catch your attention.

Don't miss: the Ancient City, a 1,200-acre open-air museum and Bangkok's Floating Market.

The vast, widespread, volcanic islands of **Indonesia** are Singapore's other near-neighbours and also make a rich cruising experience. The capital **Jakarta**, on the island of Java, is home to 7.5 million people and reflects the history of the country since the arrival of the Dutch in the seventeenth century. **Old Batavia** is a magnificently restored slice of the city's heritage, which can also be viewed in the Jakarta Museum.

Don't miss: the vast open-air museum of 'Beautiful Indonesia in Miniature'.

Surabaya is a sprawling city of some three million, with fascinating Old Arab and Chinese quarters, while **Semarang**, Java's provincial capital, boasts many splendid old colonial buildings and **Borododur**, the largest Buddhist shrine in the world. Bali is the most familiar to European visitors, a true island paradise in its own right, famous for its beaches and volcanoes. Art and culture also play a large part in Bali's make-up, with Ancient Hinduism replacing Buddhism as the main religion, and her local artisans produce much-sought-after carvings of wood and stone, gold and silver jewellery and traditional Balinese paintings. The Balinese people are also noted for their uniquely ritualistic forms of music, folk drama and dance. Your cruise ship should also provide a grandstand seat while sailing around the remains of the volcanic island of **Krakatau**, reportedly site of the biggest explosion in the history of the world (I wasn't there at the time – August 1883), while some of the smaller vessels also visit the temple-rich island of Lombok, where Muslim and Hindu cultures live side by side in a picture-postcard setting of towers, fountains and crumbling palaces, and the great National Park of Komodo Island, which boasts the world's biggest 'lizard', the 10ft **Komodo Dragon**, and is one of the great wildlife areas of the Far East. Lombok and Komodo are two of the 17,000 S**pice Islands** of this region, scattered between Sumatra and Borneo, which also include the bustling Dutch-Portuguese island of Timor and its hectic port **Kupang**, and **Sumbawa**, with its intriguing mountain villages.

Brunei, on the north-west coast of the island of Borneo, surrounded by the east Malaysian states of **Sarawak** and **Sabah**, is a richly prosperous nation run by the Sultan of Brunei, reputedly the world's richest man. The port of **Muara** serves the capital, **Bandar Seri Begawan**, a bustling city of spotlessly-clean streets and amazing sights like the built-on-stilts water village of Kampong Ayer and the **Royal Regalia Building**, complete with its gold and silver ceremonial armour and the Royal Chariot.

Don't miss: the Omar Ali Saifuddin Mosque, with its lift to the top for a really spectacular overview of the city. Excellent beaches and unspoiled jungle complete the picture for this unique country.

The **Philippines** are the other big island group of south-east Asia, no fewer than 7,017 of them offering idyllic beaches, lush green mountains and ultra-modern cities (and therefore more great shopping). **Manila** on the biggest island of Luzon is the chief port of call, a sprawling, crowded metropolis with a wealth of sightseeing possibilities. Check out the Walled City of Intramuros, the old Spanish Fort Santiago, the 200-year-old Malacanang Palace, Rizal Park, the Chinese Cemetery, the Pistang Pilipino market and Manila's Chinatown. Other excursions take in Taal, a small but active volcano in the middle of a lake, and the coral island of **Corregidor**, scene of some of the most heroic and brutal action of the Second World War. For shopping, embroidered clothes, coral jewellery, wood-carving and hand-made baskets are all local specialities. The rest of the vast archipelago has yet to be fully appreciated and integrated into many cruise schedules, but that is likely to happen before too long as the visitors discover the delights of Cebu, the 'Queen City of the South' on Visayas island (fabulous beaches and historical sights, including Fort san Pedro and Magellan's Cross), **Zamboanga City** on Mindanao (with historic Fort Pilar and rare pink-sand beaches) and **Davao** (also on Mindanao, and with great sights like the Buddhist temple of Don Wa, the Davao Museum and some spectacular tropical parklands).

Don't miss: the frequent festivals, processions and boating regattas which are a feature of Filipino life and any trip to the Chocolate Hills of Bohol.

Back on the mainland, **Vietnam** is on the cruise schedules of a handful of forward-thinking lines, and it offers a wealth of ancient treasures, historical architecture and friendly, welcoming people, with its principal attraction being **Ho Chi Minh City** (formerly Saigon). The National Museum is the door to 4,000 years of history, the Notre Dame Cathedral is a must-see novelty and the Cholon and Benh Thanh markets can provide hours of shopping interest. The ancient port city of **Danang** is another temple-rich destination, also famous for China Beach, where the American GIs used to relax, the Marble Mountains and the Cham Museum. **Nha Trang** is also a popular port of call, with some truly stunning beaches and terrific seafood to back up the historic elements, which include the seventh-century ruins of Po Nagar, the twelfth-century tower of the Cham Sanctuary and the Pasteur Institute.

Hong Kong officially became part of China on 30 June 1997, and the cruise world is among those waiting to see what long-term changes this will bring to this busiest and most beautiful of ports. Here, the modern and ancient Chinese worlds clash in a riot of sights and sounds, and you could be convinced this is the most crowded place on earth. High-rise tower blocks spring up almost as fast as the architects can draw them, twisting, narrow streets house a multitude of shopping opportunities (not to mention the huge, purpose-built shopping malls and areas like Nathan Road on the Kowloon Peninsula), temples and monasteries litter the city and surrounding hills, and Victoria Peak, with its funicular railway, offers a truly outstanding view of the lot. Mix in some superb restaurants, vibrant nightlife and fascinating museums, and Hong Kong quickly becomes a port of call that will make you want to stay for a week or longer (and several cruise lines do now offer some attractive add-on stays). It is also a base for Star Cruises' *SuperStar Leo*, voyaging to Vietnam and China.

Don't miss: the houseboat village of Aberdeen and a trip to the Portuguese colony of Macau, with its unique blend of Portuguese and Chinese culture.

China is another relative newcomer to the cruise scene map and is quickly becoming one of those destinations which every well-travelled sea-goer has to visit. **Beijing** is a once-in-a-lifetime city of cultural diversity and richness to which no guide book or film can do justice. From the ports of **Xingang** or **Tianjin**, the Chinese capital is two to three hours' journey away, but it is worth every minute (especially if your ship arranges an overnight excursion) to view sights like the awe-inspiring Forbidden City, the splendid Summer Palace and the blue-tiled Temple of Heaven. And that is just the start. The Ming Tombs, Great Wall at Badaling, Beihai Park and the Beijing Waxworks Palace also introduce the foreign visitor to a world which can be completely overwhelming in terms of its cultural experience. The more cosmopolitan city of **Shanghai** is similarly impressive for its wealth of historical sights and new attractions, like the commercial centre of Nanjing Road. Old Town's Y Yuan bazaar and Five-Star Pavilion, Yu Yuan Garden, Long Hua Temple Pagoda and the Jade Buddha all provide a glimpse of the past. The Shanghai Museum of

Art and History also delves into more than 7,000 years of Chinese events. **Guanghzou**, or Canton, has been a South China coast trading port for almost 2,000 years and offers the history of the Memorial Garden to the Martyrs, Yuexiu Park, the seventh-century Huaisheng Mosque and the Dr Sun Yat-Sen Memorial, while students of Buddhism won't want to miss Foshan, a nearby pilgrimage site of temples and pagodas filled with images and carvings of the main Chinese religion. **Nanjing** is one of China's most attractive cities, with its broad, tree-lined streets, excellent history museum and park at Xuanwu Lake that also boasts a zoo and a theatre. The imposing Mausoleum of Dr Sun Yat-Sen is another tourist trap. Dalian, the northern-most port, is a unique Chinese/Russian/Japanese mix of architecture and history, with a fine museum of natural history as well as a large seaside park and renowned local craftsmen, who fashion eye-catching crystal animals and pictures from shell fragments.

Don't miss: Beijing.

Japan completes this cruise sweep of the Far East with yet another drastic culture change and more unique sights. Four main islands – Kyushu, Shikoku, Honshu and Hokkaido – make up the bulk of the country, which is intensely mountainous, topped by volcanoes like the picture-perfect Mount Fuji on Honshu island, just south-west of Tokyo, with its small, fertile plains, rich forests – and ultra-modern cities. The massive port of **Yokohama** is the gateway to **Tokyo**, but the two form a vast urban sprawl that is both vibrant and orderly (the latter a vital feature of Japanese life). The glittering, neon-lit Ginza district is the hub of its shopping and entertainment activities, but the city's many parks and temples are equally attractive for new visitors.

Don't miss: the Imperial Palace Plaza and its timeless park filled with the local trademark cherry trees.

Nagasaki, on Kyushu island, is Japan's most western-influenced city, and offers the International Cultural Hall, with its museum homage to the awesome destruction and horrors of the 1945 atomic bomb attack, as well as some striking European architecture and picturesque surroundings. The ports of **Kobe** (now extensively rebuilt after the great earthquake of 1995) and **Osaka** offer tours to the historical capital of **Kyoto**, with its Kinkakuji, or Gold Temple, and the Sanjusangendo Temple with its Hall of 1,001 Buddhas. Shoppers here should hunt out the locally-made Satsuma pottery and inlaid jewellery. Osaka also features the sixteenth-century castle and sixth-century Shitennoji Temple. **Okinawa Island** and its port of **Naha** in the extreme south are another blend of ancient traditions and modern western influences, with its motorways and neon-lit skyline mixing freely with sacred temples and an Imperial castle. Here, the shopping bargains include bingata, a woodblock-print cloth, and lacquerware.

AUSTRALASIA
Who goes there?

Crystal, Cunard, Holland America, NCL, Orient, P&O, Princess, Radisson Seven Seas, Renaissance, Royal Caribbean, Silversea, Seabourn, Windstar

Cruise season: Year-round (November-April most commonly)

The far-flung islands of the South Pacific have been a cruise destination since the days of Captain Cook (well, sort of), and, while no one can claim to be the first to sail them these days, they do provide a significant opportunity to get off the beaten cruise track and explore some of the most truly picturesque corners of the world. And, as you travel down from the likes of Papua New Guinea to Australia and New Zealand, the geographical diversity is also among the most startling you will encounter, including as it does, the volcanic Samoan islands, the tropical splendour of north Australia, the stunning 1,242-mile Great Barrier Reef, the exotic South Pacific Islands of Tahiti, and the almost Norwegian fjord coastline of parts of New Zealand. Island life is slow-paced and informal and surprisingly rich in history, with magnificent beaches and the attendant wonders of rich marine life, wonderful deep-sea fishing and some of the best snorkelling and scuba-diving anywhere in the world.

TRAVEL TIP

When it comes to the climate here, beware. It is some of the most humid territory in the cruise world. So, when you venture out of the ship's air-conditioned interior, expect temperatures in excess of 48°C/120°F and near-100 per cent humidity.

South Pacific culture is still alive and thriving and islanders will happily exhibit their centuries-old traditions and customs for visitors. Village markets also offer a unique taste of local life, with artisans hard at work at their arts and crafts. The only real drawback is the extra cost and duration of flights to this part of the world. It couldn't be further away and, if you are travelling all that distance for a cruise, you want to make it a significant one in terms of time, hence they are often the most expensive you will find. Having said all that, it is still the least visited of the main cruise areas, and it has the added attraction of being the most untouched commercially, and therefore the most natural. It should also go without saying the beaches are truly stunning and water sports are one of the prime activities.

Papua New Guinea, the largest (unless you count Australia) and most northerly of the islands, is almost inaccessible to anything other than sea transport, hence cruising scores another big advantage here.

Tropical rainforests, rugged mountains, colourful bird and other wildlife, brilliant tropical beaches and timeless native villages add up to a scenic wonderland. A tour along the **Sepik River** can take you back hundreds of years to a region almost completely untouched by modern life, while the **Trobriand Islands** are a glimpse of tropical paradise with their thatched huts fringing white coral beaches and people who still insist on ceremonial gift exchanges and traditional music and dance to welcome all visitors. **Port Moresby** is the one sizeable port and city, boasting a lively, modern, high-rise centre, with the attractions of the National Museum and Art Gallery, War Museum, National Arts School (featuring exhibits of the islands' complex and varied tribal lifestyles) and Paga Hill, with a panoramic view of the whole area. The traditional side of life in the area is still evident in the stilt villages of Koki, Hanuabada and Tatana, so don't forget your camera. Cruise ship visitors do not require special visas, either.

TRAVEL TIP

Surprisingly for this tropical wonderland, the crime rate in Port Moresby is high and this is not the place to go wandering on your own. Ship-organised excursions are essential for visiting even the main sights, and you shouldn't stray far from the main group at places like Paga Hill and Hanuabada.

From Papua New Guinea almost as far as New Zealand stretch the islands and atolls of the South Pacific – the Solomon Islands, Tuvalu, French Polynesia, Vanuatu, Fiji, Samoa, the Cook Islands, New Caledonia and Tonga. In the mountainous, forested **Solomon Islands**, islanders travel among this cluster of six large islands and myriad smaller ones by canoe, but the apparent modern idyll covers some deep scars caused by bitter battles in the Second World War. The main island is **Guadalcanal**, which was at the centre of some of the fiercest American-Japanese fighting, and the capital **Honiara** contains a sombre War Memorial to the many thousands who died here. Today, the Solomon Islands are an independent member of the Commonwealth, with a well-developed fishing industry, and the principal attractions of Honiara include Government House, the Botanical gardens and Watapamu, a typical islanders' village. **French Polynesia** consists of some 130 islands spread over 1.5 million square miles of Pacific Ocean, and is subdivided into the five main groups of which **Tahiti** (in the Society Islands) is the main island and **Papeete**, the capital. The majority are steep, volcanic mountains, but one group, the Tuamotus, is mainly composed of low-lying atolls, strung together by often-submerged coral reefs. Papeete is a modern city with government offices, businesses, shops and restaurants. It also boasts the Gauguin Museum and some lovely one-off boutiques and sidewalk cafés along Boulevard Pomare. Organised excursions will take you to visit some of the mountains and waterfalls, or to go fishing, trekking or horse-riding. The 1990s nuclear tests by the French government – conducted flagrantly in the face of world opinion – were carried out on the tiny atoll of Mururoa and are still a touchy subject with the rightly-indignant Polynesian islanders. Other French Polynesian cruise stops include picture-postcard **Bora Bora** (discovered by Captain Cook in 1777 and probably the epitome of a South Sea island with its almost vertical basalt peaks soaring above a typical turquoise bay and fringed by the inevitable coral reef necklace), **Hiva Oa** (where the artist Paul Gauguin lived and died), **Moorea** (a larger version of Bora Bora), **Raiatea** (with its dense rainforests) and lush, archaeologically-rich **Huahine** (for the site of Maeva, a fifteenth-century settlement with restored marae, the ancestral shrines of local chiefs). Radisson Seven Seas' Paul Gauguin is now based year-round in Tahiti to offer a specialist product in French Polynesia, while Renaissance have a comparable offering, but spread over 10 days instead of seven.

Don't miss: the canoe trip down the River Faaroa on Raiatea, where the jungle provides a canopy of ferns, orchids and vanilla.

TRAVEL TIP

In Fiji, the bravest souls will surely want to raise a coconut shell full of the local herbal beverage – Yaqona – which is utterly unique in its non-alcoholic potency. The locals claim it is an aphrodisiac!

You have to search to find **Vanuatu** on many ship itineraries (try Norwegian Cruise Line – see page 135 – or Seabourn) but it is worth it to get off the beaten track even by the South Pacific's standards at sleepy harbours like **Port Vila** and **Espiritu Santo**, where you are as much of an attraction to the locals as they are to you. On Espiritu Santo, the remains of a huge Allied base, which supported the battle of Guadalcanal in the Second World War, lie rusting in the bush. The 320 islands that make up the **Fiji** archipelago boast more tropically adorned volcanic mountains overlooking impossibly blue waters, plus historical sights and the mind-boggling fire-walkers of the Fijian Cultural Center at **Pacific Harbour** on the main island of **Viti Levu**, who call on a Fijian god to help them withstand the white-hot stones. The capital **Suva** is alive with lush, flowered greenery and flamboyant trees, and the central market is a lively tropical mélange of fish, vegetable and fruit sellers. Albert Park is one of Suva's most attractive areas, with the nearby Government House and the peaceful Thurston gardens.

Don't miss: the Fiji Museum in Thurston gardens for a comprehensive view of Fijian history, including the double-hulled war canoe and replica village.

Western Samoan islanders proudly preserve their age-old Polynesian culture in the face of creeping Westernisation, and most people still live in fale, or traditional open-sided thatched houses in coastal villages. Robert Louis Stevenson lived and died here and his grave, atop Mount Vaea on the main island of **Upolu**, is visited by only the most energetic of tourists. Other points of interest in the capital **Apia** include Aggie Grey's Hotel (Aggie Grey was reputedly the model for Bloody Mary in James A Michener's novel Tales of the South Pacific), the Congregational Church and the First World War Memorial.

American Samoa comes as something of a culture shock after Western Samoa, with its bustling, brash town of **Pago Pago**. You are suddenly reintroduced to traffic and trash-cans, but there are still opportunities for quiet nature walks, sightseeing and even golf. The **Cook Islands** offer a legendary level of warmth and hospitality, with much of their culture living on in their vibrant song and dance, an opportunity to witness either of which shouldn't be missed. The main island is **Rarotonga** and the capital Avarua, where you will find wonderful little craft and produce markets with some outstanding weaving and wood-carving. The beaches, needless to say, are brilliantly white and the interiors tropically lush.

TRAVEL TIP

Haggling and tipping are both regarded as something of an insult on the South Pacific islands. Topless bathing is also a definite no-no for the ladies and even shorts may be frowned on.

New Caledonia boasts the second-largest barrier reef in the world, shining emerald and turquoise through the clear waters. The main town of **Noumea** is situated on a peninsula with numerous bays and coves providing excellent scuba-diving and snorkelling in the reef-protected lagoons. Also worth a visit are the Botanical Gardens and Zoo near the main town area. Otherwise known as the French Riviera of the South Pacific, Noumea is home to a bewildering variety of restaurants, bistros and chic boutiques selling everything from shell necklaces to incense burners. The **Tonga** archipelago (156 islands spread over 288 square miles) features more strong cultural ties, rich natural beauty and a way of life that is unique to these islands. Tongans are typically fat and friendly and are still ruled by a king, hence the sights of the capital **Nuku'alofa** include the Royal Palace, Royal Chapel and Royal Tombs. The town also has wonderful gardens and a bustling market, while the island group of **Vava'u** offers kayakers the chance to skirt palm-fringed islands and coral reefs and explore marine caves.

After cruising the exotic islands, the ports and cities of **Australia** can seem just a little humdrum by comparison, despite the country's 23,000 miles of impressive coastline, but it is purely a question of re-setting your culture dial. Here it is all about a vibrant, emerging continent, modern cities, rugged outdoor adventures, water sports and a landscape that changes from dense tropical forest to harsh, unforgiving desert. **Darwin** is the most northerly settlement, a multi-cultural town that has long outgrown its frontier roots to provide such modern-day pursuits as casinos and museums housing Second World War memorabilia. Journey into the outback to see local aboriginal art and wildlife at Kakadu National Park, including the 'jumping crocodiles' on the Adelaide River. Cairns is the gateway to the unmissable **Great Barrier Reef** but also offers a cosmopolitan, tropical air with tree-lined streets and a great mixture of indoor and open-air markets for some great shopping. Although it is the scuba-diving capital of the Reef, Cairns also hosts white-water rafting, canoeing and horse-riding. Your cruise ship should spend at least a day in the vicinity of the Reef, which is the largest living thing on earth. Composed of more than 300 types of coral, it is populated by technicolor fish and rare birds, with the combination of white surf, azure waters and cloudless skies making for an unforgettable experience. **Brisbane** is a thriving young city of sky-scrapers and colonial buildings, with the added attractions of Mount Cootha Botanical Gardens, the Queensland Art Museum, Queen Street Mall and the XXXX Brewery! Just to the south is the Gold Coast and **Surfers' Paradise**, a rapidly-expanding section of resort development with great beaches, theme parks and natural attractions like the Currumbin Bird Sanctuary.

TRAVEL TIP

My parents are big fans of the Lone Pine Koala Sanctuary just outside Brisbane for getting to meet the natives – inquisitive kangaroos, cuddly koalas and sad-faced wombats. Watch out for the koalas – they have a grip like a vice!

Sydney is surely the most photogenic port in the world with the unmistakable span of the Harbour Bridge and the outline of the Opera House, and that is just the starting point of this most impressive of cities. The historic area of the Rocks, where restaurants and museums have replaced the warehouses and convict-built streets, Darling Harbour, Sydney Aquarium, the National Maritime Museum and Taronga Zoo will all demand your attention, and that's before you go shopping or try one of the many excellent restaurants (and the local wines, of course). **Hobart**, on Tasmania, is Olde Englande Pacific-style, with handsome Georgian buildings, picturesque cottages and narrow lanes backed by lush, green hills. Here is a modern city with a good feel for its history, and the seaside wharves feature many sandstone warehouses filled with shops and cafés to help you while away a few hours in relaxed but sophisticated style. **Devonport**, on Tasmania's sleepy north coast, offers the opportunity to visit Cradle Mountain and the Lake St Clair National Park, a World Heritage site of spectacular alpine scenery, dense forests, towering sand dunes and unique flora and fauna, including the famous Tasmanian Devil (no, not the Warner Brothers cartoon, but an equally fierce marsupial carnivore that will take on – and kill – prey up to three times its size). **Melbourne** is Australia's cultural, financial and commercial centre, with a fine display of outdoor sights, including grand, tree-lined avenues, well-preserved Victorian architecture, art museums, gardens, open-air restaurants and the Royal Botanic Gardens, with the world's third oldest zoo. You can visit the State Houses of Parliament, and the Museum of Victoria, pan for gold in nearby Ballarat and take a vintage steam train ride through the countryside. Adelaide is a small, compact and wonderfully relaxed city at the centre of one of South Australia's greatest wine-producing regions, the Barossa Valley. Principal tourist sights include the festival centre, Parliament House, the University of **Adelaide** and the enclosed Rundle Mall.

TRAVEL TIP

When it comes to wine, South Australia can boast some of the most spectacular reds in the world, notably St Hallet's Old Block Shiraz and Rochford's Black Shiraz. Heaven in a bottle.

Albany, in the historic first colony of Western Australia, displays many original buildings, including the state's oldest house and post office and a memorial to the famous Light Horsemen of the tragic First World War battle of Gallipoli. Finally **Perth**, even further round on the beach-strewn west coast, completes the sweep of Aussie cities with its port of **Fremantle**, where you will find Victorian pubs, hotels and shops, more wine-growing country, the Swan Lager Brewery and Cahunu Park, another good place to see kangaroos and koalas.

Don't miss: any excursion which takes you out to the Pinnacles Desert.

If you can imagine Britain with clean cities, Scandinavian scenery, Alaskan wildlife and friendly Pacific manners, then you arrive at **New Zealand**. Wild-sculpted dunes, majestic mountains, wilderness fjords and island-studded bays are just part of the remarkable wealth of attractions on offer, which are rounded off by the opportunity for white-water rafting, jetboat rides, bungee jumping (!), hiking, whale-watching, gold-panning and horse racing, plus some spectacular ports of call. **Auckland**, or the City of Sails after its yacht-filled harbour, is a city of stunning natural beauty, set as it is over seven extinct volcanic hills and around two bays, combining the best of the old and the new, including some impressive museums brimming with Maori artefacts. Shop at the colourful Victorian Park Market, visit the Underwater World Aquarium, take a ferry across to Devonport harbour and climb Mount Eden for the magnificent view of it all. Shopping bargains include Polynesian crafts in Karangahape Road and knitwear in Queen Street.

Don't miss: either by tour from Auckland or the nearer, less-frequented port of Tauranga, the Maori homeland of Rotorua for its village and craft centre and geothermal springs, with evil-looking bubbling mud pools and geysers.

Christchurch is frequently labelled the most English city outside England (although Canada's Victoria on Vancouver Island could argue the point), a garden metropolis of parks, Gothic architecture and the spired Christchurch Cathedral all set along the meandering River Avon that somehow helps to slow the city pace down to a gentle walk. The capital, **Wellington**, cascades down pine-clad hills to its pretty harbour. Ancient timber homes and early Victorian architecture live comfortably alongside modern tower blocks. The lively waterfront and main shopping area of Lambton Quay are at the forefront of the tourist attractions, while stairs, lifts and cable cars take you from the quay to the top of Mount Victoria for a stunning scenic overview. **Napier** boasts glorious art deco buildings that rival Miami's for authenticity and scenic beauty, with the Marine Parade oceanfront another highlight for its beautifully landscaped gardens and the Nocturnal Wildlife Centre. Dunedin offers the feel of Scotland (**Dunedin** is, in fact, the Gaelic name for Edinburgh) with its Victorian red-brick buildings, mist-draped Larnach Castle and 30-acre oak woodlands of Glenfalloch, plus the panoramic views of Otago harbour. And, when it comes to the spectacular coastline, the Bay of Islands offers scenery aplenty in its sheltered waters, plus world-record-setting deep-sea fishing and the **Bay of Islands** Maritime and Historic Park. There is also a quaint cruise around the bay for a close-up of the wildlife, which can include dolphins and penguins, on the old milk-collection steamer called the Fuller's Cream trip. **Milford Sound** is pure fjord country, a valley carved out by glacial ice thousands of years ago, with improbably high cliffs and waterfalls plunging down into the gorge where seals sun themselves and penguins dive through the icy waters. Finally, no cruise around New Zealand would be complete without a look at Marlborough Sounds, a maze of inlets and labyrinthine rock formations which offered Captain Cook a haven on one of his Pacific explorations. The pretty town of **Picton** sits at the head of neighbouring Queen Charlotte Sound, and its Dunbar Wharf is home to the last sailing vessel of the old British East India Company, the *Edwin Fox*.

THE INDIAN OCEAN AND AFRICA

Who goes there?

African Safari Club, Cunard, Hebridean Island Cruises, Mediterranean Shipping, Noble Caledonia, Fred Olsen, Orient, Princess, Radisson Seven Seas, Royal Caribbean, Seabourn, Silversea, Swan Hellenic

Cruise season: year-round (November-April most commonly)

Considering the vast amounts of tranquil, inviting ocean, the eye-catching exotic ports and islands and the extra attractions of activities like safaris and other wildlife opportunities, it is surprising the Indian Ocean and its African coast are not visited by the cruise lines in any significant numbers. Even where they do visit, it is quite often just a 'passing through' segment of a longer cruise. Only the specialist, small-scale operator African Safari Club, and their homely ship *Royal Star*, and Mediterranean Shipping out of South Africa currently offer a year-round option. Stretching from the Red Sea in the north to the Cape of Good

Hope off Cape Town in South Africa, and eastward through the tropical islands of Madagascar, Mauritius and the Seychelles to India and Sri Lanka, this is a colossal area of untapped cruise potential and just a few ships currently have it virtually to themselves. The main argument against the region as a mass-market destination is its lack of a-port-a-day capability. The area is not port-intensive by any means, and some of the countries and islands are several days' journey apart. This obviously makes for more relaxed, elegant cruising, but it doesn't generally make for readily packaged one- and two-week itineraries, hence the current lack of real cruise volume. However, Fred Olsen, Cunard and Princess have all ventured into these areas in the last couple of years and the area's potential is slowly turning into real cruise growth.

Once again the attractions – apart from virtually guaranteed sunshine and wonderful beaches – are the exotica, the great geographical diversity from deserts to mountains to tropical rainforests, the fascination of culturally diverse areas like Buddhist Sri Lanka, Arab-influenced Djibouti, historical Zanzibar and tribal Madagascar, and the spectacular flora and fauna of places such as Kenya and South Africa.

India can be the start or finish of an Indian Ocean cruise, with its main port at **Mumbai** (formerly Bombay), a bustling, people-choked city of some 10 million souls that ranges from the western-style skyscrapers at Nariman Point through the history-laden colonial atmosphere around Bombay Fort to the poverty-stricken shanty suburbs where it seems impossible human beings can exist at all.

An organised tour of Mumbai, covering the main sights of the Dhobi Gatt laundries, the Gateway to India, the temples of Elephanta Island, Gandhi's house and museum, the Prince of Wales Museum and the Hanging Gardens, is probably the best way of tackling this congested city for the first time. **Cochin**, in the lush, southern Kerala region, was a Portuguese settlement back in the sixteenth century, but its history goes back much further as the proverbial land of incense and myrrh, with a 900-year-old Jewish colony (including a sixteenth-century synagogue), and ages-old local traditions and customs, including the Kanakali, a folk dance involving elaborate hand movements and ritualistic gestures.

Don't miss: the Mattancheri Palace with its fabulous mythological murals.

TRAVEL TIP

In India (and Sri Lanka for that matter) shoppers are expected to haggle over the prices of goods like Kashmir shawls, semi-precious jewellery, carpets and lovely gilded fabrics.

Colombo, the capital and main port of **Sri Lanka**, is a fascinating mix of colonial and Oriental, with much of the architecture harking back to the days of the Raj, but the sights and sounds of the bazaars, temples and local specialities like the dancing elephants are timelessly original in their local setting. The other principal sights include the Colombo Museum, the ancient shrine at Kelaniya, Victoria Park and the President's Palace. The civil conflict between the government and the Tamil region remains a serious concern, but the most recent reports on the island suggest it is still a friendly, rewarding place to visit provided you heed local tourist advice.

Don't miss: any all-day excursion to the inland city of Kandy, former royal capital of the Sinhalese kings, and one of the most sacred Buddhist sites with the sixteenth-century Temple of the Tooth.

Sailing west from Colombo brings you to the 2,000 coral islands that make up the **Maldives**, an unspoiled beach paradise featuring rare sea birds, glittering coral reefs and sea life (including giant turtles) and luxuriant vegetation. The main island is **Male**, and idyllic, palm-fringed beaches are taken for granted. Next up are the French-influenced **Seychelles**, and more tropical island splendours. The main island of **Mahé** is quite mountainous, with a pretty, ramshackle town of Victoria. It is also home to the giant Aldabran tortoise at the Botanical Gardens and to some fabulous marine life, which can be viewed on a glass-bottomed boat ride at the beach of Beau Vallon or more sedately at the National Marine Park. The island of **Praslin** offers an even richer tapestry of white beaches, dark mountains and verdant forests, with the world-famous Vallé de Mai National Park often compared to the Garden of Eden for its botanical wonders. The third Seychelles port of call is often **La Digue**, a must for all ornithologists as the home of the Black Paradise Flycatcher, one of the most rare and exotic species on the planet. You can rent a bicycle to explore more closely, or tour as the locals do – on the back of an ox-drawn cart.

TRAVEL TIP

The increase in tourism on the Seychelles has led to a consequent rise in petty crime, and visitors are advised not to take any valuables with them on beach trips.

The **Comoros Islands** offer yet more perfect, crystal-clear lagoons, lush forests and volcanic peaks, with French-controlled **Mayotte** being the most photogenic for its coral reef bays, while **Moroni** features the Karthala Volcano and a wonderfully pretty harbour, and offers magnificent diving off the west coast. The massive Indian Ocean island of **Madagascar**, and its tiny attendant Nosy Be, are a naturalist's paradise in much the same way as the Galapagos Islands are in the Pacific. Unique eco-systems, fascinating wildlife like the Madagascan lemurs, and fragrant plants like the ever-present frangipani and bright yellow-flowered ylang-ylang make it an unforgettable visual spectacle. On **Nosy Be**, visit the lemur preserve of **Nosy Comba** to have one of these cute monkey-like animals eat a banana right out of your hand, or just relax a million miles away from everyday cares on the beaches at **Tanikely**. The mixture of

≋≋≋ TRAVEL TIP ≋≋≋

As in much of tropical south-east Asia, the climate in Madagascar can be pretty fierce, especially as the winter season in the northern hemisphere, when many ships make the journey south, coincides with the summer down here. Expect temperatures above 32°C/90°F and enervating humidity levels.

African and Indonesian cultures is well exhibited on the main island, but it is best to stick to ship-organised excursions from the main port of **Diego Suarez** as the locals, who tend to speak French rather than English, are notoriously unhelpful.

To the east of Madagascar lies the tiny volcanic island of **Réunion**, a rugged, tropical gem that is well worth seeking out in cruise itineraries. Impossibly spectacular scenery, including the lunar-like **Plaine des Sables** around the active volcano cone, French-creole hospitality, the bustling port of **St Denis** with its colonial flavour, and the inevitable sun-soaked beaches make for quite an unexpectedly intense experience. A new cruise terminal was completed in 1998, making Réunion one of the hottest destinations to visit.

Mauritius, to the east of Madagascar, is the other island destination of the Indian Ocean, a charming, carefully controlled tourist environment where no building can rise higher than the indigenous palm trees and visitor numbers are restricted to annual quotas. Consequently, the atmosphere is of tranquil, unspoiled beauty at the same time as delivering a high level of modern comfort. An island tour is a pure delight, starting from the harbour of **Port Louis** with its markets and gift boutiques, and taking in the Royal Botanical Gardens, the spectacular beach at Grand Baie and the Casela Bird Park, with dozens of rare species.

A relative newcomer to this region is the Arabian Gulf port of **Dubai**, which completed its first (and totally state-of-the-art) cruise terminal in 2001 – marked by a visit from *QE2* – and aims to become the hub of the Middle East cruise world. As well as the new facilities (with more than 50 cruise ship visits in 2001), the 'City of Merchants' boasts superb shopping in a series of malls (some of the best in the world at these prices – check out the Bur Juman Centre or the Wafi Mall), the stunning gold and spice souks, or markets, great golf, water sports and beaches, a safe environment (with English widely spoken) and an impressive tourist infrastructure offering other adventures into the Arabian hinterland like the popular desert safaris, sand-skiing and visits to a Bedouin village. Dubai is also increasingly a centre for world-class spectator sports in golf, tennis, athletics and horse-racing.

Coming to mainland **Africa** provides another fascinating geographical experience. Starting in the north with the country and city of Djibouti, at the strategic meeting of the Gulf of Aden and the Red Sea, this poor semi-desert land boasts the world's hottest climate (averaging 30°C/86°F and often exceeding 40°C/104°F), some impossibly contorted desert rock formations and a mixed Arab-African culture, plus the French influences of 96 years as a colony. The port city of **Djibouti** fully highlights this crossroads feel of the Middle East and Africa, especially in its pulsating Arab markets. **Kenya** is at the heart of this region, both for its city and port of **Mombasa** and for the delights of using it as a base to explore the hinterland, with its massive landscapes and rich wildlife. The heavily Arab-influenced Old Town area of Mombasa is a real delight as the winding streets give way to colourful mosques, lively markets and elaborately-carved houses. Shop for woodcarvings, highly-patterned native cloths and soapstone chess sets.

Don't miss: the sixteenth-century Portuguese fortress of Fort Jesus.

Most cruises out of Mombasa will also offer the option of a pre- or post-cruise safari or other journey inland to see the delights of the **Masai Mara** region. The vast low-level forests and grasslands are home to all the major species of African wildlife, including lions, elephants, leopards, buffalo, rhino, impala, wildebeest, zebras and gazelles. **Tanzania** offers more spectacular game parks and other natural wonders, like the stunning ten-mile wide, 2,000-foot deep crater of **Ngorongoro** with its swarming animal populations, **Lake Manyara** at the entrance to the Great Rift Valley (and the archaeological treasure of Olduvai Gorge), **Manyara Park** with the greatest concentration of elephants in the world and the **Serengeti National Park**, a 5,600-square-mile expanse dotted with rocky outcrops, acacia bushes, forests and small rivers, not to mention the small matter of millions of zebras and wildebeest, plus lions, cheetahs, giraffes, hyenas and other typical African inhabitants. This is *the* place for wildlife. The main ports are the city of **Dar Es Salaam** on the mainland, a lively, modern, often chaotic centre, designed mainly to handle cargo, and the island of **Zanzibar**, the most common cruise ship harbour. The latter, the nineteenth-century centre of the Arab slave trade and spice industry, is a real tourist trap, with its crowded bazaars, narrow stone streets and strong-scented spice shops. Other sights include the Arab Fort and Dhow harbour, the ruins of the Maruhubi Palace, the Palace of the Sultans, the site of the notorious slave market (now a small cathedral) and the house where Dr Livingstone lived before setting out on his last expedition into the continent. Almost inevitably, there are some more splendid white-sand beaches, although swimmers are strongly advised to heed the warnings about the fierce currents which make the east coast quite treacherous.

South Africa has long been a cruise-ship destination, but it is only since the end of apartheid and the onset of democratic rule that its possibilities as a tourist destination have been fully appreciated, and the country expects to enjoy a major holiday boom in the new Millennium – so get in first! Having travelled widely in Southern Africa (my family lived there for seven years) I may be a touch biased, but to my mind it is the perfect blend of natural wonders, scenic cities and blissful climate, with the added attraction of more good wildlife-watching opportunities, great beaches and some outstanding wines in the Cape region. The only real worry for its long-term prospects is the increase in crime in the major cities, which has already made parts of Johannesburg no-go areas. Cruise-and-stay options should become big business in South Africa, though, centred on the two great ports of **Cape Town** and **Durban**.

TRAVEL TIP

Hikers will find the Cape a real paradise, with 140 trails over the top of Table Mountain alone. The Cape of Good Hope itself offers some rewarding hikes, plus the chance to view the meeting of the two great oceans, the Atlantic and the Indian, and the line of marker buoys that mark the join, stretching into the distance.*

The former is right up there with Hong Kong, Rio de Janeiro, Sydney and Istanbul as one of the great scenic ports of the world, with its backing of awesome Table Mountain. It is worth getting up early for the sight of sailing into port with that unforgettable backdrop. The city itself will keep you more than fully occupied for a day, with St George's Cathedral, the Victoria and Alfred Waterfront (where new shops and cafés mix with working fishing boats and ships under repair), the seventeenth-century Castle of Good Hope, the beaches of Hout Bay, Clifton Beach and Sea Point Promenade, plus the must-do chance to take the cable car to the top of Table Mountain for a breathtaking overview of the area (but not on windy days, which are rather frequent). Start to travel to the immediate hinterland and more delights are in store: the awesome scenic route of Chapman's Peak Drive, the Cape of Good Hope Nature Reserve, the beaches of Fish Hoek, the nautical charm of Simonstown, and the magnificent, mountain-framed scenery and charming picture-postcard Cape Dutch homesteads of the Cape winelands, typified by the historic town of Stellenbosch, the 'Town of Oaks'.

Don't miss: the chance to sample the local wines, and, from October to December, the Cape of Good Hope Nature Reserve when it bursts into vivid bloom as part of the richest floral kingdom in the world.

Durban is the Indian Ocean gateway to South Africa and the largest city in the province of Natal, a lively mix of Zulu, East Indian and European cultures. A quick drive through Durban reveals this heritage in the shape of the Indian Market, Zulu Arts centres and Zulu dancing, as well as the many modern shopping complexes, the Botanical Gardens and the exciting entertainment venues in the harbour.

Journeying out of Durban brings you to **Natal National Park** and more African wildlife, while the Valley of a Thousand Hills is truly spectacular and offers the chance to learn all about Zulu culture at Assagai Safari Park. Port Elizabeth, the fourth-largest port, is a more elegant, relaxed city than Durban, and can boast a variety of readily accessible scenic attractions which have earned it the nickname of 'the ten-minute

---

*Surely you didn't fall for that old gag? Marker buoys indeed! Everyone knows the meeting of the two oceans is easily spotted because the Atlantic is two feet higher than the Indian.

TRAVEL TIP

You can watch the tugs and pilot boats buzzing in and out of Durban's Small Craft Basin from the BAT Centre, which consists of a lively restaurant, theatre, and gift shops centred on the arts.

city' (because none of them is more than ten minutes away). The possibilities include rich bird and floral reserves, early morning and late afternoon game park drives, a snake park, an oceanarium, museums, arts and craft galleries, vintage steam train outings and boat excursions along the pretty coast. **East London** completes the line-up of South Africa's cruise ports and is part of the 'Romantic Coast', a near 300-mile stretch of long, unspoiled, safe, clean beaches in resorts like Haga-Haga and Lagoon Valley, tangled dune forests and evergreen nature reserves. The beaches of **Nahoon Reef** and **Eastern Beach** are ideal for surfing, while nature lovers will enjoy the Umtiza Forest, with its unique Umtiza trees filled with chattering monkeys, and the **Gonubie Bird Sanctuary**. Back in town, check out Latimer's Landing, a major new waterfront development featuring restaurants, flea markets and gift shops.

TRAVEL TIP

For all the fact South Africa has some marvellous scenic wonders, its sheer size dictates it also has some pretty boring stretches. Steer clear in particular of the featureless Little Karoo Desert, the vast expanses of Orange Free State's maize fields, and the coast route through the mist-prone Transkei, between East London and Durban, which is like driving through Wales on a wet day.

Don't miss: Mpongo Park, a 20-minute drive from East London, where you can dine above the resident hippos after a day of watching antelope, rhino and other typical wildlife in action.

ANTARCTICA AND SOUTH AMERICA
Who goes there?

Antarctica:
Abercrombie & Kent, Clipper Cruise Line, Hapag-Lloyd,
Noble Caledonia, Orient, Society Expeditions

Cruise season: December-February

South America:
Abercrombie & Kent, Clipper Cruise Line,
Costa, Crystal, Cunard, Hapag-Lloyd, Noble Caledonia,
Mediterranean Shipping, NCL, Fred Olsen, Orient, Princess,
Royal Olympic, Seabourn, Silversea, Society Expeditions.

Cruise season: September-April

Linking these two rather disparate destination areas together does make some sense as they are both the preserve of specialist operators who often offer unique views of and excursions to the ports of call. South America is also a genuine geographical link to cruising in the incomparable Antarctic Ocean since the main starting points for South Pole voyages are the southernmost ports of Chile and Argentina.

South America is a unique blend of European culture, native heritage and African traditions and rhythms that lives for Carnival time, the chance to dance the night away in exuberant, evocative style. It is a continent of swarming cities, impenetrable jungles and lonely outposts like the Falkland Islands and Straits of Magellan. You can shop in exclusive boutiques in Montevideo and Buenos Aires or native craft markets; dine out on exotically spiced foods; enjoy fabulous colonial architecture and modern sky-scrapers; and learn about a major ecological system on the verge of breakdown because of the devastation of the rainforests of the interior. It is a continent that is both exciting and heartbreaking at the same time.

The principal attraction of South America, though, is the **Amazon River**, 3,900 miles long and up to 30 miles wide in places, it can more than cope with the medium-sized cruise ships that aim to explore this region and it positively engulfs the small expedition ships, which are the only ones to get you a real close-up experience of the jungle. The majority offer the Amazon cruise from the port of Belem at the mouth of the great river as far as Manaus some 1,000 miles from the Atlantic Ocean, but Abercrombie & Kent and their little adventurer the *Explorer* are notable for journeying some 1,000 miles further up to Iquitos in Peru, providing a far more intimate view of this mind-boggling world of improbable waters and impenetrable forest. Considering that for much of the time the banks are just distant blurs on the far horizon and what wildlife there may be is practically invisible, it is nevertheless an intensely rewarding cruise as you still get to visit some fascinating ports of call along the way, including the **Breves Narrows**, a labyrinth of narrow channels and one of the most scenic areas with its stilt houses and fishermen in dugout canoes; **Alter do Chao**, the Altar of the Earth, a white-sand beach offering great swimming and a small village where you can taste the local drink guarana, made from caffeine-rich seeds; **Santarem**, a trading port full of all manner of floating craft; **Boca de Valeria**, a close-up view of a genuine Amazon village and its people, who all want to be photographed or bargain for beaded necklaces and other local curios; **Anavilhanas**, a tiny port on an island archipelago beloved of the great marine biologist Jacques Cousteau for its brilliant sights and abundant wildlife, including river dolphins, turtles, sloths and the scarlet ibis; the **Wedding of the Waters** at Manaus, where the two rivers of the dark-stained Rio Negro and coffee-coloured Solimoes (as the Amazon is known in its upper reaches) meet and are flowing so fast they go side by side for nearly four miles before finally merging; and **Manaus** itself, a duty-free port and sprawling city of some 1.5 million people that was briefly the richest city in the world at the turn of the century because of the rubber boom, and still boasts a nineteenth-century Opera House, art deco Municipal Market, Indian Museum and Natural Science Museum full of all South America's nasty beasties which (hopefully) you never got a close-up of on the river.

TRAVEL TIP

Haggling for goods in the craft markets and stalls is expected – and so are pickpockets and other petty thieves in most of Brazil's cities. Take good care of your wallet and handbag, and never take valuables on to a beach, especially in Rio, where crime is a serious problem.

Travelling south along the coast of **Brazil** brings you to other fascinating ports like **Fortaleza**, the country's fifth-largest city, most famous for its lace industry and with a wonderful handicrafts centre in the converted old city jail, the Centro de Turismo, where you can shop for leather, wooden carvings and sand paintings in bottles as well as hand-made lace; **Recife**, an immaculate city with great shopping at the Pernambuco Culture Center, another prison-turned-craft-market, and pretty churches and bridges; **Salvador**, with its historic Baroque-styled Pelourinho District from its colonial days, dozens of churches (nearly 200 in all) and superb public market of Mercado Modelo; **Santos**, the largest port in South America and gateway to the impossibly crowded, smog-laden city of São Paulo; and, of course, huge, scenic **Rio de Janeiro**, home of the spectacular annual Carnival (the weekend before Ash Wednesday), magnificent museums, world-famous beaches like the Copacabana and Ipanema, the world's largest football stadium, the Maracana (holding well in excess of 100,000), sleek, high-rise developments and poverty-ridden shanty towns huddled on the steepest slopes surrounding the city. The setting, of course, is breathtaking, with the huge Guanabara Bay dotted with rocky, palm-covered islands and surrounded by steep, domed mountains like the famous Sugar Loaf and Corcovado with its giant statue of Christ, and, in keeping with the great crowded city centres of the world these days, notably New York, Tokyo and Cairo, you'll either love it or hate it.

Don't miss: the cable car ride to the top of Sugar Loaf for the stunning view over the city and the bay.

After Rio, the **Uruguayan** capital and main port of **Montevideo** is a positively restful experience. Heavily influenced by European culture, it is a vibrant, modern city full of art deco buildings, heroic statues and elegant monuments, the fascinating Prado District and the Rambla, or riverfront drive.

Don't miss: any excursion to a local ranch for a demonstration of those traditional gaucho (cowboy) skills and a barbecue feast.

The neighbouring port of **Punte del Este** is the up-market beach resort area for Montevideo: set on a peninsula lined with white-sand beaches, it attracts South America's jet-setters to the calm waters of the west side, the large waves of the east, or just to shop, play golf or go deep-sea fishing.

TRAVEL TIP

Buenos Aires offers some tempting European-style shopping on pedestrianised Florida Street, but it is a long walk from the harbour. Taxis are relatively cheap (a ten-minute ride shouldn't cost more than £3–£4), but many take only two passengers.

You can't usually visit Montevideo without paying a visit to **Buenos Aires**, the cultural heart and political capital of **Argentina**, a sprawling, sophisticated city of broad avenues, parks and flowers. Sample the fare of the many open-air pavement cafés or shop for the immaculate leather goods of Avenida Lavalle, tour the ornate opera house Teatro Colon or, for a real taste of South American experience, visit a local dance parlour to learn the tango. Other famous landmarks are the Casa Rosada, the former palace of Juan and Eva Peron, Eva's Tomb and the Obelisk.

Puerto Madryn is Argentina's other main port, and is usually the gateway to the fabulous wildlife preserve on the Valdes Peninsula, with its collection of birds, the 13,000 or so amusing sea elephants and offshore whale-breeding grounds. The port also boasts some fine seafood restaurants. Those patriotic souls who fancy a visit to the bleak **Falkland Islands** can also do so on a South American itinerary out of Montevideo. Be warned, the wildly dramatic, windswept cliffs, hills and beaches (home to numerous waterfowl and sea-birds) are rarely warm, so you will need to have packed a couple of sweaters (a similar effect can be gained much closer to home in the Shetland Isles, and at least they have plenty of whisky there!). Still, the wildlife can be quite rewarding, with the tiny Magellan's penguins, black-browed albatross, kelp geese and rare Peal's dolphins all adding up to a naturalist's delight.

Going further south still brings you to the two most southern ports, Chile's **Punta Arenas** and Argentina's **Ushuaia**, the southernmost town in the world (population: 20,000 hardy souls). The months of December and January are just about the only time of the year that the vast, rocky wilderness of **Tierra del Fuego** and its famous point of Cape Horn are anything like hospitable, but again they offer a unique experience, especially for nature-lovers. At Ushuaia you can take a catamaran trip to see the teeming wildlife of the Beagle Channel or visit Fagnano Lake with its peat bogs (see, it's the Shetlands again) and beaver dams, and dine in a charming country inn. Punta Arenas is another frontier-like town, where local museums, housed in what used to be mansions, honour the region's cultural and natural history. Dine on unique shellfish and other seafood, and shop for wood and shell carvings in the duty-free zone. The hardiest of sailing aficionados will also want to savour the newest cruise experience being offered by NCL, Princess, Seabourn, Silversea, Royal Olympic, Fred Olsen and Orient – the chance to sail right round Cape Horn and up into the truly spectacular Chilean Fjords, which make Alaska and Norway look tame by comparison. Sailing between the fishing towns of **Puerto Natales** and **Puerto Montt**, you can enjoy the magnificent sight of the Torres Del Paine, where the glaciers are topped by sheer rock spires, and condors soar overhead, and you can do it in supreme comfort and style, soaking up scenery that could be the moon for all its similarity to anywhere else on earth. This, truly, is one of the last great cruise frontiers and will appeal to anyone with a thirst for adventure in their soul.

And talking of frontiers brings me neatly to the last serious cruise area of the world, **Antarctica**. Whether it is the awe-inspiring natural beauty of one of the world's most forbidding regions, the abundance of stunning wildlife or just the feeling of achievement at having cruised where only a relative handful have gone, the adventure experience of Antarctica is at once exciting, educational and uplifting. Nothing in your normal life will feel quite the same after you have gone ashore by Zodiac landing craft, trodden the ice of the great frozen southern continent or looked a giant penguin in the eye. In fact, no pictures or words can really do it justice and the appeal of cruising this icy wilderness will be either instantly obvious or totally off-putting.

TRAVEL TIP

Remember this is still an expedition, for all the creature comforts of ships like *Marco Polo*, and, as such, the route and ports of call are subject to weather, ice and wildlife conditions and can be changed at short notice. Despite the drawbacks, these are among the most popular cruises anywhere, and it is vital to book early to get on.

Round trips from Ushaia or Punta Arenas, or the grand Antarctic circumnavigation all the way to New Zealand are on offer. On the round-trip itineraries, expect to visit the likes of **Hope Bay**, with its huge Adelie penguin rookery, **Deception Island**, a volcanic caldera where the bravest souls can swim in the steam-heated waters, spectacular **Paradise Harbour**, dotted with floating icebergs, and the gentoo penguin rookery of **Port Lockroy**, surrounded by spectacular mountains. The circumnavigation route (lasting in excess of 20 days) comes within 736 miles of the South Pole at the American **McMurdo Station**, the largest research facility based on the continent and home to hundreds of scientists, and also takes in **Cape Evans**, **Cape Royds** and Cape Adare, where the stark huts bear witness to the incredible hardships suffered by the first Antarctic explorers.

A word from the wise

Captain Ben Haas, a former skipper of Orient Lines' *Marco Polo*, summed it up for me when he explained: 'My first opportunity to cruise Antarctica was unreal. During the months of preparation, a picture formed in my mind of what to expect. But, when the first Antarctic iceberg appeared in our sights, it was quite different from what I had imagined. Massive, brilliant white and blue (and completely flat on top like a magnificent, illuminated condominium); nothing had prepared me for such an awesome sight. The ice has a mesmerising effect (you just cannot get enough of it), in every shape and hue. In Antarctica, the days are so long and wildlife is amazing. During the cruise season, in the window of the short austral summer, the sea is surprisingly calm and the weather is usually bright and sunny. I always wanted to make the long voyage from the Antarctic Peninsula by way of the Ross Ice Shelf to New Zealand, and, in the *Marco Polo*, I achieved that ambition. For me, one of the most interesting aspects was the lectures from our team of experts, who brought it all to life and took us into the huts where explorers like Shackleton and Scott had wintered. It makes you feel quite small.'

TRAVEL TIP

Although the vistas are always icy, don't pack as if for sub-zero temperatures (it will usually be around 13°C/55°F during the day). Most ships will supply the necessary all-weather parka, but do take a lightweight waterproof jacket and over-trousers, comfortable, waterproof boots and plenty of film. Specialist publications also advise taking small gifts for the scientists who show you round their research stations – current magazines, books, fresh fruit and souvenirs from your home town.

And, in addition to the comical, fearless penguins (which, having no previous experience of Man, are interminably curious), you should also see giant elephant seals, leopard seals, humpback whales and killer whales, as well as countless seabirds. Don't get the idea, however, you can rush off and trample around this great wilderness unhindered. Groups are carefully supervised to maintain environmental controls, and the local wildlife cannot be interfered with in any way.

Well, that about wraps it up for the whole wide world of cruising. I am often asked where my favourite cruise areas are, but the simple truth is I just enjoy cruising. All the different regions have their attractions and it isn't difficult to get the best out of them by doing your homework and getting stuck in. Whether it is Barbados or Brisbane, Alaska or the Amazon, they all have a rich and rewarding experience to offer. Hopefully, by reading this book you will have gained a better understanding of what it is all about, but there is simply no substitute for first-hand experience. Just get out there and cruise!

CHAPTER SEVEN

HOLD THE
FRONT PAGE

Here is a last-minute round-up of cruise news that was too late to squeeze into the main sections. **Royal Caribbean:** the big American line have announced their first British-dedicated cruises in summer 2002, with *Splendour of the Seas* being based in Southampton for a series of eight cruises from 3- to 14-nights to Norway, the Canaries and Spain. The venture, to include British-orientated entertainment, cuisine and even beers, begins on May 5 with a 4-night voyage to Belgium and Holland. Four cruises will be themed, either 'Discovering Gardening' or 'Discovering Food and Wine' with celebrity guests, lectures and demonstrations. *Splendour* then moves on in late June to her base in Venice to complete a European-dominated summer (from the passenger point of view).

Thomson Cruises take a bold step in 2002 by bringing back the *IslandBreeze* into their fold, thus giving them a three-ship fleet once again. The 31,793-tonner had been sailing as *Big Red Boat III* for now-defunct Premier Cruise Line after two seasons with Thomson, but she had built up such a following, the quick-thinking British tour operator have got her back in their colours for a summer in Majorca with alternating 7-night western Mediterranean cruises. *IslandBreeze* is a veteran of 1962 vintage but has been well looked after and still offers a great range of amenities, good open deck space and a classic feel (although her lower level cabins leave something to be desired).

P&O will become the UK's largest fly-cruise operator to the Caribbean in winter 2002 when their new *Oceana* takes up duties for them. The 77,000-ton ship (from Princess Cruises) will be adapted for UK passengers and operate five different two-week cruises from Fort Lauderdale. Ports of call will include Cristobal in Panama and Costa Maya in Mexico, plus their private Bahamian island.

Princess Cruises have announced that their 1,590-passenger *Crown Princess* will be leaving the fleet in summer 2002 to join newly-formed German cruise line A'Rosa, offering voyages to the Baltic, Canada and New England and the Caribbean. Meanwhile, **Seabourn** have sold off the two *Seabourn Goddess* ships to a Norwegian operator to concentrate on their trio of *Legend, Pride* and *Spirit.*

THE DAILY EXPRESS BRITISH CRUISE AWARDS

So we come to our annual celebration of the Best of the Best in the British cruise industry, the *Daily Express* **British Cruise Awards**. This innovative scheme aims to provide extra insight into the real value of cruising as well as highlighting the pinnacle of excellence in each of the main categories. Since the *Daily Express* became the Awards' principal promoter, this yearly presentation has taken on huge significance in the UK travel world.

First, let's introduce the Panel of 25 experts who represent a full industry cross-section and are renowned for their insight into the vast range of products. They are: **John Ball**, travel writer, cruise specialist, consultant editor of *What Cruise?* magazine; **Mary Bond**, editor of *Seatrade Cruise Review;* **Jennifer Brown**, former senior sales and marketing executive for Royal Caribbean Cruise Line and Star Cruises in Europe, now a travel and cruise industry consultant; **Sue Bryant**, travel writer and editor of new magazine *Cruise Traveller;* **Gary Buchanan**, specialist cruise writer, maritime historian and author; **Ian Buckeridge**, sales and marketing director of cruise agents The Cruise Line Ltd; **Chris Coate**s, partner in Cruise & Maritime Services, who are a specialist cruise ship charter broker; **Bob Duffett**, former general manager of Norwegian Cruise Line UK, founder of the PSA's training arm PSARA and now a cruise consultant; **Kevin Griffin**, managing director of specialist agent The Cruise People Ltd and chairman of the Guild of Professional Cruise Agents; **Lucy Huxley**, cruise correspondent of the essential travel trade newspaper *Travel Trade Gazette*; **Peter Milne**, an experienced cruise consumer of many years standing; **David Mott**, the former shipping correspondent of *Lloyd's List,* now a freelance cruise writer; **Paul Mundy**, founder and retired director of specialist cruise agents Paul Mundy Cruising; **Ken Page**, former director of the PSA; **Patricia Piacente**, American-based president-owner of cruise agents Talk About Travel; **Tony Ripper**, director of specialist cruise agents The Cruise Advisory Service; **Ted Scull**, a renowned US-based cruise writer and author; **John Shakespeare**, a specialist cruise consultant with the Offshore Cruise Club; **David Short**, a director of Page & Moy, specialising in cruise product; **David Simpson**, founder and owner/operator of the cruise internet service Seaview; **Simon Veness**, travel writer and author of *Choosing A Cruise,* editor of *World of Cruising* magazine and Awards Panel co-ordinator; **Carolyn Voce**, a cruise consumer and principal research assistant with *Choosing A Cruise*; and **Peter Wild**, founder of GP Wild International, the world's leading cruise analysts.

And so to business. Each Panel member has a say in compiling the Awards' Nominations list, which allows for all ships with at least six months' unbroken service up to June 2001. The voting is then done on the basis of each panelist listing a first and second choice in each category, with 3 pts for a first-place vote and 1 pt for second. The winner of each award is then simply that which polls most points, with a Highly Commended certificate going to the runners-up. Here's how the votes were cast.

BEST STANDARD SHIP

1998 winner: *Victoria* (P&O)
1999 winner: *Victoria* (P&O)
2000 winner: *Black Prince* (Fred Olsen)
(Highly commended: *Ocean Majesty,* Page & Moy)

2001 Nominations: *Black Prince* (Fred Olsen), *Carousel* (Airtours), *Olympic Countess* (ROC), *Ocean Majesty* (Page & Moy), *Emerald* (Thomson)
Highly commended: *Black Prince* (Fred Olsen)

2001 winner: *Emerald* (Thomson Cruises)

BEST SUPERIOR SHIP

1998, 1999: Not classified
2000 winner: *Mistral* (Festival)
(Highly commended: *Victoria,* P&O)

2001 Nominations: *Sunbird* (Airtours), *Black Watch* (Fred Olsen), *Pacific Princess* (Princess Cruises), *Costa Allegra* (Costa), *Mistral* (Festival)
Highly commended: *Black Watch* (Fred Olsen)

2001 winner: *Mistral* (Festival Cruises)

BEST PREMIER SHIP

1998 winner: *Oriana* (P&O)
1999 winner: *Vision of the Seas* (Royal Caribbean)
2000 winner: *Oriana* (P&O)
(Highly commended: *Voyager of the Seas,* Royal Caribbean;
Marco Polo, Orient Lines)

2001 Nominations: *Disney Magic* (Disney CL), *Aurora* (P&O), *Voyager of the Seas* (Royal Caribbean), *Norwegian Sky* (Norwegian Cruise Line), *Crown Odyssey* (Orient Lines), *Olympic Voyager* (Royal Olympic Cruises)
Highly commended: *Voyager of the Seas* (Royal Caribbean),
Crown Odyssey (Orient Lines)

2001 winner: *Aurora* (P&O)

BEST DELUXE SHIP

1998 winner: *Century* (Celebrity)
1999 winner: *Rotterdam* (Holland America)
2000 winner: *Hebridean Princess* (Hebridean island Cruises)
(Highly commended: *Seabourn Goddess II,* Seabourn)

2001 Nominations: *Song of Flower* (Radisson Seven Seas), *Caronia* (Cunard), *Millennium* (Celebrity), *Amsterdam* (Holland America), *Grand Princess* (Princess Cruises), *Hebridean Princess* (Hebridean Island Cruises), *R8* (Renaissance Cruises)

Highly commended: *Millennium* (Celebrity Cruises), *Caronia* (Cunard)

2001 winner: *Hebridean Princess* (Hebridean Island Cruises)

BEST ULTRA-DELUXE SHIP

1998 winners: *Silver Cloud* (Silversea – Small), *Crystal Symphony* (Crystal Symphony (Crystal Cruises – Large)
1999 winners: *Silver Cloud* (Silversea – Small), *Crystal Symphony* (Crystal Symphony (Crystal Cruises – Large)
2000 winner: *Silver Cloud* (Silversea)
(Highly commended: *Crystal Symphony,* Crystal Cruises)

2001 Nominations: *Crystal Symphony* (Crystal Cruises), *Silver Shadow* (Silversea), *Seabourn Legend* (Seabourn), *Deutschland* (Peter Deilmann), *Seven Seas Navigator* (Radisson Seven Seas)

Highly commended: *Crystal Symphony* (Crystal Cruises)

2001 winner: *Silver Shadow* (Silversea Cruises)

BEST FAMILY SHIP

1998 winner: *Oriana* (P&O)
1999 winner: *Oriana* (P&O)
2000 winner: *Disney Magic* (Disney Cruise Line)
(Highly commended: *Oriana,* P&O; Voyager of the Seas, Royal Caribbean)

2001 Nominations: *Disney Magic* (Disney Cruise Line), *Aurora* (P&O), *Voyager of the Seas* (Royal Caribbean), *Carnival Destiny* (Carnival), *Grand Princess* (Princess), *SuperStar Leo* (Star Cruises)

Highly commended: *Aurora* (P&O)

2001 winner: *Disney Magic* (Disney Cruise Line)

BEST SPECIALIST SHIP

1998 winner: *Hebridean Island Princess* (Hebridean Island Cruises)
1999 winner: *Minerva* (Swan Hellenic)
2000 winner: *Minerva* (Swan Hellenic)
(Highly commended: *Star Clipper,* Star Clippers; *Hanseatic,* Hapag-Lloyd)

2001 Nominations: *Minerva* (Swan Hellenic), *Clipper Adventurer* (Clipper Cruise Line), *RMS St Helena* (Curnow), *Royal Clipper* (Star Clippers), *Hanseatic* (Hapag-Lloyd), Norwegian Coastal Voyages
Highly commended: *Royal Clipper* (Star Clipper)

2001 winner: *Minerva* (Swan Hellenic)

BEST RIVER CRUISE OPERATOR

1998/1999: Not held.
2000 winner: Peter Deilmann
(Highly commended: KD/Viking River Cruises)

2001 Nominations: Peter Deilmann, KD/Viking River Cruises, Swan Hellenic, European Waterways, Thomas Cook, Bales Worldwide
Highly commended: KD/Viking River Cruises

2001 winner: Peter Deilmann

BEST BROCHURE

1998 winner: Cunard
1998 winner: Silversea
2000 winner: Silversea
(Highly commended: Hebridean Island Cruises)

2001 Nominations: Hebridean Island Cruises, Seabourn, Silversea, Cunard, P&O, Fred Olsen, Radisson Seven Seas
Highly commended: Fred Olsen, Silversea Cruises

2001 winner: Hebridean Island Cruises

WHAT CRUISE INDUSTRY CONTRIBUTION AWARD

1998 winner: Holland America
1999 winner: Disney Cruise Line
2000 winner: Dover Cruise Port
(Highly commended: P&O, Passenger Shipping Association)

2001 Nominations: Passenger Shipping Association (for their continued investment in consumer promotions and statistics), Royal Caribbean International (for their Southampton showcase of *Voyager of the Seas*), Cunard (for their awareness campaign for *Queen Mary 2*), Princess Cruises (for Southampton showcase of *Golden Princess*)
Highly commended: Royal Caribbean

2001 winner: Passenger Shipping Association

INDEX

References to tables and ship names are given in italics. Cruise lines have (C) after their name.

Abercrombie & Kent (C) 176, 242
Adventure of the Seas 16, 18, 156–9
Aegean Spirit 181–2
Africa 238–41
  North 185–97, 196
  see also South Africa
African Safari Club (C) 78–9, 104, 235
age profile 32–3, *34–7*, 74, 75
Airtours (C) *34–5*, 78–9, 83, 103, 105–7, 185, 204
Alaska 27, 29, 64, 71, 78–81, 183, 184, *185*, 216–17, 218–19
Albatros 177–8
Algeria 196
Amazon River 64, 242–3
America
  East Coast USA 71, *78–81*, *185*, 220–2
  Mexico 205, 209, 215
  South America 30, 64, *78–81*, 90, *185*, 242–5
  West Coast USA 71, *78–81*, *185*, 215–19
Amsterdam 71, 128–30
Antarctica *78–9*, 242, 245–7
Antigua 210
Antilles 205, 208–10, 213
Apollon 160–2
Arcadia 144–7
Arcalia Shipping (C) 176–7
Arctic Circle 197
Argentina 244–5
Aruba 204, 213
Astor 181
Astra I 176–7
Athens 191
Atlantic *78–81*, 85
Aurora 16, 19, 22, 24, 31, 44, 45, *63*, 144–7
Ausonia 125–6
Australasia 64, *185*, 229–34
Australia 71
Azur 123–5
Bahamas 29, *78–81*, 86, 204, 207
Bali 225–6
Baltic Sea 197, 200–1
Bangkok 225
Barbados 204, 205, 212
Barcelona 71, 187
Bay of Biscay 85
Beijing 227
Beirut 195
Belize 204
Bequia 211–12
Berlin 200
Bermuda *78–81*, 210, 220
Black Prince/Watch 74, 87, 138–41
Black Sea 194
boarding 94
Bolero 123–5
Bonaire 213
Borneo 226
Boston 221
Braemar 138–41
Brazil 71, 243
Bremen 179
Britain 198–9
British Cruise Awards 103, 249
Brunei 226
Bulgaria 194
cabins 19, 27, 47–53, 94–5
  choice of 27, 47–53
  staterooms 50
  suites 51

Cairo 195
Caledonian Star 179–80
Calypso 132–3
Canada 71, 220, 222
Canary Islands 64, *78–81*, 185–97
Cape of Good Hope 240
Cape Horn 245
Cape Town 71, 240
Caribbean 27–30, 64–5, 70, *78–81*, 93, 183–4, *185*, 204–15
Carnival (C) *16–17*, 18, *19–20*, *34–5*, *78–9*, *82*, 83, 92, 108–10, 204, 215, 220
Carnival Conquest 19
Carnival Destiny 14, *16*, 42–3, 52, 60, 108–10
Carnival Pride/Spirit/Victory 16, 18, 108–10
Carnival Triumph *16*, 43, 108–10, 206
Caronia 119–20
Carousel 105–7
Cayman Islands 209
Celebration 20 108–10
Celebrity (C) *16–17*, 18, *34–5*, 80–2, 83, 92, 111–13, 185, 204, 215, 220
Century 45, 111–13
children 2, 13, 30, 44, 50, 67, 91, 96
Chile 245
China 223, 227–8
Clipper Adventure 177–8
Clipper Cruise Line (C) *78–9*, 178, 204, 215, 220, 242
Colombia 213–14
Columbus 179
Comoros islands 237
Cook islands 232
Copenhagen 201
Corfu 191
Corsica 188
Costa Allegra/Altantica/Classica 114–16
Costa (C) *16–17*, *34–5*, 76, *82*, 83, 197, 204
Costa Cruises (C) *78–9* , 92, 114–16, 184, 185, 242
Costa Marina/Riviera/Romantica/Tropicale 114–16
Costa Victoria *16*, 43, 114–16
Crete 191
Croatia 190
Crown Princess 148–51
cruise consultants 89–92
cruise experience
  boarding 94
  disembarkation 99
  embarkation 92–3
  exploring ship 95–6
  final evening 97
  first day 96
  first evening 96
  first port of call 97
cruises
  adventure 39–40
  age profile 32–3, *34–7*, 74, 75
  anniversary packages 40
  art auctions 58
  assessing standard 42–50
  British/American 9, 11–14, 64, 77
  cabins 19, 27, 47–53, 94–5
  children 2, 13, 30, 44, 50, 67, 91, 96
  choosing the right 9, 21, 25, 91–2, 183–4
  daily programme 22
  deck games 24, 45, 84
  deluxe 75
  destination 39–40
  for disabled 88–9
  discounts 29, 92, 93
  entertainment 58, 73, 77
  European style 77

facilities 22–5, 42–50, 84
fly- 12–13, 64–5, 84–5, 93, 97
food 26, 41–2, 59–63, 74, 75, 77, 95
formality 33, 38
future of 14–16
gambling 46
Gentleman Host programme 41
health and beauty 24, 43–4
lifeboat drill 95–6
medical care 46–7
mix 'n match 76–7
modern face of 10, 13–15
money ashore 70–1
money on board 45, 95, 98
newcomers 38, 65, 74
non-smoking 110
on-shore excursions 21–2, 26, 29, 63–5,
    68–72, 74, 75
photography 46–7, 94
ports of call, best 71–2, 75
premier 74
ratings 73–76, 77, 82, 102
relaxation 24–6, 84
safety 95–6
service and tipping 28, 53–7, 98
settling up 98
ship-speak 100–2
shopping 45–6
short vs long 85–6
for singles 86–8
specialist agents 89–92
standard 73–4
superior 74
themed 24
top 10 largest lines 82, 83
travel agents 10–11, 13, 68, 89–92
types of 66–8
ultra-deluxe 75–6
as value for money 10, 11, 27–9, 74
and weather 64
weddings 40–1
Crystal Cruises (C) 17, 34–5, 76, 80–2, 83,
    116–18, 197, 204, 215, 223, 229, 242
Crystal Harmony 45, 60, 62–3, 116–18
Crystal Symphony 25, 45, 52, 116–18
Cuba 205, 208
Cunard (C) 17, 20, 34–5, 80–2, 83, 119–20, 185,
    197, 204, 220, 223, 229, 235, 242
Curacao 204, 213
Cyprus 86, 194–5
Daily Express British Cruise Awards 4, 103, 249
Damascus 195
Dawn Princess 16, 43, 148–51
Dead Sea 195
deck games 24, 45, 84
Delos 191
Denmark 197, 201
Deutschland 180
disabled 88–9
disembarkation 99
Disney Cruise Line (C) 16, 34–5, 65, 82, 121–2, 204
Disney Magic/Wonder 16, 121–2
Dominica 211
Dominican Republic 204, 208
Dover port 198
Dubai 238
Dublin 203
Durban 240–1
Dutch Antilles 213
Dutch Islands 204, 205
East Coast USA 71, 78–81, 185, 220–2
Ecstasy 108–10
Egypt 195

Elation 108–10
Emerald 19, 172–4, 208
Enchantment of the Seas 16, 43, 156–9
Estonia 197, 200
Europa 179
Europe
    northern 78–81, 185, 197–204
    southern 183–97
European Vision 19, 45, 77, 123–5
Explorer of the Seas 8, 16, 18, 42, 45, 156–9, 176,
    205, 242
Falkland Islands 244–5
families 2, 13, 30, 44, 50, 67, 91, 96
Fantasy 108–10
Far East 29, 30, 64, 70–1, 78–81, 184, 185, 223–8
Fascination 108–10
Festival (C) 17, 18, 34–5, 78–9, 82, 83, 123–5,
    185, 197, 204
Fiji 231
Finland 197, 201
First Choice (C) 34–5, 78–9, 125–6, 185
Flamenco 123–5
Florida 12, 65, 71, 204, 205
fly cruises 12–13, 64–5, 84–5, 93, 97
food 26, 41–2, 59–63, 74, 75, 77, 95
Fort Lauderdale 92, 205, 206–7
France 188
Fred Olsen (C) 36–7, 78–9, 83, 103, 138–41, 185,
    197, 204, 235, 242
French Polynesia 230
Funchal 176–7
Galaxy 16, 45, 111–13
gambling 46
Gentleman Host programme 41
Germany 197, 200
Gibraltar 187
Golden Princess 16, 18, 47, 148–51
Grand Princess 15, 16, 25, 43, 47, 52, 60, 148–51
Grandeur of the Seas 16, 43, 156–9
Great Barrier Reef 233
Greece 70, 86, 190–2
Grenada 204, 208, 212
Guadeloupe 205, 211
Guernsey 71, 199
Guild of Professional Cruise Agents (GPCA) 90
Haiti 208
Hanseatic 179, 184
Hapag–Lloyd Tours (C) 80–1, 178–9, 184, 197,
    220, 242
Harwich 199
Hawaii 78–81
Hebridean Island Cruises (C) 80–1, 126–7, 185, 197
Hebridean Princess/Spirit 126–7
Holiday 108–10
Holland 197, 199–200
Holland America Line (C) 17, 34–5, 80–2, 83,
    128–30, 185, 197, 204, 215, 220, 223, 229
Holy Land 195
Hong Kong 71, 223, 227
Horizon 111–13
hotel vs cruise costs 27–9
Ibiza 188
Imagination 108–10
India 185, 236
Indian Ocean 64, 78–81, 85
Indonesia 223, 225
Infinity 16, 18, 111–13
Inspiration 19, 108–10
Ireland 203–4
Island Cruises (C) 19, 131–2, 185
Island Escape 19, 131–2
Israel 195
Istanbul 71, 192–3

Italy 71, 189
Jakarta 225
Jamaica 30, 204, 208
Japan 223, 228
jargon, on-board 100–2
Jason 177–8
Java 225
Jerusalem 195
Jordan 195
Jubilee 20 108–10
Kenya 104, 236, 239
Ketchikan 214
Komodo Island 226
Korea 223
Krakatau 226
La Compagnie des Iles du Ponant (C) 177
Lanzarote 196
Lapland 203
Latvia 197, 200–1
Le Levant/Le Ponant 177
Legend of the Seas 43, 156–9, 223
lifeboat drill 95–6
Lombok 226
London 191
Louis Cruise Lines (C) 78–9, 82, 83, 132–3, 185
Maasdam 128–30
Madagascar 236, 237–8
Madeira 71, 197
Majesty of the Seas 156–9
Majorca 71, 187, 188
Malaysia 223, 224–5
Maldives 237
Malta 190
Marco Polo 39–40, 245, 246
Martinique 210
Mauritius 236, 238
Mayreau 212
medical care 46–7
Mediterranean 13–14, 27, 28, 64, 78–81, 83, 183–97
Mediterranean Shipping Cruises (C) 17, 78–9, 133–5, 185, 204, 235, 242
Melbourne 233–4
Melody 133–5
Mercury 16, 45, 111–13
Mexico 86, 205, 209, 215
Miami 12, 92, 205–6
Middle East 185–97, 195
Millennium 16, 111–13
Minerva 20, 32, 171–2, 199
Mistral 58, 74, 77, 123–5
Monarch of the Seas 156–9
Monte Carlo 188
Monterey 133–5
Montreal 222
Montserrat 210
Morocco 196
Mykonos 191
Nantucket Clipper 177–8
NCL (C) *see* Norwegian Cruise Line
New Caledonia 232
New Zealand 78–81, 229, 234–5
Newfoundland 221
Noble Caledonia (C) 180, 235, 242
Noordam 128–30
Nordic Empress 156–9
North Africa 185–97, 196
North Cape 197, 198, 203
North-West Passage 80–1, 184
Norway 16, 27, 71, 197, 201–2
Norwegian Coastal Voyages (C) 180
Norwegian Cruise Line (C) 16–17, 18, 78–9, 83, 83, 92, 135–8, 184–5, 197, 204, 215, 220, 223, 229, 242

Norwegian Dream 31, 63, 135–8
Norwegian Majesty/Sea 135–8
Norwegian Sky 16, 18, 28, 43, 63, 135–8
Norwegian Star 16, 18, 135–8
Norwegian Sun 16, 135–8
Norwegian Wind 63, 135–8
Nosy Be island 237
Ocean Majesty 180
Ocean Princess 19, 43, 148–51
Oceana see Ocean Princess
Oceanic Clipper 177–8
Odessa 194
Odysseus 160–2
Olympic Countess/Explorer/Voyager 160–2
on-shore excursions 21–2, 26, 29, 63–5, 68–72, 74, 75
Oriana 8, 13, 43, 45, 47–9, 60, 61, 98, 144–7
Orient (C) 36–7, 68, 78–9, 82, 83, 185, 197, 223, 229, 235, 242
Oslo 71, 201
P&O (C) 16–17, 19, 36–7, 78–9, 82, 83, 103, 144–7, 185, 197, 204, 229
Pacific Princess 53, 74, 148–51
Page & Moy (C) 91, 180
Panama Canal 78–81, 205, 214
Papua New Guinea 229–30
Paradise 108–10
Passenger Shipping Association Retail Agents (PSARA) 90
Paul Gauguin 152–4, 231
Penang 224–5
Peru 242
Peter Deilmann Cruises (C) 181
Philippines 223, 226
Phuket 225
Port Canaveral 205
Port Everglades 205
port lectures 68–9
Portugal 187
Princesa Amorosa/Cypria/Marissa/Victoria 132–3
Princess Cruises (C) 16–17, 18, 36–7, 78–9, 82, 83, 148–51, 184, 185, 197, 204, 215, 220, 223, 229, 235, 242
Princess Danae 176–7
Puerto Rico 204, 208
Purser's Desk 26, 45, 95, 98
QE2 8, 15, 19, 27, 32, 38, 67-8, 119–20, 198
QM2 14, 17, 20, 119
Quebec 222
R1/2/3/4/5/6/7/8, R8 154–5
Radiance of the Seas 16, 18, 156–9
Radisson Diamond 27, 152–4
Radisson Seven Seas Cruises (C) 17, 19, 36–7, 80–1, 82, 152–4, 185, 197, 204, 215, 223, 229, 235
Red Sea 195
Regal Princess 148–51
Renaissance Cruises (C) 80–1, 82, 154–5, 185, 197, 204, 229
Reunion 238
Rhapsody of the Seas 16, 43, 133–5, 156–9
Rhodes 191
Riga 200–1
Romania 194
Rome 189
Rotterdam 128–30
Royal Caribbean International (C) 16–17, 18, 19, 36–7, 78–9, 82, 83, 92, 156–9, 185, 197, 204, 215, 220, 223, 229, 235
Royal Clipper 167–9
Royal Olympic Cruises (C) 18, 78–9, 82, 83, 160–2, 184–5, 197, 204, 242
Royal Princess 148–51
Royal Star 104, 235

Russia 70, 197, 201
Ryndam 128–30
safety 95–6
Saga Cruises (C) *36–7*, 68, *78–9*, 85, 162–3, 185, 197, 204
Saga Rose 87, 162–3, 185
St Croix 209–10
St Helena 58, 178
St Helena Line Ltd (C) 178
St John 209–10
St Kitt's 210
St Lawrence Seaway 222
St Lucia *28*, 29, 210, 211
St Martin (St Maarten) 210
St Peter Port 199
St Thomas 204, 209–10
St Vincent 211
Samoa 231–2
San Blas Islands 214
San Francisco 71, 217
Santorini 191–2
Sardinia 189
Scandinavia 64, 197
Sea Princess 16, 43, 148–51
Seabourn (C) *36–7*, *80–2*, 83, 163–5, 184, 197, 204, 215, 220, 223, 229, 235, 242
Seabourn Goddess I/II 163–5
Seabourn Legend/Pride/Spirit 163–5
seasickness 26, 50
Seawing 105–7
Sensation 19, 108–10
Serenade 132–3
Seven Seas Mariner 19, 52, 152–4
Seven Seas Navigator 152–4
Seychelles 236, 237
ship-speak 100–2
ships
    background noise 52
    big vs small 84
    largest *16*
    new *17*, 18–19
    passenger crew ratio 104
    size 14, 25, 42–3
    space ratio 25, 73, 75, 84, 103
    staffing 54–8
Sicily 189
Silver Cloud/Whisper/Wind 165–7
Silversea Cruises (C) 19, *36–7*, 68, *80–1*, 165–7, 184–5, 197, 204, 215, 220, 223, 229, 235, 242
Singapore 71, 223–4
Society Expeditions 242
Solomon Islands 230
Song of Flower 152–4, 199
South Africa 71, 235, 236, 238–41
South America 30, 64, *78–81*, 90, *185*, 242–5
South Pacific 71, *78–81*, *185*, 230–2
Southampton 198
Sovereign of the Seas 156–9
space ratio 25, 73, 75, 84, 103
Spain 187–8
Spice Islands 226
Splendour of the Seas 18, 43, 156–9
Sri Lanka 236–7
Star Clipper 167–9
Star Clippers (C) *78–9*, 167–9, 184–5, 204, 223
Star Cruises (C) *16–17*, *78–9*, *82*, 83, 169–70, 223
Star Flyer 167–9
Statendam 128–30
Stella Solaris 160–2
Stockholm 201

Suez Canal 195
Sumatra 223
Sumbawa 226
Summit *16–17*, 18, 111–13
Sun Princess 16, 43, 148–51, 205
Sunbird 25, 74, 105–7
sunburn 27
Sundream 105–7
SuperStar Gemini 169–70
SuperStar Leo 16, 169–70, 223, 227
SuperStar Virgo 16, 169–70, 223
Swan Hellenic (C) *20*, *36–7*, *78–9*, 83, 103, 171–2, 185, 197, 223, 235
Sweden 197, 201–2
Syria 195
Tahiti 71, 229, 230–1
Tallinn 200
Tampa 205
Tanzania 239
Tasmania 233
Tenerife 196
Thailand 223
Thomson Cruises (C) 19, *36–7*, *78–9*, 83, 103, 172–4, 185, 204, 242
Timor 226
tipping *28*, 53–7, 55–6, 98
Tobago 205, 213
Tonga 232
Topaz 172–4
Tortola 210
Transocean Tours (C) 181
travel agents 10–11, 68, 89–92
Trinidad 205, 208, 212
Triton 160–2
Tunis 196
Tunisia 196
Turkey 70, 71, 191–2
Ukraine 194
Uruguay 244
USA
    East Coast 71, *78–81*, *185*, 220–2
    West Coast 71, *78–81*, *185*, 215–19
Vancouver 71, 218
Veendam 128–30
Venezuela 204–5, 208, 213
Victoria 58, 74, 144–7
Vietnam 223, 227
Virgin Gorda 210
Virgin Islands 183, 205, 209–10
visas 70
Vision of the Seas 16, 43, 156–9
Volendam 128–30
Voyager of the Seas 8, 14, *16*, 18, 25, 42, 45, 51, 84, 156–9, 205
Voyages of Discovery (C) 182
weddings 40–1
West Coast USA 71, *78–81*, *185*, 215–19
Westerdam 18, 128–30
Wind Song/Spirit/Star/Surf 174–6
Windstar *80–1*
Windstar Cruises (C) *26–7*, *80–2*, 83, 174–6, 185, 204, 223, 229
working ships 68
world cruises 68, *78–81*, *185*
World Renaissance 160–2
Yorktown Clipper 177–8
Zaandam 128–30
Zanzibar 239
Zenith 111–13